This book was
donated by . . .

Friends Corner
Book Shop

in honor of
our volunteer:

Camille DeCampos

DRAMA HIGH

DRAMA HIGH

THE INCREDIBLE TRUE STORY OF
A BRILLIANT TEACHER, A STRUGGLING TOWN,
AND THE MAGIC OF THEATER

Michael Sokolove

RIVERHEAD BOOKS

New York

2013

RIVERHEAD BOOKS
Published by the Penguin Group
Penguin Group (USA) LLC
375 Hudson Street
New York, New York 10014

USA · Canada · UK · Ireland · Australia
New Zealand · India · South Africa · China

penguin.com
A Penguin Random House Company

Library of Congress Cataloging-in-Publication Data

Sokolove, Michael Y.
Drama high : the incredible true story of a brilliant teacher, a struggling town,
and the magic of theater / Michael Sokolove.
p.   cm.
ISBN 978-1-59448-822-1
1. Volpe, Lou.   2. High school teachers—Pennsylvania—Levittown—Biography.
3. English teachers—Pennsylvania—Levittown—Biography.   4. Theatrical
producers and directors—Pennsylvania—Levittown—Biography.   I. Title.
LA2317.V65S65   2013   2013019393
370.92—dc23
[B]

Printed in the United States of America
1   3   5   7   9   10   8   6   4   2

BOOK DESIGN BY AMANDA DEWEY

*Penguin is committed to publishing works of quality and integrity.
In that spirit, we are proud to offer this book to our readers;
however, the story, the experiences, and the words
are the author's alone.*

For Ann

CONTENTS

DRAMA HIGH

TRUMAN'S 2001 PRODUCTION OF
LES MISÉRABLES. THE SCENE IS
"AT THE BARRICADES" IN ACT 2.

PLACES

Harry S Truman High School, set on a slight incline, is a monument to utility, neither inviting nor forbidding. Buffered on three sides by athletic fields, the school rises to just one story. Its exterior is brick—not red brick but a dull yellowish hue, the color of putty. A framed black-and-white photograph of the nation's thirty-third president occupies a wall just inside the front entrance. Several trophy cases commemorate the school's mostly unsuccessful athletic teams, and a big bulletin board lists the colleges that current seniors have been admitted to, along with the dollar amounts of scholarships they were awarded.

From there, the building unfolds into a grid of long hallways, lined with lockers, that come together to form lonely interior courtyards. An energetic janitorial staff buffs the floors each afternoon to a high gloss. The classroom clocks tell the right time.

Lou Volpe's classroom, far from the main entrance, is furnished with old couches and living room chairs, donated stuff that otherwise might have gone to Goodwill or landfills. The bookshelves, windowsills, radiators, and all other flat surfaces are piled high with anthologies of plays, copies of scripts, and videotapes and sound tracks of Broadway productions. Several mobiles hang from the ceiling, some low enough that a tall person has to duck around them. It is distinctly his room, even without the huge banner that says, in red block letters, LOU IS BACK. The sign appeared out of nowhere some years ago—tacked up to the rear wall when Volpe arrived one morning—and he knew not to ask too much about its provenance, though word did eventually filter down that some students had pilfered it from a local used car lot and that "Lou" was apparently one of the salesmen. "I really hope this other Lou doesn't miss it too much," Volpe says with a mischievous grin when I ask him about it one day.

As we talk, he is walking a circular route around the classroom, straightening and fluffing the upholstery on the couches and chairs, a ritual he performs numerous times a day, always in a clockwise direction. It is September 2010, about a week into a new school year. The final afternoon bell has just sounded, and the room is beginning to fill up with students arriving to audition for the fall play.

"Yo, Volp," a boy says as he walks past. "Hey, Krause," he adds with a nod to Tracey Krause, a former student of Volpe's and now a teacher at the school and his indispensable assistant director.

Another boy breezes in and comments on Volpe's attire, a frequent topic of conversation, and what looks to him like peace signs on Volpe's belt. "Yes," he says, "I got this belt at Woodstock. I was there, you know." The student laughs, knowing that Volpe would never have been anywhere near the mud and chaos of Woodstock.

Most students walk in and silently take seats. They have already endured a seven-hour school day. They plop down on the furniture and enter that resting mode of teenagers in which they are neither fully asleep nor awake but are nonetheless utterly aware. The more crowded the room gets—meaning the more competition there will be for parts—the quieter it becomes.

The play being auditioned for on this day is called *Good Boys and True.* It is a daring choice for a high school, but a typical one for Volpe—a searingly intense drama in which a secretly recorded sex tape is discovered at a high school and a golden-boy athlete is implicated. In the play, the school's football captain has picked up a girl who works at a food court in a shopping mall, and on that day, the first time he meets her, without her knowledge he films them having sex together. The videotape is found in a locker and then viewed by his teammates. The boy's face is obscured, so his identity cannot be known for sure.

The story moves forward in a series of painful unravelings—the school is scandalized; a family fractures; a gay relationship is revealed; a deep friendship between two boys rips apart. It is the kind of material that grips high school actors and audiences but terrifies school administrations. Volpe will be the first to put this drama on a high school stage.

Some fifty students wait in the classroom to compete for just six parts—three female, three male. Volpe speaks for a moment before they begin. "I hate to use the word *relevant*, but this play is," he says. "It feels very *now*. Like it's something that could happen here, or just about anywhere."

The initial event in the play has the same effect as someone throwing a stone into a pond, he tells them. A calm is disturbed, even if it does not attract much notice at first. Ripples flow outward. It's one of Volpe's favorite analogies. Another is the concept of doors opening—one door opens, revealing a secret of some kind, then another and another. Once opened, the doors cannot be closed. It is how he sees theater and life, including his own.

He makes clear what it will take to win a role. "We're going to need to see how far you can go. We need to see the fire. If it's anger, if it's pain, you can't be afraid to go to that place. I'm not talking about shouting. I mean something you find deep inside."

Everyone understands. Volpe plays are full emotional commitments. And they are competitive. Nobody gets a pass into a Truman production. You can be a lead in one play and get left out of the next. It happens all the time. "Volpe and Krause love the 'new,'" is how one of the girls in the room that day puts it. "They love that new blood, that undiscovered talent, so you've always got to watch your back for what's coming up behind you."

Just a week or so earlier, in New York, I had visited with Nicole Sabatini, a student of Volpe's in the mid-1990s. We sat in a coffee shop in the basement of 30 Rockefeller Center. A slightly built former dancer, she worked upstairs as a vice president at Bravo. "A lot of us had an idea who Mr. Volpe was even before we got into high school," she said. "You wanted to be part of what he created. You looked forward to it. My first year I auditioned for *Little Shop of Horrors* and didn't get a part, but he told me it was going to be a good three years for me, that he was impressed by me.

"I got leads in two musicals after that. Then in my senior year, I didn't get a part in the drama, and then it got picked for the Main Stage at the national festival [the annual International Thespian Festival, a massive high school gathering each summer at the University of Nebraska]. I went to the festival as a stage manager. I had one job to do—press 'Play' on a cassette player to turn on some music. I'm not gonna lie—it hurt. But it was a big lesson for me. I had done my best at the auditions, but it wasn't good enough. It happens sometimes when you're around other people who are talented."

The auditions are cold readings—Volpe or his assistant, Tracey Krause, calls out page numbers and students read the lines—but, in fact, nearly everyone has already gotten ahold of scripts and studied the story and parts. Some have read the play in their theater classes. "That was good, very good. Thank you," Volpe says after a nervous tenth-grade girl finishes her reading.

The auditions move quickly, except when Volpe slows the pace with observations about the material. "The setting here is a private school, very privileged," he says. "I wanted you to see how the other half lives."

The dialogue includes talk of colleges, elite schools where a couple of the characters have applied. One of them is Dartmouth. Confronted with it on the page, the Truman students pronounce it *DART-mouth.* "It's *DART-myth,*" Volpe points out a couple of times, but they keep making the same mistake. Oberlin College and Vassar are equally baffling.

Volpe and Krause select ten students for callbacks the next day. Again, Volpe appeals to them to reach for intensity. "This is not a director's play. I can only stage it so much. It's an actor's play. It's up to you to elevate it."

Two boys step forward to read a scene. One is Zach Philippi, a six-foot-two, athletically built senior who has been in just one previous play. He is a baseball player, all-county, even a possible pro prospect. The other is senior Bobby Ryan, a little shorter and more slightly built, but also an athlete, a lacrosse player. He has been acting at Truman since his freshman year. Volpe gives them a scene from near the end of the play, with Philippi taking the role of the golden boy who has made the sex tape that caused the scandal. He accuses his best friend (Ryan) of informing on him to school authorities. The character played by Ryan is gay. The one played by Philippi ostensibly is not, though they have been sexually intimate.

"If I kicked the shit out of you, would you answer me then?" Philippi asks as the scene builds.

"Go ahead," Ryan says, opening his arms wide and putting his face forward, as if he wants to be hit. "Do it. Beat me to a pulp. Do it! I know you're not scared to. I know you get off on shit like that."

The scene is a denouement, ugly and raw. "Do you know what they call you behind your back?" Philippi shouts, and then rattles off a series of vulgar expressions.

The boys have moved so close to each other that their noses almost touch. It is just an audition, but riveting nonetheless. "That's good," Volpe says. "That's good." There is some polite applause in the room, mostly from the girls, who will not have to compete for these two parts.

Sitting in a corner of the room by herself is Mariela Castillo. Earlier in the day, she had gotten into a screaming argument in the school corridor with her boyfriend of two years, a varsity basketball player. She has her earbud in and her knees curled up under her. Volpe considers Mariela a triple threat—an accomplished singer, dancer, and actor. "And," he adds, "it doesn't hurt that she's absolutely stunning-looking." But even though Mariela has been one of his stalwarts, she seems disengaged and in no shape to rise to the occasion and win a part.

Castillo does not volunteer to come forward—she just sits there, radiating bad energy—and Volpe has to finally call on her after most of the others have auditioned. He asks her to read lines from the mother of the golden boy, a difficult role for any high schooler because she will have to play the part of an adult. Castillo is wearing tight jeans and a snug-fitting T-shirt. Before she goes to the middle of the room, she pulls on a tailored blue blazer that she had set down beside her. She ties her hair back, puts on a sophisticated-looking pair of eyeglasses. She takes a breath and seems to collect herself.

"The scene on pages twenty-nine and thirty," Volpe instructs. The passage comes in the play after the football coach has shown the mother the sex tape and she confronts her son—a person she no longer recognizes. Castillo reads the lines with a cool, simmering anger: "I saw a boy, I saw you, lead that girl onto, what? Not even a bed, onto a mattress, on some floor . . . I saw you slap her . . . I saw you force her face onto the mattress . . . I swear, you were *enjoying* it."

Makeup and wardrobe would make Castillo even more convincing as a forty-five-year-old ER surgeon, which is what the mother is. But on this first reading, she calls forth distress, sadness, barely controlled rage. She seems to pull these layers from deep within, just as Volpe asked.

On a mid-November afternoon in 2001, a black stretch limousine set out from Manhattan, passed through the Lincoln Tunnel, and headed south for fifty miles on the New Jersey Turn-

pike before crossing over the Delaware River and into Pennsylvania. Among its passengers—and the person for whom the trip had
been organized—was Sir Cameron Mackintosh, the West End and
Broadway producer of *Cats, The Phantom of the Opera,* and *Miss Sai-
gon,* blockbusters that grossed hundreds of millions of dollars and
afforded the producer a lavish, jet-setting lifestyle. He split his time
between his apartments in London and New York, farmhouse in
Provence, seaside home in Malta, and fifteen-thousand-acre estate
in the Scottish Highlands. Queen Elizabeth knighted him on New
Year's Day 1996 for "contributions to musical theatre."

Cameron Mackintosh was headed to Levittown, Pennsylvania, and Truman High for a Lou Volpe production. Mackintosh's
traveling companions—business associates who had arranged this
excursion—had fervent hopes for its success, but were uneasy. It
was once written of Mackintosh, "His gut is famous." Meaning that
he knows what he likes and what he doesn't and how to make
that known.

By the measures that seem to matter most, Truman High is,
at best, second-rate. Its students do not excel at standardized tests,
and few of them ever go off to Ivy League colleges or other
prestigious institutions, unless you put the U.S. military in that
category—the school sends plenty of its graduates straight into
the Army, Navy, Air Force, and Marines. The neighborhoods it
draws from are often called blue-collar, but that is an outdated
notion, one based on steady union jobs at U.S. Steel and other
nearby industrial giants that are two decades gone. Parents of
Truman students work at warehouses and call centers, and some
supplement their incomes with shifts at fast-food restaurants.

When Truman makes news, it's usually for the wrong reasons,
like when the class president couldn't give his graduation speech

and an empty chair was put in his place because he was the target of a gang hit and no one wanted gunfire at commencement. In the local lexicon, Truman High, in otherwise prosperous Bucks County, is "on the wrong side of Route 1." It's where you do not want to be and where you'd leave if you hit the lottery.

The high school has one principal mark of distinction: Volpe's astoundingly successful drama program. Younger students know of him long before they reach Truman and hope to one day be in his shows. He is like the winning football coach in some down-on-its-luck Ohio or Texas town—a beacon, a sign that grand achievement is possible, albeit unlikely. Schools with vastly greater financial resources, boasting higher-achieving students born to wealthier parents, cannot match the quality and accomplishments of Truman Drama. No high school in American can.

Volpe had joined Truman's faculty at age twenty-one, and the night Cameron Mackintosh was to arrive was three decades into his career. He had said more than once, "I just want to be remembered." He hoped that something that occurred in his classroom or at a rehearsal—maybe something he said, an interaction between students, some spark of learning—would be carried forward and help someone live a richer life. He wanted his students to come to some deeper understanding of themselves, for their lives to be more fulfilling, because they had once passed his way.

And he *was* remembered. When Truman graduates stopped by the school to visit, it was always a good bet that they were looking for Volpe. He was a kind of local celebrity in the way that a longtime educator can be—always recognized by someone at the supermarket—but he never sought or expected any wider acclaim.

As the limousine approached Truman, it passed by a factory complex, the old 3M plant—Minnesota Mining and Manufacturing. It is now called the Bristol Commerce Center, the sort of Orwellian name given to a place where commerce has ceased to exist. No cars were in the vast parking lot. No cars are ever in the lot. Out to the left side of the road was Bloomsdale, a ramshackle, all-black enclave that its residents, employing an advanced sense of irony, had long called "Hollywood."

Mackintosh and his entourage were now entering Levittown proper, the postwar suburban colossus. The town's main intersection, called Five Points, is dotted with check-cashing agencies and pawnshops. Most of the 17,000 homes, mass-produced by developer William Levitt in the mid-1950s, are still standing—in defiance of predictions that the ticky-tacky structures would not last—but many are in need of a new roof and a coat of paint. Levittown has never been a pretty place, even in its best days. It is a suburban prairie, an expanse of flat terrain once farmed for potatoes before it was planted with house upon house and little else. If you visit in spring or summer, you might ask, *Does anyone in this place ever plant a flower?* As the town has aged and everything has become weathered and faded—the houses, the old cars and pickups in the driveways, even some of the people—it can seem like Levittown is receding back into the earth.

At the intersection of Green Lane and Mill Creek Road, the limo turned into the Truman High parking lot and was directed into the spot closest to the front door, the principal's space. A sort of pre-theater buffet, cold cuts and soft drinks, had been set out for Mackintosh and his traveling party in the guidance office. Volpe scurried in briefly to meet the famous producer, but he had a cast to ready for a show and, in any case, was far too nervous to eat. As he would recall, "I was delirious. I was hysterical. I thought, *How am I going to make it through this night?* I was running all around, trying to keep the kids calm, but they were fine. I was the one who was a mess."

Some of the other teachers gamely made conversation with Mackintosh, but the chasm was too vast. What were they going to say to him? *How are things in Malta?*

L evittown is not technically a city or any kind of municipality. The Levitt-built houses sprawl over three Pennsylvania townships—Bristol, Middletown, and Falls, as well as a tiny jurisdiction called Tullytown Borough—and the children who live in them go to one of three different public school districts. Truman is part of Bristol Township, referred to as the lower end of Levittown—a designation that applies both geographically and demographically.

Mackintosh had come to Levittown on a quest: to see if Volpe and Truman could stage his musical *Les Misérables* at a high enough level to persuade him to make it available to other high schools. Plays that get into the bloodstream of high school theater are lucrative sources of revenue for their creators and heirs—annuities that throw off income for generations without end. Mackintosh, of course, hardly needed the money himself. And he was known to be fastidious about not granting permissions until he could be confident his shows would be produced to a certain standard.

It was Steve Spiegel, then president of Music Theatre International, the leading licensing agent for Broadway productions, who made the decision on what high school would be asked to pilot the play. He needed someone who could collaborate with MTI to pare down the show, simplify some of the music and set, while still pulling off a production that would impress Mackintosh. Spiegel had seen some Truman High shows at festivals, and he had also traveled to Truman, which was not far from his home in Princeton, to see Volpe's work. "I could have called any of twenty-five thousand high school drama directors," he would recall. "That's about how many there are."

The party from New York took up two rows, front and center, on the sixth and final night of *Les Mis* at Truman. Mackintosh had not made the trip just to bless the production. It didn't work that way. It had to please him. The Truman stage was small and primitive, the fly space above it nonexistent. Generations of Volpe's students had heard him say, "If all we had was a bare stage with one light bulb, we could still do theater." They had more than that, but not much more.

Michael Kammerer, a senior, played the reformed convict Jean Valjean, and he was among those in the cast who, at Volpe's behest, had gone trash-picking for elements of the set. ("Any of you with a car, round up three people and go," were Volpe's instructions. "Get what you can, and we'll sort it out when you get back.") Kammerer had a rounded, soft look, but he managed to play Valjean with a degree of ferocity. He was typical of the students in Volpe's productions in that his life had been composed of more struggle than ease, though his circumstances were more complicated than most. He had come out as gay in tenth grade. His parents were divorced. His father had remarried numerous times, so he had half siblings and stepsiblings in multiple states and one in the Philippines. His mother was also remarried—to a man who did not like to hear him sing show tunes—so he practiced his vocals in the garage or sometimes while cutting the grass, so the power mower would muffle his voice.

From the stage, Kammerer could easily identify Mackintosh's

group, about twenty people in all. They didn't look local. He thought to himself: *Here is this famous guy from New York, and he's sitting on these awful wooden seats in our crappy auditorium. I hope he and his friends don't get splinters in their asses, because that would be really embarrassing.*

When I drive into Levittown, I come in from the south, up I–95, and I navigate a cultural divide of my own. I was born in Levittown, spent my whole childhood there, and was Lou Volpe's student near the beginning of his now four-decade-long career. He was my teacher, mentor, and friend, and he was central to what I would become.

I live now in Bethesda, Maryland, among people whose levels of income, education, and importance are still a marvel to me. We're less than a half mile from the National Institutes of Health, and my zip code has one of the highest concentrations of graduate degrees per capita in the United States. I've done well in my career, but within a couple of blocks of my home are two Pulitzer Prize winners. If I extended the radius another two dozen blocks or so, I'd take in numerous other Pulitzer recipients, as well as the chief justice of the U.S. Supreme Court. People on the Listserv of our public high school are always posting off-topic queries that seem to me like boasts: "Our family is going to Bali for spring break; can anyone recommend a good dive shop?"

The Levittown of my youth, and of Volpe's early years in teaching, was the great suburban dream before the invention of the dream's antidotes—video games, cable TV, the Internet. Levittown had no Main Street or downtown, no culture, not a single thing of visual interest. Its poverty was of a particular kind—lack of imagination, color, zest.

Rather than a childhood of wonder, I remember long stretches of boredom, that dull ache when you wish that it were already the next day, or that you could be someplace else, or that the boys you wanted to play baseball with had been home when you knocked on their doors. Some afternoons, I would just plant myself on my father's big overstuffed chair, a serially reupholstered splendor, its indeterminate color faded by cigar smoke, and listen for the Philadelphia *Evening Bulletin* to land with its thump against the screen door. By age twelve, I was a devotee of the political columnist Mary McGrory and the muckraker Jack Anderson. I looked at the horse-racing results because I liked the names of the horses and at the ads for the burlesque clubs because I liked the names of the dancers (Cella Phane, Pearl Harbour, Bermuda Schwartz, and so on). My comprehension of the adult world came from reading Dear Abby.

Several of the earliest memories I can summon make me think I was trying to carve out a rugged, Huck Finn–like existence in spite of the place. We explored in the one small wooded area within walking distance, looking for the hobos rumored to have made encampments. Where they would have been hiding was never clear. We climbed trees, sometimes first hammering two-by-fours into them to use as steps. We fished in an algae-choked lagoon known as the Black Ditch (its official name was the more stately Queen Anne Canal), and when the water froze over in the winter, we played ice hockey, using tree branches as sticks. One day, chasing an errant puck onto a patch of ice warmed by the sun, I fell through a crack into the frigid muck and had to be yanked by my elbows back to the surface.

We seemed to get everything wrong. Our favorite tree for climbing was called the Big Oak, which I later found out was a maple. All the streets in Levittown began with the first letter of their sections. I lived in Violetwood on Vulcan Road, which was intersected by Verdant Road—*VUR-dunt,* as in green or lush, but I never heard anyone, even my parents, call it anything but *ver-DANT.*

I had an older second cousin in the Navy, stationed in Europe, whom I met only once in my childhood. He came to stay with us and left behind a bottle of Old Spice cologne in the upstairs bathroom I shared with my brother and sister. It stayed there for years, second shelf of the medicine cabinet—milky-white bottle with the iconic line drawing of a sailing ship, a totem of our exotic visitor. As a teenager, I spent summer nights coasting around on my bicycle with friends, often well past midnight, miles in every direction. We told ourselves we were looking to meet girls, but I think we were trying to get somewhere that didn't look like everywhere else. We were not coming back to this town, any of us, once we left.

In the midst of this suburban void, my own flat Earth, I encountered Volpe. I was sixteen years old, and he was my eleventh-grade English teacher. Volpe was in his mid-twenties and just starting off in his career, but he wasn't one of those hippie teachers who talked about the Vietnam War, whole grains, and yogurt. I don't recall thinking of him as especially young, even in relation to the other teachers. He seemed fully an adult. He wore his jet-black hair stylishly long, but not too long, and you could tell he cared about how he looked and dressed.

My education to that point had been adequate. Levittown was a factory town, and the schools proceeded along a factory model of efficiency. We put in our shifts, and all the necessary information was drilled into us. It was the tail end of the baby boom in a heavily Catholic community, back when Catholics still listened to Rome on matters of birth control. My family, with its three children, seemed abnormally small. A family on a neighboring block had twelve children. It was routine for families to have five or six kids. Our class sizes were large—mid-thirties, sometimes close to forty—and many of our teachers were stretched to their limits just trying to keep us all from teetering over into chaos.

When I look back now on what first drew me to Volpe, I think it was just that I loved to hear him talk. He had a beautiful way of speaking—sentences and whole paragraphs just seemed to flow extemporaneously, organically. He seemed literary, to the extent we knew what that was, but not spellbound by his own voice. Just as naturally as his words poured forth, they stopped, and he asked what we thought. The class went back and forth like that day after day, and when the bell rang it was always a surprise and an intrusion.

Volpe's most pronounced quality was passion. He was so madly in love with the material he was teaching that I was swept up. I wanted to read the books he assigned to see if I could get the intense pleasure that he did from them. In his class that year, we read *The Great Gatsby, The Scarlet Letter, Invisible Man, Catcher in the Rye, The Sun Also Rises.* He gave us entry-level Bellow—*Seize the Day*—and Flannery O'Connor's *Everything That Rises Must Converge.* We read *Who's Afraid of Virginia Woolf?* and *A Streetcar Named Desire.* It was, at the time, the classic American canon, but also what Volpe felt like teaching and what he thought we would like.

I still remember the simple question he asked me not long after I started in his class. "Has anyone ever told you that you're a good writer?" I had just turned in a paper on Herman Melville's *Billy Budd,* a book I did not particularly like and definitely didn't understand, but I had attempted to make some original point, God knows what, and Volpe applauded my boldness. And, in fact, no one ever *had* pointed out that I wrote well. I don't think I had ever been expected to do much writing. I was an athlete, interested mainly (or solely) in whatever sport was in season. If I wrote well, I probably did so without any evident sense of pride or ownership.

In the spring we studied *King Lear* and *Hamlet.* Then about ninety of us, our three sections of honors English students, spent a weekend with Volpe and a couple of other teachers at the American Shakespeare Festival Theater in Stratford, Connecticut. It felt like an incredible extravagance. Seeing two plays a day. All of us together at a roadside motel.

Volpe was married then, and he and his wife, Marcy, had just had a son. The following year, as we moved toward graduation, he would invite some of us for dinners at his home, and Marcy would serve up big bowls of pasta with garlic bread. It was a different era. We talked about books. It felt grown-up and fun. It was a step out from our barren world and into a more enchanting one.

My father, a lawyer with a small-town practice, was the only college-educated adult I was aware of among all the parents of my friends and classmates. He had a second-floor walk-up office in the neighboring town of Bristol. My mother was his secretary, and they ate lunch together every day at a local diner, each with a copy of the tabloid *Philadelphia Daily News* spread out in front of them. On Sunday nights, they bowled. They hovered—happily, I'd say—between the hardscrabble Philadelphia neighborhoods they came from and a more cosmopolitan life they aspired to. When their monthly book group met at our house, I sat at the top of the stairs in my pajamas and eavesdropped. They read some popular psychology—Eric Berne's *Games People Play* sticks in my mind, because my father still quotes from it—and bestsellers like Leon Uris's *Topaz.* At home, we would occasionally get a knock on the door from a neighbor, and my father would step outside to talk, then drive off to bail someone out of jail.

Not long after I left for college, my father became a judge and my parents moved up-county, out of Levittown, across the Route 1 divide—and I didn't have many occasions to go back. But I talked (and later e-mailed) with Volpe every couple of years, and I followed his growing list of accomplishments. His productions kept being selected for the Main Stage at the International Thespian Festival. Only a handful of high school productions each year are judged worthy of this honor, so Volpe's drama troupe was like a college basketball team that keeps making it back to the Final Four—except that Truman was nothing like the big powerful teams that qualify for those repeat visits.

As well-regarded as Volpe's program had become, the *Les Mis* experience and the visit from Cameron Mackintosh catapulted it to a whole new level. When the show was over that night, Mackintosh was called up onto the stage, where he accepted a bouquet of flowers, took a bow, and said to the more than eight hundred people packed into the auditorium, "This is why I do what I do. It's not for the blockbusters. It's for this—to get theater into schools and into all levels of culture."

To everyone's shock, he did not jump right back into his limo and hightail it back to New York. He stayed for the cast party in the school cafeteria. Michael Kammerer was talking to friends when Mackintosh approached. The famous producer told him he was good in the role, even if his voice did crack once or twice in the higher registers. The two of them laughed, as if they were professional colleagues. Kammerer thought to himself, *How many real actors would want to be in this conversation?*

The whole cast felt as if they were in a dream. No one, in their experience, chose to come to Truman. And here they had put on a show, and Cameron Mackintosh, the most powerful man on Broadway, was celebrating with them, shaking their hands, telling everyone that they had been "brilliant, just brilliant!"

After *Les Misérables,* Music Theatre International came calling again (not for the last time), and in 2007, Truman became the first high school to stage a production of *Rent,* a show most high schools still will not touch because of its subject matter: AIDS, addiction, homosexuality, and homophobia. Allan Larson, the father of the late playwright Jonathan Larson, made the trip to Levittown and sat in the same unimproved auditorium and on the same wood-plank seats as Mackintosh had.

T hree years after Truman's staging of *Rent*—and thirty-six years after my own high school graduation—I was asked to give the commencement speech at Truman High. The high school my own children attended held its graduation ceremonies at Constitution Hall, near the White House. Built in 1929 by the Daughters of the American Revolution, it is a grand, historic venue, but one that I never liked for that purpose because it was just a rented space; it wasn't theirs. My own graduation had taken place on the high school football field.

Having grown up in a place I was dying to escape, then landing in one where I sometimes feel like an imposter, hardly makes me unique. Mobility, reinvention, identity: These themes are central to the American story, and, in fact, were threaded through the literature I read in Lou Volpe's classroom. (I had particularly liked Theodore Dreiser's *Sister Carrie,* not generally considered a terrific book. But Carrie Meeber got out! Out of her prison of a hometown in rural Wisconsin, into the clamor of big-city Chicago and ultimately New York. That it all ended badly for her did not make much of an impression on me.)

On the night of Truman's 2010 commencement, I parked across the road in the open field we knew as Booz's Farm, where my mother used to buy tomatoes, sweet corn, and melons from a stand at the intersection. Bloomsdale (Hollywood) was right down the hill, and the parents and siblings of its graduates walked by on the shoulder of the road on their way to the ceremony. I was led to a seat on a stage set down on about the ten-yard line, with the Blue Ridge section of Levittown—Butternut Road, Balsam Road, Bittersweet Drive—just behind me.

My mother had died about eight months earlier, and my eighty-four-year-old father, in a natty seersucker suit, sat in a reserved section with the school board president, an old friend. It was a cloudless seventy-five degrees. The sun was still in the sky, the humidity blessedly low. I felt happy, and oddly at home.

I had been told to speak for no more than five minutes, though three minutes would be better, which seemed perfect to me. At my son's high school graduation a week earlier, I had listened as a self-important cable news commentator droned on for thirty minutes about the future of the media in a digital world. At Truman that night, I passed along some gentle guidance, advising the graduates not to let go of cherished possessions that might seem childish now that they were passing into the adult world—their baseball gloves, skateboards, stuffed animals, favorite books. Thinking of the many hours I spent coasting around Levittown, talking with my friends and plotting our futures, I said they should hang on to their bicycles—or if they didn't already have one, buy one. I said something about how everyone should have a passport, which even as the words left my mouth seemed too exotic.

Volpe was up onstage that night, among several teachers who took turns calling out the names of graduates. I tried to remember details of my own graduation night. Had he been the one to call out my name? Had I thanked him? Had I even said a proper good-bye?

I know that he gave me a gift, a collection of Shakespeare's Sonnets. Inside the front cover, in a note dated June 3, 1974, he wrote, "As a prospective English major, I felt you couldn't survive without the Sonnets." He added, "Sure!" maybe just in case I was naive enough to believe the Sonnets were something I'd have to consult daily, like some kind of guide for living or dating. But I have kept the book, through many years and many moves, always on a prominent shelf, and have never once held it in my hands without thinking of Volpe and rereading his words.

I am my lawyer father's son, a journalist, rational. I don't say that everything happens for some divinely inspired reason. But as I stood at the podium facing the Truman High Class of 2010— including several who were children of my own high school class-mates—there was providence in the moment.

I had considered writing about Volpe many times, but other projects always got in the way or I found some reason not to. But from the moment I received the out-of-the-blue invitation to return to Levittown and give this speech, I knew it had happened for a reason: to let me know that it was time to tell the story of Lou Volpe and the magical things he does at Truman High.

BOBBY RYAN (LEFT) AND ZACH PHILIPPI
IN *GOOD BOYS AND TRUE.*

GOOD BOYS AND TRUE

Not everyone, of course, starts with an equal chance of being cast in a Volpe play. If a part calls for a handsome boy or a beautiful girl, Volpe doesn't put someone ugly in the role. (Does the basketball coach, out of a sense of political correctness, play a five-foot-five kid at center?) Volpe is a compassionate person, but he casts on merit, not out of empathy. At one audition, a boy with a great voice and big stage presence tries for a part. He seems like a good prospect. But he is known to have a rap sheet that includes convictions for assault, including one with a deadly weapon. After his reading, Volpe says to Krause that he hopes the kid gets his life turned around, but there is no way he is giving him a role. "It's more than I want to handle," he explains.

After everyone has read at the callbacks for *Good Boys*, Volpe tells the ten who are left, "It breaks my heart that some of you are

not going to be in this play. That's not bullshit. You were all astonishing. But there are only six roles."

The next morning, he posts the casting choices on the wall outside his classroom. Mariela Castillo, Zach Philippi, and Bobby Ryan
have won parts, along with Wayne Miletto, a would-be anchor of
Truman's defensive line except that he quit football for theater;
Britney Harron, a rarity among Volpe's actors in that she has taken
years of private lessons, in voice and dance; and Courtney Meyer, a
dazzling actress and sometimes lost soul whom Volpe and Krause
worry over when she is not under their watch. All six of them are
seniors and closely bonded as friends. Volpe is thrilled they auditioned well and held their places, as it were, because he considers
them one of the finest classes of actors he has ever directed, a special group that comes along no more than once a decade. (Miletto
and Harron won parts in *Rent* as ninth-graders, when *they* were the
"new.") He chose this play, in part, to show off their strengths, but
he could not just hand them the roles. He needed them to step up,
and they did.

"We're gonna have a great time," Bobby Ryan, the clown in the
group, says to the others on the first day they gather as a cast. "We've
got some chocolate flavor," he says, referring to Miletto, who is
black. "We've got some Latin flavor," he continues, looking at Castillo. "Hey, Mariela, are you gonna bring in some of those great rice
and beans your mom cooks?"

Mariela was part of a salsa duo with her older sister and likes to
say proudly that she is "one hundred percent Puerto Rican." She
shoots Bobby a wicked look. "I made those fucking rice and beans.
What do you think, I can't cook?"

Volpe does not demand decorum in any traditional way, just
excellence. As he begins to speak to the cast, Britney Harron, a diva

since he first encountered her as a freshman, is stretched out on one of the couches, her feet up, her eyes half open. But she is attentive in her own way, and Volpe doesn't care. He lays out the rehearsal schedule—basically, every day after school—and then tells them, "This is not a Nebraska play. It's too much on the edge of the knife for Middle America," by which he means that no matter how high the quality of performance they achieve, the adjudicators who make the selections for the International Thespian Festival will find the material too disquieting to honor with a Main Stage selection. "So I don't even want you to let that enter your minds," he continues. "We're going to create this play, this piece of art, and take it as far as we can take it, and we're going to be happy about that."

But he is just trying to tamp down expectations, and everyone knows it. Volpe wants to take *Good Boys* to Nebraska. That was the goal from the moment he chose it. He likes to shake things up. Likes to push the limits. If he could get *Good Boys* to Nebraska, it would create a stir. The kids in the audience would love it; some of the teachers would hate it. It would be a sensation.

Three of the cast members had been on the Main Stage two years before, as sophomores, performing a quirky play called *The Rimers of Eldritch* in a massive theater packed with an audience of 2,800. They wanted to go back, and the rest of the cast wanted to get there for the first time. (*Rimers* is a Lanford Wilson play, "a dark, brooding contemplation of a small ghostly town frozen in time and place, the mid-century in the Middle West," as *The New York Times* described it—so, in other words, a pretty good introduction to the level of work Volpe demanded.)

The schools chosen for Main Stages in Nebraska tended to be from well-heeled communities that poured money into their theater programs, like Grosse Pointe, Michigan, or the Woodlands, outside

Houston. A high school in Kenosha, Wisconsin, an outer suburb of Chicago, was another frequent Main Stage qualifier. When the Truman kids got to Nebraska, many of the other students they encountered just assumed that they came from one of these lucky kinds of places.

"Who's your diction coach?" a student from another school asked Bobby Ryan after the performance of *Rimers*.

"What's a diction coach?" he said.

If *Good Boys and True* was judged worthy, the trip to Nebraska would occur after graduation, during "beach week," when Truman's seniors traditionally cram into houses in the tacky Jersey Shore town of Wildwood. "But none of us would care about missing that," Bobby says as they get started with rehearsing. "Everybody in this cast—me and Wayne; Zach, Brit, Mariela, Court—we're all, like, best friends. We've been through everything together. Good stuff, bad stuff, relationships that got started and didn't end too good, you name it and we've survived it. We're like a family. If we did go to Wildwood, we'd all be in a house together, but if we get a Main Stage, it'd be like the same except we'd be having our beach week in Nebraska."

Going to Nebraska would also mean extending their time with Volpe by one week, a prospect the cast relishes. Each of them feels close to him. He is their teacher and friend—and for some, a father figure—but they had started out feeling intimidated by him, which shocked me at first. Afraid of Volpe? I never knew anyone who felt that way and couldn't imagine it. But he has an aura around him now and he controls something of value: parts in his productions. "It's our Broadway. That's how we think of it," Tyler Kelch, a tenth-grader, says. Kelch is not in the *Good Boys* cast, but is hoping to go to Nebraska as part of the stage crew. "It would be, like, the coolest thing ever." (I would learn that was a signature phrase of Tyler's— "coolest thing ever.")

Antonio Addeo, a Truman student from 2004 to 2007, was one of Volpe's most gifted actors in recent years. As a freshman, he won a lead role in Truman Drama's rendition of *Parade*. He has found some success in New York—he has an agent, gets auditions, and has been cast in small productions, though not yet Broadway. He hooked on to a touring show of the musical *Academy* that went to Seoul and won South Korea's version of a Tony for best play. "I've been auditioning in New York for two years now, and nothing was as stressful as my audition in ninth grade," he says. "It loomed that large to me."

He remembers hearing about Truman's drama director as far back as seventh grade, when he started performing in middle school shows. "People would say, 'Do you think he'll come to see our play?' Somebody would say they saw him walk through the door and everybody would freak out about it. The way he was talked about, I thought, *Who is this Volpe? I really want to meet him*. To me, he was like a mythic figure."

Good Boys is Bobby Ryan's fifth show at Truman. He auditioned for *Rent* as a freshman but didn't get a part. He was too scared to do well in his audition, then "cried like a baby" when he wasn't cast. The memory of once being kicked out of a Volpe rehearsal for being disruptive is still seared into him.

"That's it!" Volpe shouted at him one afternoon. "I'm tired of it. I don't even want to see your face anymore. Get out of the auditorium!" He added, for emphasis, "I don't know who this new Bobby Ryan is, but I don't like him. If you find the old Bobby Ryan, tell him I miss him."

The rebuke went straight to Bobby's gut. "The thing is, you can have fun and make jokes, but when it's time to be on task, you have to be on task," he says. "I realized I didn't like who I was being. I was being a real dick, getting in the way of the work being done. I almost threw up when I walked out the door. When you disappoint Volpe, it's like the worst thing in the world."

The Lou Volpe I had known in my youth was self-effacing. I wasn't even sure he would be comfortable with the idea of this book and the attention it would bring to him. But nearly four decades had passed, half a lifetime for both of us. The Volpe I have now come to know can be self-regarding, though it is a trait he tries his best to keep in check. He is accomplished, celebrated, still a good-looking guy. His cleverness, over time, has sharpened into a rapier wit. I have discovered, to my delight (and, yes, relief, since we have been spending a great deal of time together), that I still love to listen to him talk.

At a rehearsal, as another opening night draws near, he tells his cast, "You have become so good that every mistake you make has a spotlight on it." That seems to me such an economical yet elegant way of giving praise while making a demand.

He can be amazingly unflappable in the face of the surprising and bizarre things that occur in schools, and sometimes deadpan in ways that make me laugh. A student on the way into class approaches him at his desk, glances up at some posters of Sesame Street characters, and asks, "Mr. Volpe, did you know Big Bird?" It doesn't seem to be a joke, but it isn't clear whether he is asking if Volpe knew the late Jim Henson—if he knew the person inside the Big Bird costume—or if this student perhaps thinks Big Bird is real.

Volpe blinks twice, as if momentarily trying to decide. "No, I didn't know Big Bird," he finally answers. "But thank you for asking me that." He tidies up a pile of papers on his desk, takes a seat, and starts class.

In another class, he asks students to bring in an object of some personal meaning and say something about it. A girl comes in clutching an urn with her father's ashes and gives her talk, a bittersweet story of loss and memories, then puts the urn in his classroom closet for safekeeping—where it stays for a week. And then another. "Rebecca, honey, you know I still have those ashes?" he finally reminds her one day. "Oh, okay, thanks, Mr. Volpe," she says.

There are a great many ways, and more all the time, to put numbers on what occurs inside a school. One is the so-called Challenge Index, a mathematical equation invented by respected education writer Jay Mathews that divides the number of Advanced Placement and other college-level tests given at a high school by the number of its graduating seniors. It's very simple. The more tests given—and the more students enrolled in rigorous courses—the higher the ranking a school achieves. (This puts a lot of faith in the AP program, which is costly for students and revenue-generating for the College Board, the nonprofit that administers the tests.) At Truman High, close attention is paid to the PSSA (Pennsylvania System of School Assessment)—standardized tests mandated by the state. Truman's scores rise and fall from year to year—along with the anxiety levels of the administrators and teachers who are held responsible—and usually land just a hair above or below the "acceptable" line.

Volpe teaches according to no index or formula. He never expounds on education theory or education reform. His career and, in fact, his life, have followed no grand plan. When I return to

Levittown in 2010, he is teaching theater, not English—a full day of theater classes, four levels of them. Some who take his classes are honors students; others won't make it to college, either because they are not academic enough, they don't have the money, or they will get pregnant and have babies. Volpe's mission is the same as it has always been—to fill up his students with art, literature, and beauty and put material in front of them, rich in content and complexity, that no one else will. He has done this right through the age of No Child Left Behind and of unyielding educational metrics, which seems to me an act of utter subversion and unwavering conviction of purpose.

Over the decades, without much acclaim beyond his community and the world of high school theater, Volpe has transformed lives, thousands of them. He is like that person you never heard of who wins one of those MacArthur genius awards for creating astonishing success in the most unlikely of settings. His drama program, in its infancy when I was his student, started on its upward trajectory just as Levittown began going to pieces—as cultural poverty morphed into economic despair, as the jobs died, unions withered, families came apart, and even the churches emptied out.

His choices of plays have challenged his students, the school, and the still socially conservative community it serves. In the two years I spend with Volpe and his students, I sometimes wonder: Has he pushed it too far? Am I looking at the thing that is finally going to bring him down? His students walk right along with him, on a high wire, the "knife's edge," as Volpe likes to say. They come to believe in what he believes—not in art for art's sake, but in art as a way of fully embracing, and understanding, life.

They are not yet adults, but in that middle stage, late adolescence, coming of age. They have relationships that matter. Some of them have sex. They have seen enough—parents whose marriages blow apart, homes foreclosed on, family vehicles repossessed in the middle of the night, classmates who commit suicide—to know that life is not a Disney movie. Volpe expands their worldview and shows them that struggle and suffering are universal, but so are hope and resilience. "We deal with all the topics that out in the real world make people uncomfortable," Courtney Meyer, a member of the *Good Boys* cast, tells me one day. "That's one of the big reasons to do theater, right?"

Volpe brings ideas back to Truman from everywhere. On a trip one summer to Spain, he visited the Museo Reina Sofía in Madrid and was captivated by Pablo Picasso's *Guernica*, a painting commemorating the brutal bombing of a Basque town by German and Italian warplanes in 1937 in support of the Fascist leader Generalissimo Francisco Franco. He stood and looked at the painting for a long time, then sat on the floor in front of it for what seemed like hours. He had never been so moved by a work of visual art.

What called out to him from *Guernica* was both the terrible tragedy of what had occurred and the enormous power of art to explain and ultimately defeat man's most evil impulses. The fact of the painting itself, it seemed to him, was an answer—a defiance of the world's darkest forces. The mural was disturbing, of course, just like some of the plays he presented at Truman, but he found it ultimately hopeful. That year's major production at Truman was called *Confronting Guernica*. It was an original piece, written by Volpe and a Truman art teacher named Bill Double.

At a theater festival I attended with Volpe and his students, another highly respected high school drama director, Mark Zortman of York High School in central Pennsylvania, observed, "The rest of us do high school theater. Lou does theater."

It's not all darkness and tragedy. Volpe loves theatricality of any kind—all the magic and illusion that can be created onstage. He likes putting sound effects into comedies, the sillier the better, and he reacts to them like a delighted little boy. Every time he hears the crash or exaggerated sneeze or breaking glass at just the right moment is the first time he hears it—even if it's really the sixth performance of a show, after two months of rehearsals, and therefore the two hundredth time. I got used to sitting next to him in the Truman theater and having him nudge me with his elbow in reaction to his own trickery and whisper, "I just love that!"

Volpe's goal is not to send his students into the world of arts and entertainment, but many have been inspired to go into those occupations—among them, dozens who have acted professionally; two Emmy Award winners; a movie producer; numerous drama, dance, and voice teachers; set designers and other technical theater professionals; a television newscaster; a vice president at Bravo; the front man for a heavy metal band favored by mixed martial arts fans; the founder of a community theater in California; and the general manager of Madame Tussauds wax museum in New York.

The student who leads his tech crew in 2010 and 2011, Robby Edmondson, walks right out of Truman after graduation and into a job operating the light board at the Prudential Center in Newark for professional hockey and basketball games. The pay is $20 an hour, good money for a Levittown kid right out of high school, and it helps pay his tuition at the University of the Arts in Philadelphia. Volpe also pays Edmondson to continue to help out at Truman productions in the year after his graduation, until a richer high school nearby lures him away with an offer of $12,000 for three months' work. "Good for Robby," Volpe says. "He really needs that money."

He keeps no running list of the whereabouts or exploits of

his former students, which sometimes frustrates me because I want to know about them. He mentions one Emmy winner, but forgets about the other one. (Both of them, Bob Schooley and Jim Schumann, are producers at Nickelodeon.) It isn't a matter of favoritism, but just that he lives in the present and is focused on his current students. "Oh, have I never told you about her?" he says after I tell him I have received an e-mail from Elizabeth Cuthrell, his former student and a highly regarded screenwriter and independent film producer in New York. (Her movie *Jesus' Son*, which she adapted from a collection of stories by Denis Johnson, made the 1999 top-ten lists of Roger Ebert, *The New York Times*, and the *Los Angeles Times*.) "Stunning," he says when I ask about her. "Brilliant. Homecoming queen."

In talking to many of Volpe's former students and his current ones, I am struck by how many believe that he knows them better than they know themselves, that he knows, at the very least, where a particular light switch is located and reaches inside and turns it on—just as he did with me when he asked if anyone had ever noticed that I could write. "He saw something in me that I would have never recognized in myself," Sheri Cunningham, a Volpe student in the mid-1990s, says. It is a version of what I would hear dozens of times from other Volpe students through the generations. In fact, it is rare to talk to a former Volpe student who does not volunteer a story just like that.

Elizabeth Cuthrell recalls being fourteen years old, a high school sophomore, and in the grip of turmoil and unhappiness in her home life when she first encountered Volpe. "Lou steered my life away from something dark and devouring, and toward something unimaginably happy," she says. "He took me on. From tenth to twelfth grades, he recited to me a mantra about how I could do anything. The recitation wasn't literal, but it was in the subtext of every interaction we had. He praised my writing, my acting, my dancing. He laughed at my jokes."

I sometimes look at a Facebook page devoted to Truman Drama, where Volpe's former students communicate with one another and reminisce about what the program meant to them. A student from the late 1990s, Raul Castillo, whose younger sister, Mariela, I have come to know as one of Volpe's most accomplished performers, wrote about participating in *Confronting Guernica*: "This play forever changed my life. It gave me the fearlessness that I proudly wear on my sleeve to this day, showed me how beautiful and ugly us human beings really are, and I got to wear a dance belt. Uncomfortable!"

When I visited with Ansel Brasseur, a former lead in Truman's plays, he was partway through an MFA program at New York University, a "theater boot camp," as he put it, consisting of fourteen-hour days. On full scholarship, he was one of eighteen students, whittled down from hundreds who auditioned. As an undergraduate at Cornell, he started off as a public policy major. "I wanted to just make theater a hobby, but I couldn't," he explained. "I think Volpe knew I would come back to it. It's this weird feeling I had."

Brasseur did not seek out Volpe's advice, "but I felt his presence. He's that person you encounter in your life who shows you a bravado you didn't know yourself that you had. It's a gift that he gives you."

LOU VOLPE AND HIS SISTER, ROSEMARY,

WITH THEIR MOTHER, LILY.

WE WERE AN AMERICAN FAMILY

When Volpe tells me about his younger years, I imagine them taking place in black-and-white, like in an old movie. He was born in 1948. For most of his childhood, his family lived in the far northern reaches of Philadelphia, in what is called with some inspired grandiosity the Great Northeast, a kind of suburb within the city, similar to neighborhoods in Queens where people settled after they had achieved a measure of success. But many of them did bring their old ways with them.

The adults in Volpe's household—his mother, father, and maternal grandmother—spoke Italian to one another, but not to him or his younger sister, Rosemary. His grandmother could speak virtually no English and rarely left the house. She stayed by his mother's side as the two of them cooked, cleaned, and sewed. Volpe loved being able to understand Italian, but could not speak it fluently. His mother and father spoke to their children only in English as a point of pride and a matter of definitively severing the bond to the Old World. "We were an American family," he says, "and my father was the most American person I ever knew. He went into the Marines in World War II. He only made it as far as Puerto Rico. I think it was like a vacation. But oh my God, he was a Marine for the rest of his life. He had a flag flying 365 days a year, a huge flag on a pole in front of the house. The Yankees and barbecuing and his lawn and his garden were his life. He had the best lawn in the world."

It would have been highly unusual to be a New York Yankees fan in Philadelphia, which had two major league baseball teams of its own, one in each league, through the mid-1950s. But Thomas Volpe may have believed that rooting for the Yankees made him even *more* American.

I am with Volpe at his town house in Yardley, Pennsylvania, a pleasant community about fifteen miles north of Truman High. The walls of his living room, nearly every inch of them, are taken up by theater posters of shows he has seen in New York, with one wall devoted entirely to Sondheim and a prominent place given over to his favorite, *Sunday in the Park with George*. Outside, his own American flag hangs from a pole above the front door. "I would always have a flag, wherever I live, because of my father," he explains.

It is about a month after I delivered the graduation speech. Volpe, it becomes slowly clear to me, still has much to teach me— but we are starting out on an entirely new relationship. The one we already have is, in some ways, stuck back in the mid-1970s: I still look up to him, and he is proud of my successes. But now we are two middle-aged men. I have a job to do and will not get very far forward as one half of a mutual admiration society. My interest is in learning how he became the person who built this vaunted drama program, who has endured four decades at a challenging school, who makes art that dazzles, stuns, outrages, terrifies, and delights people in a town that, without his presence, would be perfectly content with fare that runs the gamut from *Bye Bye Birdie* to *High School Musical.* We talk first about his family, or *three* families, really—the one he grew up in, the family he built with the woman he married, and his most enduring family, the one at Truman High.

Over time, one of the things that I come to see is how deeply Volpe knows his students. How couldn't he? They take chances onstage that reveal their inner selves. But it is also true that the very things they learn from being involved in theater—empathy, the ability to imagine lives other than their own; the actor's gift for giving a character a backstory, a biography beyond what the playwright put on the page—allow them to know him.

You have to "find your character," he tells them, meaning they have to imagine lives they cannot fully know. Not the prosaic biographical details, but beyond that. What is it like to *be* that person? What resides deep within, and what is missing? Volpe gives his students only hints of his personal life—tells them about the show he just saw in New York, the purchase he made at the mall—so they have to imagine the rest, intuit it, figure out what it's like to be Louis T. Volpe, high school theater teacher.

I travel with Volpe and a group of students one night to see another high school perform a musical called *The Drowsy Chaperone,* a very good show with a really dumb title. The central character, known only as the Man in the Chair, is a finicky, brilliant middle-aged man, a lover of the theater and of language. He directs an absurd play within a play, orchestrating actors onstage to whom he is invisible. The Man in the Chair is not easy to know. He keeps things hidden. He is charming and cultured and clever—but opaque. You sense that offstage, out of public view, he is lonely.

Volpe and his students love the show, and one of them says afterward, "Mr. Volpe, you're the Man in the Chair!" He does not disagree. The character was played by a gifted high school actor, someone talented beyond his years, the only student actor I would see anywhere who rivaled Truman's best. After the show, he comes walking by, and Volpe's students insist on getting pictures of him with their teacher. Volpe eagerly agrees and poses, beaming, as his students click away with their cell phones.

A t his town house, Volpe shows me pictures of his parents. His mother, Lily, had the olive-toned complexion of her forebears, who came from southern Italy, all the way down in Sicily. Her father had immigrated to America first with his oldest son, leaving his wife and other children behind until he found work. Lily was the youngest of her parents' nine children and the only one born in America.

Volpe's father, Thomas, came from northern Italian stock and was lighter-skinned, almost Irish-looking. That side of the family was more sophisticated. It had more money, a little more education. It was never spoken of, but there was no love lost between the families. They must have been together, on some occasion or another, but Volpe has no memory of it. On both sides, everyone had their own little business. "Hoagie shops, pizza parlors, things like that," he says. "It was a cliché. We were living in a cliché."

Thomas Volpe owned his own small business, a tavern called the Rex Café. "That was his little thing. It was like a corner bar, but with a back room with food and tables and a kitchen. Every once in a while, if he had to do something, or if he was getting a shipment in, he would take us down there. We would sit in the dark and look around. My sister was always so much more adventurous. One day, he was getting us sodas with cherries in them, and we went around in the back of the bar and we found a gun. And we picked it up. He saw us with that gun, and I can remember the fear in his face. He was a very gentle, calm, kind man. I very rarely saw his temper, but when I did, it was terrifying."

The kids did not see much of their father, and Lily Volpe did not see much of her husband. The Rex Café was all the way on the opposite side of the city, and he worked day and night. In the mornings, he ordered the food and liquor and stocked it. Later in the day and into the night, he served his customers. He found time to drink with his buddies at the bar. At closing time, he cleaned the place up before coming in the next day to do it all again.

Volpe's mother was "the centerpiece of the family. The hard-edged one and the ruler." She was, as well, "tenacious, bold, and risky."

She never believed that being safe was worthwhile. If either of her children had a question about what to do, and one option involved a risk and the other did not, her answer was always the same: "What's the worst thing that can happen?" She was never the kind of person to say, "You're comfortable, you have a great life, don't change anything."

So while Volpe's father worked behind the bar at the Rex Café, his mother opened the world to her two children. She took them to the public library, bypassing the little branch nearby to go instead to a big stone structure in one of the city's historic neighborhoods, a cathedral of books, where her son devoured the Greek myths and spent hours trying to discern the meanings of the various gods and goddesses. On weekends, she took them to the movies to see big Hollywood extravaganzas like *Cleopatra* and to the theater for classics like *Guys and Dolls* and *South Pacific* (which his father, the superpatriot, attended). They went almost every Saturday into the center of the city to Philadelphia's finest department stores—Strawbridge's, Gimbels, and Wanamaker's, where afternoon tea was served in its Crystal Tea Room.

Lily Volpe loved fashion and was an inspired seamstress. At first she made things just for her family—dresses for Lou's sister, Rosemary, wedding gowns for cousins and nieces. Word got out and it became a business, quite a successful one. She would do anything from putting up a hem to making a ball gown.

Thomas Volpe built a workshop in the basement for his wife's business, with big mirrors for fittings. The basement itself was "gargantuan," Volpe says, with enough room for a couch and a settee to make up a little waiting room, almost like one of the department stores. "It was beautiful. She became as successful financially, or more successful, than he was. They never shared anything about their finances, of course, but I judged it by the cars. One day, he showed up in a Cadillac, and I figured out they were doing pretty well."

Volpe and his younger sister, Rosemary, were exceedingly close as children, and still are. She lives in the Philadelphia area, about thirty minutes from him, and works as the office manager of a software firm. "Oh, you want to talk to me about His Majesty, my mother's favorite?" she says to me when I first make contact with her. She is kidding, of course, though that kind of comment within families is never entirely a joke.

She tells me that her brother's artistic eye, his tastes, his whole way of relating to the world, come through their mother. He would spend hours by her side doing art projects. Once, when she was invited to some sort of masquerade party that required a mask, "Lou and her started with a paper bag and just added elements to it—this went on for hours—and when they were done, it was like something from New Orleans. It was just beautiful."

Plenty of Philadelphians back then still called their neighborhoods by the name of the local Catholic parish. One of the biggest, and certainly the one with the most dramatic name, was Most Precious Blood of Our Lord, also known as MPB. The Volpes lived within the boundaries of Maternity Blessed Virgin Mary, or BVM. Lou went to Mass every Sunday, served as an altar boy, and attended BVM's grammar school before moving on to Father Judge High School, which had three thousand students. All boys.

From the first day of ninth grade, he thought to himself, *Jesus, this is not going to be a very good four years.* "I was different than the other boys," he says, "and I knew it and they knew it."

Father Judge was a "humorless cement box" with numerous stairwells and endless hallways that at class changes became a swirling sea of boys in matching blue jackets and red ties. The school's instructors were priests from the Oblates of St. Francis de Sales, an order dedicated to a seventeenth-century French cleric known for his sunniness and kindness who is sometimes called the "gentleman saint."

Volpe's science teacher that first year used to break Life Savers in half with his teeth and put one part in his mouth and return the other to the foil wrapper to eat later. He asked Volpe, incongruously, if he "came from a dockworker family," which he figured was intended as an insult. Always adept at turning pain into humor, he wondered later, "Did this teacher have a problem with *On the Waterfront?*" Another instructor was a terrifying man who sat in a chair atop his desk during exams to see if anyone was cheating.

Volpe considered many of his classmates to be mean-spirited and some to be outright dangerous. It was a *Lord of the Flies* atmosphere—they taunted and sometimes physically assaulted weaker classmates. "The priests—not all, but many of them—would see boys attacked and they would look the other way. And they would laugh. That part of it is absolutely burned into my brain. Some of the priests were very open about the fact that they wanted to be friends with the bullies, the leaders.

"And then you'd go to Mass, and they were parading around in their vestments, giving sermons about humanity. And you'd say, *Wow, that was well rehearsed. They should have been in the theater.* I thought about this many times after I became a teacher, and I told myself I'd never be that person who encourages or allows that kind of cruelty, for any reason."

Father Judge's football team was perennially one of the best in the city. Volpe did not miss a game, home or away, for all four years. He always did the driving, transporting friends and his sister in an ancient Pontiac with scratchy woolen seats that his father bought him when he turned sixteen—"a big, heavy, vulgar automobile that I absolutely loved." In his senior year, the football team won the city championship, beating Frankford High, the Public League representative. Volpe was among the masses who rushed onto the field and helped pull down the wooden goalposts, and for many years he kept a little chunk of one of them as a souvenir.

Several of the best players on that team were his grammar

school classmates and fellow altar boys, and they served as his protectors. "To this day, I don't really know why, but they continued to feel close to me. I was accepted by them, and they would not allow me to be victimized. They saved me, whereas other boys weren't saved."

Volpe dated in high school, went to dances, had girlfriends. He first met Marcy Hargrove at his junior prom, where they both had other dates, then didn't see her again until a couple of years later, when he was a student at La Salle College, another Catholic institution, and she came to a mixer on campus. She was smart, funny, and sharp-tongued. If she had been born a generation later, or even a half generation, she surely would have gone on to college, but she worked as a secretary.

Marcy's life had not been easy. She was adopted at birth—had never known her birth parents—and remembers the pain of being told by her adoptive parents that she was "illegitimate." Her adoptive father was schizophrenic and for a time lived at Philadelphia State Hospital at Byberry, a sprawling mental institution that was later closed by court order because it inhumanely "warehoused" its patients. Family pictures show Marcy at Sunday picnics on the grounds of the state hospital, always in a colorful summer dress and holding a cloth parasol.

She had a boyfriend when she met up with Volpe that second time, but he was in Vietnam. Volpe was going to school during the week and selling home furniture on weekends at Strawbridge's, one of the downtown department stores where he used to shop with his mother. (He had always had some kind of job since he was eleven years old and began delivering the Philadelphia *Bulletin* on his bicycle.) He was also in the ROTC, so two days a week he wore a military uniform to campus, drilled, and learned to fire a rifle. He kept his shoes shined and his brass polished. He expected ultimately to be drafted and serve—the war was in full swing, and he was nothing if not dutiful—but a high blood pressure reading kept him out of the military and Vietnam.

Marcy and Lou went to a jazz concert together, and she had a great time despite her avowed dislike of jazz. They started spending more time together. She considered him the most handsome man that she had ever been with, the best dancer, the hardest worker. They were married on July 11, 1970, about a year after his graduation, in a morning wedding Mass followed by a reception at a catering hall in Cherry Hill, New Jersey. Her bridesmaids wore dresses in lemon and lime colors. His groomsmen wore morning coats. "It was a morning wedding," he recalls. "I think I insisted on that."

Marcy was not Italian, and Lily Volpe referred to her as "the American girl," which she pronounced with a Sicilian inflection— "the *a-MEHR-ugn* girl." (This despite the fact that her day-to-day English was entirely unaccented.) Marcy took pride in her ability to hold up her end of the conversation at social gatherings with her husband's college friends and, later, with his faculty colleagues. She enjoyed the secondhand education she got from typing his graduate school papers.

The newly married couple picked up an inexpensive painting at a yard sale—a blue-eyed, blond princess standing next to a dark, bearded prince—and hung it in their living room. It wasn't a very good piece of art, but it was their own little joke. They were the prince and princess. Lou Volpe was, as well, gay, which he knew on the day he was married and, in fact, sensed long before he could give what he was feeling a name.

. . .

Volpe had spent his college years as an English major, reading novels and writing papers, which was exactly what he wanted to do—"I thought, This is great! I'm going to school and doing the thing that I love"—though hardly an approach tailored to job-seeking.

The Vietnam War, however, had taken some young Americans out of the workforce, and the school-age population was still booming, so teachers were needed. He enrolled in a couple of education courses at Temple University the summer after his graduation, having taken none at La Salle, and was granted an "emergency teaching certificate." The chairman of Truman's English department recognized a passion and potential in Volpe and hired him in November of 1969, a few months after the school year started, to teach English.

On his first day of teaching, Volpe was surprised to see sheep roaming in the field across the street at Booz's Farm. As he got to know his students, he learned that many had never been to Center City Philadelphia, where the city's restaurants, theaters, and museums were, all of twenty miles away. Their parents, in many cases, had been raised in city neighborhoods, but it was as if they had made a clean break, an escape.

But Levittown, in other respects, was not so different from the tree-lined neighborhood in which Volpe was raised. He had not, after all, grown up above his father's Rex Café in gritty South Philly, nor would he have wanted to. He sought his own kind of comfort. He was an adventurous reader and theatergoer, but less so an adventurous person. He liked the idea of being a conventional person, a schoolteacher and family man, and Levittown was full of people seeking conventional lives. "They wanted to be safe and protected and have a pleasant life," Volpe said. "I totally got that and I never looked down on it."

His work ethic was set at the same high level as those relatives of his who put in murderous hours inside their taverns, pizza joints, and hoagie shops. That first year, he got in the habit of arriving at school by six A.M., a routine he would maintain for the next forty years. He liked the dimly lit corridors of the empty building, the peace, the promise of the day ahead. He would drink his coffee, go through lesson plans, or sometimes just read a book. "I was terrified, of course, but I knew there was something inside of me that wanted to give this knowledge to people, and I really believed I could do that," he recalls. "As scared as I was, I loved it right away. Every single day in the classroom was like a celebration. It was just this wonderful feeling that I was doing exactly what I was meant to do."

His first students were in the vo-tech program—vocations and technology—and took half their classes in such disciplines as auto mechanics, carpentry, baking, welding, and hairdressing. Volpe figured if he made literature compelling enough, they would enjoy it. He never imagined he would turn any of them into scholars, "but I'd like to think I helped them in some way in the lives they went on to live."

Before he became a teacher, Volpe had no experience in theater—*none*. It is the great oddity of his career. He had never acted, never painted a set, never worked on a stage crew, never ushered or as much as sold a ticket. He loved the theater and talked about it with friends and with his mother. Voraciously read reviews and theater histories. But he was strictly a patron.

A couple of months into his first year of teaching, he was headed home at the end of a day when he heard the sounds of a rehearsal in progress in the auditorium, which was just steps from his exit to the parking lot. He opened the door and took a seat in the back row, watched for a few minutes, then continued on his way. He began dropping in several times a week, staying longer, watching with a more critical eye. There is a particular moment he remembers vividly. The cast was rehearsing *Camelot*, the musical. The drama sponsor, a woman named Joan Mott, a "very nice person" and his colleague on the English faculty, was staging a scene and blocking the actors. "And I'm sitting and watching—and this sounds so self-confident—but I said to myself, *Hmm, I wouldn't do it that way. I wouldn't have them there. I wouldn't have them say it like that.*"

The next day, he asked Mott if she needed any help with the musical. No, not on the creative end, she said, but would he want to help with ticket sales and other administrative tasks? Eager to deepen his involvement at the school, and never afraid of putting in more hours, Volpe readily agreed. At the end of the school year, Mott left the faculty to move to a farm in Maryland with her husband to raise chickens, and Volpe applied to be assistant drama director. "I thought, *Oh my God, she's buying a chicken farm. I guess she really, really doesn't want to be in education anymore.*"

Applying to be the *assistant* drama director was a classic rookie teacher's mistake. There was such a job on the books, but no one had filled it for years. If it paid anything at all, it would have been pennies per hour. If you did the math on what the drama *director* got paid and figured in all the hours required, it probably did not amount to any more than two bucks an hour.

One day that summer, Volpe came back into his house from running errands and Marcy handed him an envelope from the school district. It was from the principal. "Dear Lou," it said, "Congratulations on your appointment as drama director." The letter went on to express confidence that he would do a terrific job and take the program to great new heights. Volpe thought, *They've made a mistake. I don't know the techniques. I don't know the nomenclature. I don't know anything that I haven't seen from a seat in the audience or read in a book.* No one else, though, had applied. He became the school's drama director by default.

In his first year, he considered the vast array of material he could choose from—all of Shakespeare, of course; one of the very serious Eugene O'Neill dramas; light fare from Neil Simon; old standards like *Our Town* and *Arsenic and Old Lace.* He finally decided: *We'll do something classic. We're going to do* Antigone, *but we'll do it very modern.*

The set was all white—white pillars, white ramps, white everything. It looked like some kind of soap commercial gone terribly wrong. He costumed the actors in green plastic trash bags. Their armor was sculpted out of foil, Reynolds Wrap purchased at the local Acme supermarket. (At least no one would be able to say the new drama director didn't stay within budget.) Just one performance was scheduled. The "saving grace" was that no more than fourteen people came to watch. "It was the biggest disaster in theater, all of theater. I couldn't tell you what made me do it that way. When it was over, people did that thing where they clap, but very slowly. No one would look at me. Not even Marcy. Everyone averted their eyes."

Volpe had no choice but to get some training in the theater or endure further humiliation. He attended productions at other local high schools and made friends and mentors of their drama directors. He took classes anywhere he could find them—back at La Salle, at Temple, at Philadelphia's University of the Arts.

He started with basics—classes that made him go through exercises like picking a penny off the floor and accounting for every part of the multistep process to hammer home the lesson that every movement onstage has a purpose. He spent part of a summer at the drama school at Northwestern, where the program included a three-day-a-week, three-hour improv session with Dawn Mora, a venerated instructor. "We had to create three different characters from three generations—a child, a middle-aged man, and an old man. They had to have a background, a life, and we had to show them to her. She wanted to see everything about them. When you were finished, you were soaking wet." He learned about acting from Mora, but more so how to teach it in an atmosphere of "complete trust and honesty. She accepted nothing less."

Volpe obviously had innate talents that related to theater—an ear for language, a feel for pacing and for calibration of emotional pitch, an acute visual sense. But it was untapped and entirely untrained. From the day he started as drama director, "I knew what I wanted to do on the stage, but I didn't really know how to get there. I had to learn balance, harmony, order, design, composition. I had to learn that all good theater is a process and you must go through it totally or an element will be missed somewhere, and the end result will be nothing more than mediocre."

There is a difference between people who strive and those who merely work hard. Levittown was full of hard workers, hourly wage-earners who eagerly stepped forward for overtime shifts and spent what extra money they had to repave their driveways, build rec rooms, or buy RVs. The community in its early years was a destination; it was full of people who felt they had *arrived*. Three years into Volpe's tenure as head of the drama program, a new principal took charge. Larry Bosley was a smart man, ambitious for himself (he later became a superintendent) and for the school. He was himself a striver, and he sought to instill that ethos in the school. He told Volpe that great high schools had great theater programs that put on big, showy musicals, and that's what he wanted. Bosley directed a little more money into the program and made sure Volpe had an assistant as well as the energetic support of the music and visual arts departments.

Volpe's first musical, *You're a Good Man, Charlie Brown*, ran for three performances—a Friday and Saturday night with a matinee in between—of nearly packed houses. The next year, Volpe did *Bye Bye Birdie* and again nearly sold the performances out.

One way that high school theater bears some similarity to professional theater, or any kind of show business, is that ticket sales matter. The more money you take in, the more that you have to pour into future performances. Bosley wanted shows that stretched over two weekends so word of mouth could promote the last two shows. Volpe agreed, and he also liked the idea "because the kids have that week in between where everyone they know is patting them on the back and telling them how great they are. They put so much into it; it's nice if it doesn't end so fast."

Volpe began to dabble in somewhat edgier fare, beginning with *Pippin*, a dark and existential musical inspired by the story of Charlemagne's rebellious son. As directed by Bob Fosse on Broadway, the dancing was raucous, and the themes—Pippin's relationships with multiple women, his struggles with authority and the church—were overtly presented. "Now everybody does *Pippin*," Volpe says. "It's safe and tame by today's standards. But it was controversial then."

He toned the show down some, but the subject matter was the same. Volpe did not consider it gratuitous or overly sexualized, but neither was it dated and musty. Its themes—a young person searching for his place in the world, pushing boundaries, rejecting the established order—were ones he would come back to again and again. What could be more appropriate and compelling for high school actors and audiences? And wasn't it better to explore and work them out in a rockin' musical than in some droning, hectoring lecture from their teachers or parents?

Some of the faculty, though, were not thrilled. "A few teachers were furious, and they let me know it," he recalls. A mother who attended the play with her high school daughter complained about it in a memorable letter to the local newspaper. "I thought I was going to see Pippi *Longstocking*!" she wrote. But Pippin did sell tickets. And even those who had problems with its content could see that Truman Drama was getting better and Volpe—as the letter hiring him seemed to too optimistically predict—really was taking it to new heights.

Over the course of the two years I spend with Volpe—at rehearsals and performances, in his classroom, around the school—it never stops feeling strange to walk the corridors of Truman High and encounter decades-old memories and even vestiges of old panics. Any sighting of a mathematical equation on a blackboard still makes me queasy. When I glimpse a periodic table through the open door of a chemistry classroom, it looks like no less of a jumble.

The lunchroom brings back other memories, including the day

in eleventh grade when I walked in wearing a pair of bell-bottoms with wide pastel stripes—pink, green, blue, orange—along with platform shoes purchased from a store called the Wild Pair, and one of the school's prettiest and blondest cheerleaders looked me up and down and said, "You're kidding, right?" I said, Yes, I'm kidding. My classmate David Uosikkinen, who would become the drummer for the rock band the Hooters, wore platform shoes; I apparently believed I could pull off the same look.

A ball field at one corner of the school calls forth the end of my senior year and my last honest-to-God fistfight, a scrap with a football player named Richard Harrison, a perfectly nice guy I'd known since first grade, during a daylong game of team handball—a rough sport made even more brutal by the fact that we didn't actually know the rules. It was my very last day of twelfth grade; what were they going to do, suspend us?

Some obvious things have changed at Truman, starting, somewhat oddly, with the name of the school itself. When I attended, it was called Woodrow Wilson High School, its name since the doors opened in 1959. A few years after I graduated, a second high school in the district closed, and its student population was subsumed into Wilson. In order not to ruffle feelings and to give the impression that a "new" institution was being formed out of these merged schools, the Bristol Township School Board, a body of faithful Democrats, gave the school the name of a more recent Democratic president, Harry S Truman. It took me a while to get used to calling my old school by its new name.

Truman can be a rough place. One day when I pull into the school's parking lot, all the usual spaces are taken, and I find myself in an unfamiliar section where a space is set off by a sign that

says Reserved for Probation Officer. It is one of many little re-
minders that I am not in Bethesda anymore; I'm back home.

Volpe's informality with his students is a way of relating that
some teachers at the school do not believe they could maintain
without losing authority. When order and peace prevail at Truman,
it is because the administration and faculty keep a tight rein—or at
least that's what the adults running the show believe.

The seniors have a tradition of going out to breakfast en masse
one morning in the spring. In 2012, they show up for school
late after this event, about nine A.M. They have the book thrown at
them. Their parents are called and lunch detentions are handed
out, along with Saturday school for those with previous infractions.
"I need to get out of this place before it strangles me," says one
of Volpe's students, a girl ranked fifth academically in the senior
class. "They're making such a huge deal of this. We weren't doing
anything mean or destructive. We were at a diner, eating eggs!"

I would never have described Volpe as a tough guy. In my mind,
the teachers who fit that description were the football coaches with
the burr haircuts and quick tempers. But it turns out that he is a
very tough guy. It's the only way he could have survived at Truman,
particularly for four decades. He knows what he wants and does not
easily back down. He has not been beyond dispensing or at least
threatening a little street justice in the school corridors.

When Tracey Krause was Volpe's student in the mid-1990s, she
didn't get parts at first because Volpe wasn't sure he could depend
on her. Later, after she had found a place in his program, Volpe
discovered that her boyfriend had been physically abusive to her.
He went looking for him between classes. When he found him, as
Krause put it, "Lou jacked him up"—Levittown-speak for grabbing

someone by the collar and lifting him off his feet—"and told him it was going to stop right then and there. He did it right in B Hall. And that was the end of it. Lou scared the shit out of him."

The composition of the neighborhoods that Truman draws from has changed in some small ways. A number of students at Truman have the last name Patel, a common Indian name and one I never heard in my days in Levittown. Truman also now includes a sprinkling of Hispanics among its 1,600 or so students—from Puerto Rico, Mexico, and Central America—whereas in my day I was aware of just one, a girl from Honduras, who would marry a good friend of mine.

Volpe has a student in his drama program by the name of Rachel Greenberg. "I hope you don't mind my asking," I say to her one day, "but are you Jewish?"

"No," she replies, "I'm Irish Catholic. I think my great-grand-father was Jewish."

Years ago, the schools on the other side of Levittown, the upper end, had substantial numbers of Jewish students, but I was one of no more than ten Jewish students in my graduating class. As far as I can tell, there are no longer any Jews (other than teachers) at the school. The Reform synagogue in my part of town, which my family attended, struggled along for years as its congregation dwindled, before it finally shut its doors in 2011. The Conservative synagogue moved out of Levittown north of Route 1. Truman's longtime debate and forensics coach, Carl Grecco—he is retired as a teacher now, but began at the school even before Volpe—told me that many of his former standouts have gone on to be lawyers and doctors, among them a specialist at the Cleveland Clinic whom he has consulted on his own medical care. "At least half of them were Jewish kids," he said, "but we don't get any of them anymore. It's been years."

Minus the Jews, however, and with a few other minorities now added into the mix, the demographics of Truman remain what they always were—predominantly white working class, with an African-American population that hovers around 10 percent. In the 2010 U.S. Census, white residents accounted for 88 percent of Levittown's population.

Certain characteristics of the community have remained constant. For example, it is not a place where people generally wait to have children until they are in their late twenties or early thirties—until their careers have lifted off. Sometimes they don't even wait till they're out of high school. Tracey Krause, when one of her own children was in kindergarten, had a senior girl in one of her classes with a child in kindergarten. "We could compare notes!" she says.

When I was a student at the school, my coeditor of the high school newspaper got his girlfriend pregnant. They married and had a daughter before senior year. Volpe always had a knack for imparting life lessons without being gross or embarrassing about it. For whatever reason, I've always remembered what he said when word got back to him that this fellow was claiming that he and his girlfriend had sex just that one time. "Once people start doing that," he told us, "they don't usually stop."

One day in the spring of 2011, a young woman pokes her head into Volpe's classroom and says, "Volp, I'm having a boy!" At first I hope maybe this is a young-looking teacher, but I pretty much know that's not the case.

"Isn't that what I told you?" he answers back.

"Yeah, that's what you said, that it'd be a boy."

After she leaves, he says, "She's sassy. Sometimes she gives me a hard time, but she's very smart. One day she left a paper on her desk with some doodling, and it said, *Volpe is awesome.* I put it up on the door—she has to walk past it every time she comes in here. But she won't get through the year. She's having that baby pretty soon."

The classroom session that follows involves students prepping for a "night of theater" at Truman, not one of his ballyhooed productions, but just a one-act and a series of monologues that might, at most, attract an audience of a couple of dozen. But Volpe's coaching is no less intense and exacting. He suggests to a junior named Colin Lester that he build his monologue, which is from *Red*, a play about the painter Mark Rothko, a bit more slowly. "But I don't want you to say yes if you don't agree," he adds. "You're the one who has to present it."

Another boy performs a cut from a Paul Rudnick play that is dead-on hilarious, but marred just a bit by one mispronounced cultural reference. "I don't think you pronounce the *bat* in *bat mitzvah* like you say baseball *bat*," Volpe interjects. "It's *baht* mitzvah."

Volpe occasionally includes me, and this is an obvious opportunity. "That's right, isn't it?" he says, turning in my direction. "*Baht* mitzvah?"

Next, a junior who has won leads in previous plays reads a part from *Rabbit Hole*. Volpe feels that she, too, has built too quickly to anger. He wants her to slow it down, give it more layers of emotion.

"But you liked it the last time," she shoots back.

This seems to violate some code, an unwritten pact between Volpe and his students. His mode of directing is to use a word, a nudge, a silence, a wise-ass comment, a digression from his own life or from something that happened that day at school—anything but an overt command—to coax the performance that he wants. He might tell an actor, "You need to move more in this scene. I'm not going to tell you when, but you'll feel it." Or: "Your shoe is untied

and it was bothering me, so why don't you fix that and try it again."
It is well understood by all that the issue is not really the shoelace;
the performance was just all wrong, and the actor needs to reset
and try it again.

For all the banter that flies back and forth between Volpe and
his students, it is a collaboration that seems based on respect. Students rarely push back, because there is nothing really to push back
against. His direction, almost always, is open-ended. They need to
think more deeply. Slow down and allow moments of silence. Use
the stage more intuitively.

To recoil against such direction is to imply that a monologue
or a scene is *finished*. Perfect and complete. And if there is one
thing Volpe teaches, it's that the art of theater is always evolving—
rehearsal to rehearsal, one performance to the next. It's *live* theater. If it reaches a fixed point, it's dead. When his student says, "But
you liked it the last time," the classroom lets out a collective "oooh,"
and someone makes a catlike screech.

"Oh, you're fine, you're *great*," Volpe responds. He has been holding a printed copy of her monologue in order to follow along. He
gets up from his seat and hands it back to her. *Theatrically.* With
his arm fully extended and his palm up, as if the script were on a
serving tray. "I wouldn't change a thing. That was *perfect.* Just really
wonderful."

As she sits down and sulks, Volpe moves on to Edward Albee's
The Goat. The play is about a man who has taken up with a goat, but
is really about the nature of love. The material is right in his sweet
spot: a drama about human interaction, conflict, and betrayal. "I've
cut some parts of it out," he tells the class. "Otherwise I would be
fired and you would be expelled. It seems sick, yes, I know it does.

It's about a man who has sex with a goat, but it's really an alle-gory about love, about how it can be ruined, that there are certain things that can kill love even if you don't want it to. It's a heart-breaking play. It's not a dirty play at all. Is it shocking? Yes. Is it pornographic? No.

"Albee is what we call an absurdist playwright," he continues. "He's probably America's greatest living playwright."

A student interrupts him. "He wrote *Who's Afraid of Virginia Woolf?*, right?"

"Yes," he says, "and that is a remarkable piece of theater. But I have to tell you, *The Goat* is not as famous a play as *Who's Afraid of Virginia Woolf?*, but when I went to New York and saw this for the first time, I was knocked out by it. When I left the theater, I was just emotionally devastated in the way you are after you see something like that. I had to walk around the corner and have a cocktail."

Everyone laughs at that. Volpe is riffing, ruminating, enthus-ing. The first couple of times I saw him start down a path like this, I would look out into a classroom, or at a cast sitting on the edge of a stage listening to him, and I would expect to see eyes glazing over. I could not imagine that teenagers anywhere—and certainly not here, where so many of them were not that academic and read the Twilight series if they read at all—really wanted to listen to a man in his sixties rhapsodize about the plays of Edward Albee and the nature of love.

Amazingly, they do.

I asked Volpe once how he knew when he was connecting with students. His answer seemed like a credo any educator could use. "When the bell rings, I want them to feel like they wish the class wasn't over and they don't want to leave. If I see that, then I know we've had a great class."

. . .

Two weeks before the beginning of the 2010 school year, the principal at Truman gets moved to the lesser position of principal at one of the district's nine elementary schools—and the principal at the elementary school is put in charge of the high school. Such an abrupt job swap, on the eve of a new academic year, is not recommended in any manuals on how to run a school system, but Bristol Township has never followed what others might consider best practices. Sudden shake-ups, politics, and palace intrigue have long been routine. When I was growing up, my father took me to the barbershop around the corner one Saturday morning, but my regular barber—also the school board president—was not behind his chair. "Why wasn't Lou there?" I asked my dad later. He explained that Lou had to go to jail for a while—something having to do with school business and bribe-taking.

A week after the principals switch places, Truman's football coach quits. It is four days before the season's opening game. The murky quotes he gives to the *Bucks County Courier Times*, the local newspaper, do not really explain why, but it sounds a lot like he is trashing his players on his way out the door. The team has not accepted the "educational message" he was trying to promote, the coach says. He had enough players to field a team—though barely, with just sixteen at one practice—but apparently not the right *kind* of players. "It's about character, commitment, and having a strong work ethic," he says. "It's about the quality of individuals you send out on the field."

The new Truman principal is Jim Moore. A math teacher and baseball coach at the high school before becoming a principal at the elementary level, he is a big, gregarious man who talks very quickly, moves in an ungainly fashion, and gives the overall impression of having the metabolism of a hyperactive teenage boy. His vernacular makes him sound like he has just awakened from the 1950s. I was talking to him one day about the cost of attending the Pennsylvania state colleges favored by many Truman students, which run about $12,000 a year. "That's big dough for our kids," he said.

Moore and Volpe spent years together on the Truman faculty. Volpe likes him and is confident that Moore, whose son had been in theater at the local Catholic high school, values the drama program. He is somewhat taken aback, though, by a conversation with Moore early into his tenure. The new principal tells him, "We've got to change some things around here. I'm tired of people saying, 'Oh, yeah, Truman—that's the drama school.' I want us to be known for other things besides drama." Volpe replays the conversation a couple of times in his head. He wonders, *Am I getting insulted here? Is he sending me a coded message?* He finally just chalks it up to Moore's awkward manner and figures that what the principal meant was that he wanted other aspects of the school—its academics, its sports teams, even the long-suffering football squad—to rise to the level of Truman Drama.

One day, in talking to Moore about the drama program, I ask if Volpe's choices of material ever concern him. His answer seems supportive, if still a bit grudging. "After forty years, with his record of success, he can do what he wants," Moore says. "He's Lou Volpe."

Volpe has had to endure his school district's year-to-year tumult just like the rest of his faculty colleagues. It's tiresome. Counterproductive. Sometimes dispiriting. But he may also, to some extent, be a beneficiary of this ongoing instability. He represents constancy and success, which otherwise are in short supply. Under the radar, and without a formal charter, he had transformed Truman into something like a high school for the performing arts.

He teaches a full day of theater classes, as does Tracey Krause. A third teacher, also a former Volpe student, teaches drama to ninth-graders. The school offers three levels—Theater 1, 2, and 3—along with a class in musical theater. None of the classes are Advanced Placement offerings. (There is no such thing as AP theater.) In a more affluent community, with students gunning for admissions to selective colleges, parents might not be so happy for their children to take one of these classes, let alone four of them. They would want to know: What credentials are they gaining? Where will it lead them? Where's the proof that it will increase their reading levels and their SAT scores? But at Truman, somewhere close to half the students take at least one theater class before graduating, and those most keenly interested in theater take the whole progression.

In Volpe's classroom, thousands of books are piled into book-shelves and stacked so high on surfaces that if you remove a volume, you have to be careful the whole tower of them does not come tumbling down. The books are a reflection of one man's catholic tastes—works by Shakespeare and Sondheim; David Mamet and David Hare; Wendy Wasserstein, Beth Henley, Thornton Wilder, Yasmina Reza, Wallace Shawn, Horton Foote, Paul Rudnick, Athol Fugard, and on and on and on.

They are not for decoration; they are used. If a student is looking for a monologue to perform in a festival or for a scholarship audition, Volpe reaches into the pile, pulls something from the stack, and says, "Look in here. You might find what you want."

In the time I followed Truman Drama, I saw one of his students, Wayne Miletto, win scholarship money for his performance of a monologue from August Wilson's *Fences*. Another, Marilyn Hall, earned some college money at an audition in which she sang "Lot's Wife," a challenging, highly emotive song from Tony Kushner's *Caroline, or Change.*

Volpe's methods are far from scientific. They are not easily tested, nor have they been really monitored. A couple of generations of principals, school superintendents, and school boards have pretty much just left him alone. He is that one teacher that anyone needs to get anywhere in life. He became that by having been given room to express and expand his genius. Any system that constricts teachers—holds them to small-bore metrics, punishes them for forces outside their control, discourages their creativity and spontaneity, chips away at their humanity—is a bad system.

I don't think Volpe is exactly replicable. But a teacher like him is definitely *preventable.*

VOLPE IN HIS CLASSROOM DURING HIS

EARLY YEARS OF TEACHING.

YOU'RE CHERYL MOODY

The theater classes are the foundation of Truman Drama, an essential element of its success. Plays and musicals that Volpe puts into production are often already familiar to his students because they have studied them in class. In the professional theater world, you would say they have been workshopped.

"You're Cheryl Moody," Volpe says one day in a Theater 3 class. "I see you as Cheryl Moody." He is looking straight at Courtney Meyer—which causes Meyer's classmates to also look at her, but with alarm. She is Cheryl Moody? The girl in *Good Boys and True* who, on break from her job, sits alone at a table in a shopping mall food court, is approached by a boy she has never before met, and has sex with him that very night?

"If you're reading the play and don't think too far into it, maybe you think Cheryl Moody is just a whore," Courtney says one day after school. "That's fair if you judge her by what she did that night.

But as it goes on, you see that she's smart. She made a mistake, but she's not a pushover. Mr. Volpe knew that I could understand a girl like that. I was a little taken aback when he said that. I had to think about it, but I wasn't offended."

Volpe actually continued on for several minutes about how he saw this character in Courtney. Someone looking in from the outside might have found it inappropriate. He was referencing her real life—indirectly, to an extent, though everyone knew the subtext.

But his classroom is part of the extended community he has made. It's intimate. He knows which kids are private and buttoned up and which ones, like Courtney, have lives that are an open book. "What he was getting at meant a lot to me," Courtney says. "He was right. His point was that a person can go through pretty much anything and come out on the other side with their head held high, and I've done that. I've gone through a lot of crap, and everyone knows it."

Courtney is thin and doe-eyed and holds herself like a dancer. She lives in Croydon, a hamlet just east of Levittown along the Delaware River, which is frequently the butt of jokes among students in the local schools. Croydon's tiny front lawns are colonized by rusted-out cars sitting up on cinder blocks. Its boys have long been known as rough customers, quick to throw a punch. I sometimes thought Croydon was put on this earth to make Levittowners feel better about themselves. "I live right near Croydon Pizza," Courtney says. "You know it, right?" She laughs. "It's our icon—Croydon Pizza, known around the world."

When I started off on this book, the youngest of my three children had just gone off to college. One of them would soon be living in Texas; another, for a time, in Washington state. We were about to celebrate the birth of our first grandchild. Our kids had been boisterous, not just when they were little, but right through their teens. My wife and I did not really mourn being empty nesters, but the house now had several empty bedrooms. It felt quiet, and sometimes too empty.

The Truman Drama kids are about the same age as the children I just sent off into the world. I like being let into their lives. They often make me laugh, but I never think they're comical. I find them inspiring for lots of reasons: the intensity of work, intellect, and emotion they bring to the stage; the obstacles they overcome; the love they show one another. And I feel an obligation to them, to repay the trust they put in me by making sure I get their stories down right, with honesty and compassion. I am always aware of being older and wiser—of being a parent with parental fears—and being unsure of how life will treat them.

One Monday, I show up at a rehearsal after a holiday break and ask one of the younger kids in Volpe's program how her weekend was. Awful, she says. Her father walked out of the house and moved in with his girlfriend. "He was cheating on my mom with my mom's best friend. She's my godmother, but I never liked her. Now my dad's living with her and her five kids. He's going to pay child support or something, and we're just hoping we can stay in our house."

I try to say something helpful, but what would that be? *I'm sure your dad will come back? He'll have to pay that money and you won't have to move?*

"It's okay," she says. "I'll get through it."

I talk to Volpe's students during rehearsal breaks and sometimes after school in the easy chairs in Room B8, the theater classroom, where they have a sense of comfort. I visit them in their homes and travel with them to the high school theater festivals where they feel like stars—an unaccustomed feeling for kids from Truman. It's a sad fact that they have to go far from home for people to think they're worth much.

Courtney Meyer says one day, "I've overheard kids from other schools saying, 'Do you know if the Truman kids are here yet?' It's like we were awaited. It's totally different than back home, where kids from other schools consider us the lowest of the low. I hate to put it this way, but we're considered, like, this shit school."

When Truman High is mentioned in the Philadelphia newspapers, it's often in the context of Head Start programs, free school lunches, and other boosters to pull children up from their unfortunate circumstances. (That is, when it's not about drugs, crime, or some flare-up of violence.) Sometimes I have to ask myself: Is this where I grew up? And it isn't, really, except in a strictly geographic sense.

Courtney talks about the acclaim Truman Drama attracts, the attention it gets from New York. It's different from anything else in her life. "I wonder if I'm ever going to be part of something this big again. Realistically, I don't know."

Courtney's parents split up when she was four years old, and her father moved with his mother to a town two hours away, in the Pocono Mountains. Soon after, Courtney moved to her mother's new boyfriend's house. "That's when my little sister came along." But her mother's new relationship didn't last. "It went on for something like ten years, thirteen years, I'm not really sure, but we got to stay in the house. Her boyfriend was the one who moved out."

Courtney's mother, who grew up in Croydon, has waited tables at Georgine's, one of the better restaurants in the area, since she was seventeen years old. Her maternal grandmother worked there as well, "right up until the day she died." As Courtney sees it, the Georgine's waitresses are miserable in their jobs, but even so, she has recently started working banquets. She hadn't planned on it; it just sort of happened. She figures, in her sardonic way, she is part of a dynasty: "third-generation Georgine's."

Of the six cast members of *Good Boys and True*, Courtney is the most enigmatic and easily the most perplexing. She frustrates not only her teachers, but sometimes also her friends. "I love her to death, but I just don't get her," Bobby Ryan says. "She's Croydon, and I feel like she's gonna be Croydon till the day she dies."

A good reader and skilled writer, Courtney easily masters her schoolwork, except when she is indifferent to it. She did well in the one Advanced Placement course she took. She likes to use the word *realistically*, which I come to realize is a rationale—an excuse to not dream, or even plan ahead, because much of what she might want for herself, upon reflection, does not seem realistic. Halfway through her senior year, Courtney has yet to take her SATs, let alone think about college. She is acutely aware of her flaws. And too forgiving of them. "Yeah, everybody says to me, 'Courtney, you're so smart.' But I'm very irresponsible. I'm impulsive. It's terrible, to tell you the truth."

In ninth grade, Courtney worked the lights in a Truman production. The next year, Bobby Ryan, whom she had a crush on, convinced her to audition for *Rimers*. She blushes easily—"I could feel my face go totally red"—but felt that Volpe and Krause sensed something in her that would project onstage. "I think they liked my vulnerability," she says. "That's probably the main thing they saw in me."

The cast mate who became her longtime high school boyfriend was not Bobby Ryan, but Wayne Miletto, who in *Good Boys* plays the part of the football coach. It was an unlikely match. At Truman,

Wayne is known as a straight arrow, Mr. Responsibility. He is not a prude, or judgmental, but he knows what he wants and lets nothing deter him. Courtney admired his self-discipline, which she felt she had in short supply. "Nothing can stop Wayne. He won't let it," she says. "He's very strong. I'm sure he's told you he never has known his father. His mom got another boyfriend and had another child. He handled it. He handles everything."

Wayne, a husky guy when I first met him, was even heavier early in high school. Courtney's friends didn't get it. They figured she would be with a cuter guy—as well as someone who went out on weekends and cut loose. Courtney prided herself on her unconventionality. "I like the different people. I like the complex people. I'll pretty much date the ugliest person in the entire world if he can make me laugh and we have a good time. Looks were never important to me. My friends would be like, 'How can you be with him?' I would think, *Do you hear yourself? You sound dumb.* It made me more determined to be with him."

What was more problematic, especially back home in Croydon, was the fact that Wayne is black. He rode the school bus home with Courtney once, felt uncomfortable at comments directed at him, and told her not to expect him to ever do that again. A person she felt close to had a tattoo on his leg that said WHITE PRIDE. He saw a picture of Wayne on Courtney's cell phone one day—it was her wallpaper—and asked, "Are you dating him?" "I said, 'Yeah, I'm dating him.' He went on to say things like, 'Have fun getting AIDS. You're so dirty. You're dead to me.'"

What ultimately undermined the relationship was something Courtney did. "Like I told you already, I'm irresponsible," she says before going into the details, which by high school standards are utterly prosaic. She hooked up with another boy. "The kid I was with was totally drunk. It should never have happened. I messed up and I ruined something that was really good. It became a huge deal at school. Everybody thought I was such a bitch. I went through this period of time where I was just a blob who came to school."

Truman is sort of the no-drama drama troupe. Of course some of the students attracted to it have problems; they're in high school. At Truman, they are without privilege and—it is easy for them to feel—without prospects. But Volpe's stage is not a place for them to work out their personal issues. They hold themselves apart from the overly dramatic "drama kids" they meet from other schools, the ones who dress eccentrically and seem to revel in swaying between the extremes of depression and elation, as if the spotlight is perpetually on them.

The Truman troupe can be arrogant about these distinctions they make, but their pridefulness is an ingredient of their success. Elsewhere, the students have tangible advantages—better theaters, bigger stages, parents who buy them private voice lessons and put them in expensive theater camps. It's a lot to compete against. What Volpe's kids have is an ethos.

Stephen Sondheim once said, "It never occurs to me to write a song just for the pleasure of writing a song. It has to be an assignment." The Truman actors embrace a similarly resolute approach. At the drama festivals, they decline all invitations to play theater games at the lunch table. What they do instead is eat lunch. Truman Drama is a workplace. You throw off your troubles as best you can, square your shoulders, and reach within. "At other schools, it's kind of the misfit kids who do theater," Courtney Meyer says. "Some of them are strange, and personally, I love strange. I really do. But most of us in Truman theater are—I don't know what the word for it is—*normal,* I guess."

Bobby Ryan amplifies her point: "We're not typical theater kids, and we don't want to be typical theater kids."

The culture of Truman theater and the weight of Volpe's four-decade legacy has its drawbacks—and not just that some of the kids from other schools might resent their air of superiority. Volpe's kids can sometimes be *too* hard on themselves. When Courtney was in the grip of her turmoil over Wayne, in eleventh grade, she decided she could not participate in that spring's production (a rare light selection designed to attract a big box office, *High School Musical 2*). She did not want to bring her personal drama to rehearsals and to be around her former boyfriend every afternoon and feel that everyone was always looking at her.

This, of course, is a particular high school syndrome: the feeling that if you're in some emotional distress, other people are always focusing as intensely on your problems as you are. But Courtney felt it proper to spare everyone else her pain. It was not what Volpe counseled her to do, or what he wanted her to do, but she couldn't be talked out of it. "The thing you have to understand," she says, "is that Truman theater is tough love. It's no place for crybabies. You don't get coddled. If you have something in your own life you can't handle, you shouldn't be there."

The author of *Good Boys and True* is Roberto Aguirre-Sacasa, a versatile playwright and TV writer who in 2011 was commissioned by the producers of *Spider-Man: Turn Off the Dark* to rewrite parts of the troubled, $100 million Broadway musical after it had been savaged by critics. (And after numerous actors involved in the

high-flying show had come crashing down and suffered injuries.)
Aguirre-Sacasa had been a writer for HBO's acclaimed *Big Love*, a
drama about a polygamist Mormon family. In 2011, he signed on as
a coproducer and writer of NBC's *Glee*.

The son of a Nicaraguan diplomat, he set *Good Boys* in a world
he knew well: a posh suburb of Washington, D.C., and an elite high
school he called St. Joseph's Preparatory School for Boys. The two
characters at the center of the story, Brandon Hardy (played by
Zach Philippi) and Justin Simmons (Bobby Ryan) are best friends.
Even within their bastion of privilege, Brandon is royalty—second
generation at St. Joseph's, football captain, the son of two doctors.
Justin is the first of his family to attend St. Joseph's, a nonathlete
and more on the school's social periphery. He has not come out as
gay, but his sexuality is an open secret.

Brandon seems to have left the sex tape, his secretly recorded
session with Cheryl Moody, in a football teammate's locker—
accidentally on purpose, as it is said. He wants it to be discovered in
order to validate his masculine credentials, an important consideration at an all-boys school when your best friend is gay and he has
given you blow jobs—including once at the St. Joseph's pool, where
they fear classmates may have witnessed them.

Not only do Brandon's teammates see the tape, but copies are
made and circulated at other high schools and around the community. TV news crews descend on St. Joseph's to cover the episode
and question what kind of warped values the school must be incu-
bating. After Brandon can no longer deny that he is the one in the
tape, his friend Justin confronts him with the theory that he orchestrated the whole episode as an elaborate subterfuge. After all, if the
great golden boy Brandon Hardy is seen by his mates having sex

with a girl, then he could not possibly be gay. "Christ, what did you imagine?" Justin asks. "One scandal—a better scandal—replacing another?"

Good Boys, though wordy in parts, is nonetheless a great play for high school actors and audiences. Three of the six parts—the two boys and Cheryl—allow high schoolers to play high school-aged roles. The other three—the football coach (Wayne Miletto), Brandon's mother (Mariela Castillo), and his mother's sister (Britney Harron)—demand that students portray adults. The subject matter—the power and peril of sex, secrets and lies that spin out of control—speaks to high schoolers. A great many teenagers, after all, feel themselves to be just one mortifying misstep from being found out for something—by their parents or friends or by anyone who can see too deeply into their true selves. "It's universal, doing something really regrettable that comes back to bite you in the ass," Bobby Ryan observes. "Either you've been in that situation or you know someone who has."

Courtney Meyer appreciates that the play feels real. "They weren't just holding hands and going to the school dance together. People our age, where we're from, we get that. The choices you make have big consequences."

Aguirre-Sacasa has said that his drama first presents as a whodunit and evolves into a "*why*dunit." The plot partly tracks his own life. "The irony is, I *did* play football," he said in a 2008 interview. "And I definitely knew I was gay, and there was definitely no talking about that. There were no 'out' students; there were kids who seemed effeminate. I guess I was maybe one of them. I was living a straight life, playing football—and then doing plays. So I didn't feel like that much of an outsider, except that I knew that I was fundamentally different from most of my classmates."

For all its focus on sexuality, however, the play is as much about class, privilege, and power, subjects virtually unexplored in America's classrooms, as it is about sex. Cheryl Moody is a public school girl who works in a dreary mall job to earn money for college. She has goals, but you sense it is no sure thing she will attain them. As Brandon approaches, she is on lunch break, reading a textbook and eating french fries—which he leans over and samples without asking. When he introduces himself, she says, "I know who you are." She has been to his high school games and knows he is the vaunted captain of the St. Joseph's football team.

He takes advantage of her, in large part, because he can.

The Truman stage is the one place Courtney does not put limits on herself. She can twist a one-syllable word in a way that seems to give it layers of meaning. She approaches building a character, the art of constructing a story beyond what the playwright has written on the page, as if she is writing fiction, and she thinks her way through parts as well as any actor Volpe has ever had. "You have to think of who your character is, who her friends are, if she has a good relationship with her parents or not, what motivates her," she says. "The script gives you some idea, but you have to figure out the rest of it yourself. Then everything you do onstage, the way you say your lines, how you move, is based on that."

Courtney finds the experience of acting almost impossible to describe. Some of what she feels seems to her almost contradictory. Onstage, she sees more deeply into herself, but not in a way that is narcissistic. The self-focus actually connects her more deeply with other people—the other actors, people in the audience, even the fictional characters in the plays. Life in Croydon does not often uplift her. Taking the job at Georgine's felt like a death sentence. But theater is not an escape. In some ways, it is the opposite of that—it brings her closer to the true self she thinks she might be, or could become. "When you act, it's like you have so many more ways of seeing, and more parts of you are alive than in real life. Everything you are comes out."

When Courtney read for the part of Cheryl Moody, Volpe knew immediately he was right when he figured she was the one for the role. "I was like, *Oh my God, here she is already.* There was such a mix of loser/fighter/feminist/teenager in the reading. As she developed the role, it only got better. Her character was never sentimental, and it could have been. She was so intelligent and yet so victimized. She didn't want sympathy; she wanted justice."

Volpe has been Courtney's teacher and director for three years. She exasperates him, as she does everyone who roots for her success, but he loves her mind and courage. "She crosses every social boundary in the building, and that is very rare," he says. "She can talk to the really smart kids, to some of the very tough white kids, to the minorities. She has friends who are going to great colleges and are straight and narrow and do just what their parents say. And she has friends that smoke pot every weekend. She is honest and she is totally nonjudgmental, which is amazing for a kid who is eighteen years old.

"She really is one of the best high school definitions of a feminist I've known. She commands a lot of respect for that, but she also gets a lot of whispers down the hallway and name-calling. She deals with it. She doesn't let it bother her."

Volpe does not like to typecast his actors, though in high school it is sometimes unavoidable. His actors are young and can draw from only limited life experience, so sometimes he has to reach for an actor who he knows will have some understanding of her character. It provides something like a head start in the role. And even professional actors borrow from their own lives. It can't be the only attribute an actor brings to a role, but it doesn't hurt.

Uta Hagen, who originated the role of Martha in *Who's Afraid of Virginia Woolf?* on Broadway in 1963, would later write, "Martha is the daughter of a professor whom she adores; she lives in a college town; and as the play opens, she and her husband are returning from a faculty party. I *am* the daughter of a famous professor whom I adored; I *was* raised in a university town; I *did* attend many faculty parties. Consequently, those things were real to me and directly usable for that particular aspect of my work on the part."

Courtney is able to make the initial misstep of Cheryl Moody's—going off with Brandon—fathomable. "She understands what it means to be seduced by a beautiful young man," Volpe says. "She allows her character to believe the lie. Her voice has so many tones to it. She can be seductive and naive all in one sentence." At one point in the play, Cheryl Moody is confronted by Brandon's mother, who comes to apologize, but also to try to understand how a young girl could have had sex with a boy she had just met. Cheryl responds, "Mrs. Hardy. Have you *seen* your son? Do you *realize* what he looks like?" The mother says that, yes, her son is handsome. No, Cheryl replies, "he's *sexy*."

In building the character, Courtney decides that the most important thing is to make it about more than just a physical attraction. "I don't want to play her as just a slutty girl," she says. "There are millions of slutty girls. They're not interesting."

Brandon Hardy's parents are both doctors. It's not clear what Cheryl's parents do, but clearly something much lower down the socioeconomic scale. Courtney imagines her character as naive, and also somewhat socially isolated. She's popular, perhaps, but closed off—she has no close confidante to help her assess reality. None of this is in the playwright's script; Courtney is writing a backstory based on what she imagines and what she knows of real life. "Yeah, there was a sexual thing," she says, "but every time people feel a sexual attraction they don't jump into bed together. It has to be more than that. She goes in for a different kind of fantasy. She thinks if she sleeps with Brandon, that will get her out of the world she's in and into his world. Yeah, that's totally stupid. The audience can see that. It's never going to happen—she's not the same class as him—but she doesn't see that until it's too late, and she didn't have anyone to tell her that."

L. J. CARULLI AS ANGEL

IN TRUMAN'S 2007 PRODUCTION OF *RENT*.

IT'S A *PLAY*, DUDE

In the early years, as Volpe was learning and still getting started, one show—and one student—changed the program forever and set it apart from probably ninety-nine percent of the other high schools in America. Without this student, whose name was Michael Massari, *Good Boys and True* would have looked different. It might not have been possible, or at least not as credible and visceral. It is a play that needed to be cast from the full range of the school's population, particularly the full range of males.

"I really was a strange one," is the first thing Massari tells me after I track him down in Florida, as if this were something that must be stated at the outset.

Massari was a young man of disparate parts, not all of which fit together neatly. He was a vegetarian, perhaps the only one in Levittown at the time. (He volunteered the precise date of when he last ate meat—May 12, 1972, at fourteen years old.) A championship wrestler. A self-identified pacifist. A bicycle racer who went on long solo training rides in the mornings before school. A hard-hitting linebacker and captain on the football team who left the field and refused to return when a brawl erupted in his final high school game. "It shocked and saddened me," he says. "I couldn't justify going back out there." He was even an honorary stoner. "My eyes are deep-set and kind of don't open all the way, so they thought I was one of them."

Massari was also religious. His family belonged to a Baptist church, and he sang in its choir and believed in the doctrines. He founded Truman's chapter of the Fellowship of Christian Athletes, and friends could depend on him to get them home safely from parties because he did not drink. His rationale for vegetarianism came from Genesis: "And God said, Behold, I have given you every herb-bearing seed, which is upon the face of all the earth, and every tree, in which is the fruit of a tree-yielding seed; to you it shall be for meat."

In the fall of 1976, Volpe announced his choice of a musical for that year: *Godspell,* a show that began as the late playwright John-Michael Tebelak's master's thesis at Carnegie Mellon University and opened with great success on Broadway in 1971. It is a distinctly 1960s take on the Gospel of St. Matthew, a sort of period piece within a period piece that was initially criticized for its flower-child vibe and hippie-dippie costuming.

Massari had not previously been involved in theater, but was driven to seek a specific role—he wanted to be Jesus. "I knew nothing about theater, but I was drawn in when he picked *Godspell,* and I thought I had a little advantage because I connected with the material," he recalls. "This wasn't *Hello, Dolly!* It was stuff I was involved in intensely in every aspect of my life." He particularly liked the persona of Jesus as imagined by the musical's creators. "In *Godspell*, Jesus stirs the pot. He's a rebel, and I was a rebel." Other inducements were calling Massari to the stage, too. "I really liked the girls. It seemed to me there were always beautiful girls involved in drama, and they looked so good onstage when they were all made up."

Another lure was Volpe himself, his English teacher. "Intellectually, he just absolutely had a door wide open for those of us who were looking for that. Most teachers didn't even know where to find that door. I wanted to be near him. That was a big part of it."

Volpe was at first shocked to find one of the school's top athletes among those competing for parts, then delighted by Massari's voice and natural ease. He put Massari through a short improv—told him that he had come downstairs on Christmas morning looking for a special gift he had requested. "I remember it so vividly," Massari says. "I went through the motions like I was unwrapping it, and all the sudden he says, 'It's a pogo stick,' and I started playing with it. I'm hopping around and he says, 'You just broke your mom's favorite lamp.' I had no inner eye to know how good or bad I was, but I liked it right away, and Lou saw enough to know that even though I was green, I had something he could shape and mold."

Volpe cast Massari as Jesus, but right away, a major obstacle emerged: the wrestling coach. It was midseason; Massari had run up ten wins in his first eleven matches, and he seemed headed for a strong performance in the state tournament. Letters from college coaches landed regularly in his mailbox at home, holding out the prospect of scholarships. Everyone saw him as a wrestler, even if he saw himself as more than that. This was all occurring thirty years before the hit television show *Glee* popularized the notion—which even now is more an *idea* than a reality in most high schools—that a top athlete would participate in drama. Volpe was still a young teacher, not that far removed from staging *Antigone* in garbage bags and tinfoil. Wrestling was, at the time, a premier sport at the school, coached by a Truman grad who had gone on to compete in college. The coach's brother was a school legend who wrestled at the U.S. Naval Academy.

To make matters worse, Larry Bosley, the principal who had been such a partisan for theater, had already moved on. "The coaches were furious, and I would not have pressed it," Volpe says. "I was so terrified of those people. But this boy wanted to be in the musical. I don't know if he was a born-again Christian—we didn't even hear that phrase much back then—but the religiousness of it was really motivating him. He was Jesus, and he would not be denied."

Massari didn't consider his quest unreasonable, nor did he fully grasp how many steps down the ladder the drama program ranked from a powerhouse athletic team. "I figured, why shouldn't I be trying different things? I do multiple things all the time."

Volpe arranged to alter the rehearsal schedule so his Jesus would miss only a small portion of each week's wrestling practices. But when Massari informed the coach he wanted to do both, he was told that even if he did manage to maintain his prowess on the mat, he would be setting a bad example, as a senior and a captain, by not showing total commitment. "He laid this decision on me, and all I could think of is, *I really want to wrestle. I'm good. I've got schools looking at me. But I want to do this other thing, too, and I know I can because I'm working out on my own, I'm in amazing shape, and I eat a lot healthier than anybody in the whole school."*

Massari approached his guidance counselor for help, but already knew not to expect an ally. The counselor had recently tried to redirect him from his focus on English to more of a science and math orientation so he could take something practical, like engineering, in college. The wrestling coach had been on him to eat meat. "It was like everybody was trying to man me up," he says.

A meeting was scheduled to break the standoff. Massari's mother came to school and sat down at a conference table along with her son, Volpe, and the guidance counselor. After a few minutes, the school's athletic director entered with news: The coach was boycotting the meeting, "holding the line," they were told. His rationale was restated: Massari could not be allowed to set a precedent. He had committed first to wrestling and was bound to it. "I offered to run extra laps on the smelly dirty track above the pool; anything they asked I would have done," Massari says. "But he totally hard-lined it, so that was the end of it. I never wrestled again." (Massari, in adulthood, was finally able to reconcile his two passions. He teaches theater at a magnet school in Florida and coaches at a youth wrestling club.)

Volpe sat there, stunned by the whole scene. He had really been nothing but a bystander. The only way he could have changed the outcome was to have aligned with the coach and told Massari he could not play Jesus, but he was not about to do that. And even if he had, the hardheaded Massari would not have wrestled. "It was, like, my first big controversy," Volpe says. "I was young. I actually had very little to say about it. He was just refusing to do what they wanted. I couldn't stop him and I didn't want to, but I can't honestly say it was a fight I was looking for."

. . .

As the years went on, Volpe assumed numerous additional roles at Truman. Senior class advisor. Sponsor of the prom and Truman's chapter of the National Honor Society. When students went on class trips to Disneyland—to Europe, when Levittown was more awash in money—he went along. Virtually nothing of social or academic import occurred at the school without his involvement. With all these windows into the lives of students and the close attention he paid, he has become an authority on high school sociology. He knows what has changed over time and what will never change. A high school, he believes, is composed of "the three A's": the highly academic kids, the artists, and the athletes. "The athletes are always the center ring. That's the hierarchy of the building. They are the ones who will inherit the earth. It has always been thus, and always will be."

Volpe tells me that when I was his student, I had been in the school's center ring. I assure him that I definitely had not felt that way. "Believe me, you were. You and Bruce and Darryl and Don were all in that center ring," he says, naming my three closest high school friends.

The four of us were all varsity athletes—all bonded around Volpe—and we all became writers or editors. None of us participated in his theater program, which at the time existed on a smaller scale and attracted just two of the A's—artists and the nonathletically inclined academic kids. I was a baseball player of meager talent but with enough know-how to play second base for the varsity team, and a somewhat more skilled basketball player who was too short (and slow) to amount to much. I got cut from the varsity squad in my senior year. The coach's verdict utterly crushed me. I'm not proud of this, but it is likely that I cried harder and longer after being left off the team than at any time in my life, before or since. It was a death.

Volpe, a day or so later, asked me if I would want to play the role of the shy younger brother in his upcoming play, Neil Simon's *Come Blow Your Horn*. In those days, he did not audition kids so much as entreat them. He did not present this offer as a salve; he knew better. But he understood I was hurting, and this seemed like an opportunity for both of us. I needed a distraction, and he needed an actor. I refused. As I recall, it wasn't even a conversation.

For many years, I regretted the narrow-mindedness of my decision, but I focused only on the most obvious aspect: If I had taken Volpe up on his offer, I would have more quickly become comfortable speaking in public and would never have experienced those lost-in-space moments, common to fearful public speakers, when all you can hear is the sound of your own disembodied voice. But that is just a practical, nuts-and-bolts regret. What I know now is that I would be a different person, or at the least a better version of myself, more rounded, more fulfilled, more in touch with myself and everyone around me.

In so many ways, theater teaches the opposite of what I learned in sports, in which the model is that there is no self, no emotional landscape or core. Team sport is all about grit and team, about submerging self. To look within, to feel or imagine, is not encouraged. At the time, I couldn't conceive of myself being up onstage. It wasn't something my crowd did. As far as I was concerned, it was not an activity fit for a sports-playing boy.

Massari came along just a couple of years behind me. I some-

how didn't know him, even though his family lived in the same section as I did, just a couple of streets over. (Maybe while we were
climbing the Big Oak, he was taking long training rides on his bicycle.) "What happened with Michael Massari changed the drama
program completely," Volpe says. "An athlete was in the show. It was
unprecedented, and it was shocking."

Students, particularly determined ones like Massari, can make
a difference. He was steps ahead of Volpe, leading his teacher on a
path that, at the time, he would not have walked on his own. Massari was the first of many Truman athletes, male and female, to act
on Truman's stage. Most—though not all—of them kept playing
their sports. They worked it out with their coaches, because as the
shows got better and the drama program gained more status, there
was *pressure* on those coaches to make accommodations. Massari's
decision to just bolt from his sport in response to his coach's in-
transigence had not gone unnoticed; in future years, if a coach set
himself up as an obstacle, he knew that he risked losing a member
of his team.

Volpe came to love working with the athletes. If he had a choice
between equally raw kids, he usually preferred them. They pos-
sessed a sense of kinetics that translated to the stage. They showed
up for rehearsals on time, had a sense of discipline and teamwork,
and were not likely to wilt under pressure. The better they were in
their sports, the more that Volpe found those qualities carried over
to theater. About a quarter of the huge cast of Volpe's *Les Mis* was
composed of male athletes—football players, soccer players, wres-
tlers. "They all wanted to be in the show," he says. "They were the
guys on the barricades, in the vests. It was very macho."

What the athletes also gave him was an ability to reach into every slice of the school's population, into every self-defined and self-limiting clique. He liked to say that he could run his program with fifteen kids if he had to. If they were all punk rockers with pink Mohawks and multiple piercings—maybe with one chess club geek thrown in—he could make that work. But it wasn't what he preferred. "You hate to play off the popularity of one set of students, but when you get these very recognizable people at the school, the ones in the center ring, it validates drama to every other student. It creates a big gravitational pull."

The three boys in *Good Boys and True* are the heirs and beneficiaries of Michael Massari. If you watched them walk down the school corridor together, you would figure they were buddies from the football team. They have a swagger about them. It is the signature style of a Truman Drama boy, a point of pride. "When we travel," Courtney Meyer says, "the girls from the other schools are always excited to see us because we're the only school that brings cute straight guys."

This is not strictly true. But it has become part of the Truman mythology, the ethos—that in every regard, its theater program is different. "We're ass-backwards," Robby Edmondson, the lighting director, observes. "Here, the cool kids, the popular kids, whatever that means, are the theater kids, and the football players are the ones *trying* to be cool."

Just the presence onstage of boys like Zach Philippi, Bobby Ryan, and Wayne Miletto challenges traditional notions of high school sociology. And for the boys themselves, their immersion in theater, and with Volpe, is liberating. They don't surrender anything—not their friendships, video games, the rough-and-tumble sports some of them play, or even their macho posturing. They still have all that, but it's like Volpe has issued them passports into the rest of their souls.

In his own high school years, Volpe had been protected by his football-playing friends, his fellow altar boys from Maternity Blessed Virgin Mary. At Truman, it's like he's repaying a debt. His students don't know this—they know precious little of Volpe's biography or his life outside the school. Volpe himself doesn't talk about the parallel, and I don't know the degree to which he is fully conscious of it. But a couple of generations later, he is giving those same kind of boys a gift. "The only word I can use to describe it is *powerful*," says Philippi, who came into Truman theater two years after his friends Ryan and Miletto. "I've danced onstage. I sang onstage. It totally *changed* me. There's more parts of me than I realized before."

Bobby, Zach, Wayne, and the other boys who take to the Truman stage do not sit around having long discussions about the nature of masculinity in America at the dawn of a new century, but they couldn't act the roles in the shows that Volpe favors without encountering some basic questions: What does it mean to be a male in America? What are the boundaries? How will you regard yourself and how will others regard you if you seem to cross those boundaries?

Michael Massari, of course, had not totally upended the social order at Truman. Nor can all that transpires in the wider culture—from Stonewall to *Will & Grace* to *Brokeback Mountain* to *Glee* to a U.S. president declaring his support for legalized gay marriage—change every mind in Levittown. By virtue of its demographics, Levittown—older, whiter, less educated than the nation as a whole—

is a late adapter, not an early one. It is well fortified against new ideas. It is part of what makes Volpe's accomplishments all the more surprising.

The age-old question—can a boy access his softer and more artistic side and still be a genuine boy?—still has currency in corners of the high school and within some of the families. "Oh, there are some kids who are diehards," Volpe says. "I've had boys say to me, 'I'm not a fag, so I'm not taking your class,' or 'I'm not trying out for your play.' And I say fine. No problem. I'm not here to change the world.

"But there are many other students who were hesitant or even critical, and they give it a try and tell me later, 'I loved it! I wish I had done it earlier.' And those are some of my favorite moments as a drama teacher. Maybe that kid was in the back of the ensemble and he wasn't even good, or he was an abomination. I don't care. He was onstage and he was having a ball, and I'm absolutely thrilled because I've taken that kid to a place he never imagined and may never be again."

Zach Philippi has a line he delivers as his character Brandon Hardy's comfortable world begins to crash in on him: "You know what I am, right? I'm a goddamn demigod." That is a pretty good definition of Zach at Truman. He is an honored athlete blessed with a sunny temperament and an easy smile. In baseball, he plays shortstop and pitcher. In his senior season, he will be named first-team all–Suburban One, the sports league consisting of the biggest high schools in Philadelphia's northern suburbs, and he'll compete in the Carpenter Cup with the area's top high school prospects at Citizens Bank Park, the Phillies' home field. Classmates vote him onto the Homecoming Court.

Everyone wants to be around Zach, and from freshman year forward, he's just about always had a girlfriend. I happen to notice one day what a friend has posted on his Facebook wall: "If I could die and come back to life," it says, "I would come back as Zach Philippi."

His life is vexing in some other ways. His household includes two older sisters, both of them with babies who sometimes keep him up at night and make studying, to the extent he wants to do that, difficult. He cares for the babies at times, but has laid down the law at diapers. "I've done one, total," he tells me. "Piss, not poop." He feels within his rights to set limits. "They brought this on themselves. They can deal with it."

No one's status at Truman has anything to do with their parents' occupations. People in Levittown have a job or they don't, and that is about the extent of it. Thomas Philippi, Zach's father, awakens at three-thirty A.M., six days a week, and thirty minutes later is behind the wheel of a sanitation truck for Waste Management, Inc. His route is "commercial municipal trash," emptying dumpsters at schools, hospitals, retail establishments, and apartment complexes. He coached his son's baseball teams from the time Zach was six years old all the way up to when he was eighteen, the year that Zach's American Legion team captured the Pennsylvania state championship. His life is his work, his kids, and Zach's baseball. When Zach first got interested in theater, Tom Philippi was not happy. "He would call him a fag," Zach's mother, Maureen, says. "He didn't like it. I remember he kept saying, 'Zach, you're killing me.'"

Zach and Wayne Miletto have been close since grammar school. In one of my conversations with Wayne, I posit that one very minor benefit of not having a father at home is that at least there is no one to hassle him about his participation in theater. He smiles and says, "Yeah, except that Zach's father used to get on me, too. He'd be like, 'Oh, you're going to prance around onstage.' I just laugh at it, but it was harder on Zach, because that's his dad."

Bobby Ryan faced no such opposition at home, but as word gets around Truman that he is playing a gay character in *Good Boys and True*, a few kids attempt to give him a hard time. Between classes one day, one boy is especially persistent about it.

"What's up, Bobby?" he says. "So you're gay now?" Bobby at first just laughs. But the boy keeps at it, suggesting his involvement in theater will, or already has, made him gay. Bobby finally responds, "You know what? You're a fucking idiot. I'm playing a character. You get that concept, right? It's a *play*, dude."

B obby's mother earned an online degree after her children got older and now works in accounting. His father was employed for many years at a manufacturing plant operated by Crown Cork & Seal, which makes beverage cans. After he got laid off, he took a dispatching job with Atlas Van Lines. By the time Bobby is a senior at Truman, his father is working as an electrician, "but he's not trained as an electrician, so he works as an apprentice," Bobby says.

This is a common thing in Levittown. Lots of people work hard at skilled jobs but lack something—a degree, a credential, sometimes a union card—that would give them better pay and more job security. "He never really went to college," Bobby says, "so he's bounced from job to job, but I don't worry about it because he's really smart."

Bobby is smart, too, though not as academic as his older sister, a high school valedictorian and the rare Truman graduate to advance to an elite university. (She's studying bioengineering at Rensselaer Polytechnic Institute.) He is a habitual procrastinator, a champion of the art form, whose approach to schoolwork is to get started at the last possible moment and give it just enough attention to stay on the honor roll. He actually got a C in theater one quarter because he didn't do his Shakespeare monologue. "I'm not going to give him an A just because he's a great actor," Volpe says. "He didn't do what he was supposed to do. Sorry. That's the way it is."

When he's onstage in performances or even during rehearsals, Bobby feels like he's in another realm entirely, a different state of consciousness. Everything else falls from his consciousness, like a computer screen going dark—but in a good way. "All the problems in the world, all my anger, my teenage angst, if that's what it's called, my insecurities. Nothing else makes that happen."

He is a little luckless in romance at Truman. He got interested in Britney Harron—"me and Brit were talking," as he puts it—but didn't move quickly enough, and she ended up with a long-term boyfriend. He wanted to be with Courtney, but she became Wayne's girlfriend. (Bobby does, however, end up going to the senior prom with Courtney after he "forks" her front lawn—uses plastic silverware to make a heart with his initials in the middle of it to signal his intentions that he wants to be her date. "I was honestly going to go by myself," Courtney says. "Bobby or Wayne were the only ones I would have wanted to go with. But after I realized I was not going with Wayne, I came home from work one night and I see all this crap in my yard, and then I figured out what it was—and that it's from Bobby. You can't say no, right? It was the cutest way anyone was ever asked to a prom.")

Bobby's strength as an actor is comedy. He is high-energy and at times even manic in a Robert Downey, Jr.–like way. His body is so naturally kinetic that even when he is silent and nearly still he can make an audience laugh with just a slight gesture or facial expression. He spent his first two years at Truman watching Antonio Addeo, who was known to bring rehearsals to a sudden halt by breaking into impromptu, hilarious bits—including dead-on impersonations of Volpe—and Bobby reminds people of Antonio.

But Bobby is intensely serious about his craft. Volpe finds him especially rewarding, the kind of student who gives constant feedback—affirmation that as a teacher or director, he is getting through. Bobby doesn't even have to say anything. "I see his mind turning in every conversation we have. He takes everything in that I'm saying—he listens, he really does—but he always has his own thoughts and his own insights into characters and scenes."

To make *Good Boys* work—and to get it to Nebraska—Volpe is going to have to coax performances from actors of vastly different abilities and styles. Close as they are as friends, Zach and Bobby are not much alike in their approaches. Partly, it's that Zach is new; this is just his second play. But it's more than that. "Bobby thinks like an actor," Volpe says. "Zach does not think like an actor. He's getting there. I believe he will someday. But right now, he's much more inclined to want me to tell him what to do and then try to carry that out." What they have in common, Volpe continues, is "they are still boys. And they enjoy being boys. It's what is so appealing about them, what makes them so likable and perfect for these parts."

By *perfect*, Volpe means not just in their roles—but also in the impact that playing those roles will have across the school. Volpe is rarely overtly political, and almost never at school. He is a crusader only for theater. But he hates bigotry and closed-mindedness of all kinds. He never says he is going to do a particular play to *open* minds, but that is often a secondary consideration, and an important one.

He considers Zach "as close as you can get to the standard for what a macho male teenager is at Harry S Truman High School." By playing a character who may be gay and, at the very least, has been the recipient of oral sex from his gay friend, he believes that Zach is making a statement. "He is unafraid of this. People are going to see that, and Zach being Zach, it has an impact. He has a gay uncle who is out, and he's close with him. Zach knew and dealt with gay before *Good Boys and True,* and it does not scare him."

Zach is utterly comfortable with the exterior presentation and accoutrements of his character. When he pulls on his costume—navy blue private-school blazer, freshly pressed khaki pants, and Oxford cloth shirt—he looks just like the same revered young man he is at Truman, just cleaned up and transported to a leafy prep school campus. But the character he plays is dark and manipulative. His own self-doubts and character flaws cause him to inflict harm on others. The audience should not see it at first, but Brandon Hardy's golden looks and charming manner are a façade. He's not without sympathy, but he's a fraud.

I watch afternoon rehearsals in the auditorium, usually sitting with Volpe and Krause about eight rows back. The actors walk in a few minutes after the final bell, and after a few minutes of conversation—often raucous, frequently profane—they put their cell phones in their backpacks and walk up onstage. Volpe rarely has big sit-down conversations with his actors. His notes are given after rehearsals to the whole group, or in offhand and often indirect conversations. He needs Zach to embrace being a character who is unlikable—something that does not come easily even to veteran actors.

"You're a good person, Zach," Volpe says as the six cast members sit on the edge of the stage after a rehearsal one afternoon. "You know that. Everyone loves you. You love yourself." After everyone (including Zach) stops laughing at this little dig, Volpe continues. "It's going to take time, I know it will, but you have to find the evil in this character. I know that's a strong word, but think about what he has done."

I sometimes listen to these moments, as a production is still in formation, and worry how Volpe is ever going to pull things together. To take on such edgy and controversial material and fail would surely be far worse than presenting a production of *Beauty and the Beast* that falls just a little flat. One is a disappointment, the other a possible debacle. But Volpe never seems concerned. "Zach is not the best actor in the world, and he knows that," he says. "But there's an elegance about him that fits this part like a glove, and he has such a dynamic sense of commitment. He's like a bulldog."

High school directors cannot, of course, search far and wide for talent. They work with whomever they find in the building. But what they have in greater measure than their professional counterparts is *time*, because they don't have to pay their actors or rent rehearsal space. "People say, 'Why do you have such a long rehearsal process?' And it's true that they could certainly learn the lines in a shorter time," Volpe says. "But that's not what it's about. It's the process of them understanding who they are in that play and who they are in that role."

Volpe started rehearsing *Good Boys and True* in September, and it will not be performed at Truman until the week before Thanksgiving. The play begins with the Brandon Hardy character onstage by himself, leading a tour of (unseen) new students at his fancy prep school. It's a monologue, not short, so for Zach to blow it would get the play off to a very poor start, and probably also spook the rest of the cast. Volpe knows where Zach needs to get to, starting with that first monologue. The character has to project entitlement, a whiff of corrosive self-regard. His smile, as he leads the younger boys around campus, should perhaps have a hint of a sneer underneath. He can't immediately make himself detestable—that would ruin everything—but something in his manner must hint at trouble ahead.

These shadings are what set Truman Drama apart. Volpe never doubts that his kids can grasp the complexities that he sees in their roles and deliver performances worthy of the program's high ambition and its legacy of excellence. "Just wait and see," he says of Zach. "He's going to be very good. He may be great."

Volpe's challenge with some of his actors is to get them to project, to come out of themselves and show anger, sadness, joy, bewilderment, dismay—whatever the scene and part demand. Others need to be reined in, but he is always careful about that. He never wants to make an actor self-conscious or cautious. From his courses at Northwestern and elsewhere, and from studying the legendary acting coaches like Constantin Stanislavski, he knows the principles of restraint and control.

Stanislavski wrote that an actor should try to imagine an artist undertaking a "delicate pencil sketch." He needs a clean sheet of paper, no extraneous marks. No smudges or spots that would mar the drawing. The same principle applies in acting, he instructed. "Extra gestures are the equivalent of trash, dirt, spots."

Volpe translates such lessons in a much more concise way for his student actors. "You go out there as far as you want, and I'll stop you if it's not right," he tells them. It's his way of inviting them out onto a ledge but assuring them he won't let them fall. As for extra gestures, overacting—any trash, dirt, or spots—he can clean those up in time. Bobby Ryan, more than most, takes this to heart. "I have, like, a deal with Volpe," he says. "I don't want any guidelines in advance. I just want endless possibilities. I take it as far as I want, and if he tells me I've crossed the line, I don't question it. I know he won't say that if it's not the case."

Good Boys is a serious drama, at times relentlessly so, but Bobby's character is not without comic elements. As a gay outsider at a traditional boys' school, Justin Simmons masks his pain with laughs. When Bobby looks at the script, he notes a scene in which the stage direction says, *Justin is electric in this scene.* He doesn't really appreciate the explicit direction, even from the playwright, but the notation does tell him something. "He's got emotions going in all directions," Bobby reasons. "He deals with it by being funny and outrageous. I look at my part as controlled energy. The character might seem out of control, but as the actor I've got to be totally *in* control."

While *Good Boys* is in rehearsal, Bobby and Zach spend a lot of time together away from school, just like always—they play video games and Ping-Pong, work out, talk about school and girls. They talk about their parts, sometimes even ad-libbing lines that are not in the script. Both of them believe that what they are to each other offstage makes playing the parts far easier. Their friendship is not casual. It has an intensity to it. They have had a lot of good times, but also heated fights. "We trust each other. I don't see how you could do these parts without that," Bobby says. "We both know that we're not gay, but the similarity to those characters is that we're really close."

As senior year begins, Bobby and Zach have been at odds over a girl whom Zach used to date. "I started talking to her," Bobby explains. "We wound up losing our friendship over it for a little while. Being in *Good Boys* brought us back together." (I come to realize that when Bobby says he is "talking" to a girl, it means they have actually gone beyond the talking phase.) Onstage, they work to figure out how to play both the anger and the tenderness that exists between their characters—and how physical to be. There are times in the play when it seems that one of them might throw a punch, and others when it looks as if they might kiss.

Bobby says he's not sure himself what they might do. "Every time I'm onstage, it's like a clean slate. Volpe always says he's seen *Sunday in the Park with George*, like, a million times, but every time it's different. I totally get that. As an actor, every time you go out there, you create something new, and sometimes you don't even know what it's going to be."

Volpe, it seems to me, is always subtly arming his students with qualities and skills that do not come to them naturally. Wayne Miletto likes control and routine. That is how he is going to power himself through life, almost certainly with great success. But adults know that life frustrates meticulous planners and makes a mockery of control, so onstage, that is what Volpe takes away from Wayne.

My first encounter with Wayne, who plays the role of the coach in *Good Boys*, takes place a month before rehearsals begin. A big, solidly built guy with a barrel chest, he greets me at the front door of his family's Levittown rancher, extends his right hand, and says in a deep baritone, "Nice to meet you. I'm Wayne." My first impression is that he seems like he's about thirty-five years old. As we talk, he projects an uncommon self-assurance; not a high school boy's bluster, but a quality deeply ingrained.

Wayne's home life, like that of so many of the Truman kids I meet, has not been serene. All over Levittown and the smaller, nearby communities that feed into Truman, it isn't usually poverty I observe, but rather the steady, low-simmering tumult of economic and family instability. People lose jobs, move, get married and un-married, get sick, fall behind on bills, have more kids. Once the apotheosis of suburban constancy, Levittown is now an example of those same suburbs coming apart at the seams. "When I was five, my uncle down the street was having trouble with his house, so my mom offered him ours," Wayne tells me. "And then we moved into a house with my other aunt and uncle. After that, we moved into Brittany Springs Apartments. I was going to Catholic school, but after we moved, my mom took me out of that." When I ask him about his father, he says, matter-of-factly, "I've never met him." He lives with his mother and two younger sisters, including one born just ten months ago, from his mother's current relationship.

Wayne is not one of the Volpe actors who began thinking about performing at Truman in grade school. He was a football player. He began playing football at the pee-wee level, grade school, and he was good. As he enters his senior year at Truman, he weighs 230 pounds on just a five-foot-ten frame, and he doesn't look fat—just solid. "I know," he says. "I still look the part. Everybody says, 'You play football, right?'"

He did play at Truman through his sophomore season. What happened after that was a little like the Michael Massari situation, except that Wayne called the shots, not the coach. Football had started to feel boring and routine. The "product," as he calls it, was not as good as theater. He told Zach, with whom he had played football since they were little kids, "I'm done. I'm not having fun." Zach understood, but some of the other guys didn't. Big Wayne, of all people, giving up football to devote himself to theater? It made no sense. "They were like, 'Nobody quits football for theater.' And I said, 'Yeah, they do—I'm doing that.'"

Wayne first told an assistant coach who was his football mentor. "It was sort of heartbreaking. This was a person who really helped me out, and he says to me, 'Dude, I really need you. I'm low on guys, and the ones I have aren't that good.' And then he starts saying that I could really go somewhere with football, play in college and all that."

Wayne then sought out the head coach and told him, "I know this isn't the thing you want to hear, but there's no time for football in my life anymore. My heart is in theater." The coach either did not hear him correctly or pretended not to. "Okay," he said after Wayne had just quit his team. "I'll see you in the weight room this afternoon."

Wayne had to ask Volpe to get involved. Even all those years after Michael Massari, Volpe did not relish confrontations with coaches, even one he knew he was going to win. As Wayne put it, "I hesitated, because I know he doesn't like to butt heads with people." But somebody had to help Wayne get his point across.

Volpe told the coach he knew Wayne well enough to understand what a valued team member he was. He knew the football team was short on players. "But please, you have to stop struggling with him," he said. "He's not going to change his mind."

Freed of football, Wayne became a fully committed theater kid. On the first day we talked, he had just returned home from six weeks at a summer performing arts camp in upstate Pennsylvania. It was called the Performing Arts Institute at Wyoming Seminary. He auditioned to win his place, then found out it cost almost $6,000. "I sent a nice e-mail. I said, 'I'm honored, but the money is not there for me, so I can't accept the offer.'" The camp director responded that he would make a place for him if he could pay $900, which Wayne pieced together from his mother and his earnings at a restaurant job.

The camp consisted of twelve-hour days—classes, choir practice, rehearsals. He landed a lead in a show, the part of Valentine in *The Two Gentlemen of Verona*. Every night there was some kind of performance, including classical concerts performed by instrumental students. "The whole experience was a big mind-blower," he says. "Everything about it. All the talent up there, all the different stuff going on, all the stuff we were exposed to. I was never into classical music, but after listening to their concerts, I started to download it on my computer. I downloaded some jazz, too. Miles Davis, stuff like that."

Among all of Volpe's students, Wayne is the best at describing his teacher's directing, maybe because he sometimes struggles with it. In tenth grade, he won a part in *Blood Brothers*, a musical about fraternal twins separated at birth. Wayne played the narrator, who at different points in the musical just sort of appears onstage and interjects commentary. Volpe did not give him any blocking; he told him to listen to the show and pop up wherever it seemed to make sense at that moment. "I tried to do that," Wayne says. "I mapped out to myself how much time I had between scenes to get to a different spot. And I'd say, *Okay, you've got thirty seconds, or two minutes,* and that's what I did. I would come out of sidewalls. I would go backstage and emerge somewhere else. I'd show up on one side of the stage, or down the steps."

Volpe would like where he placed himself during one rehearsal, and then, at the next one, say it was all wrong—even though he had retraced his steps from the previous day and arrived in the very same spots. When Wayne expressed his frustration, Volpe said, "Feel the mood of the play and move with it. Just watch the show and think about where the narrator would overlook it, where he would be hiding. Why would it be the same place every time?"

He told Wayne to imagine he was in one of those Where's Waldo? books. His job was to surprise the audience, and to do so, he had to be unpredictable to the rest of the cast, and even to himself. Volpe kept talking to Wayne right up to opening night. He was trying to get him to let himself feel some discomfort onstage, to give in to a sense of not knowing precisely what would come next. "It's like when you played football," he said at one point. "The same play might be called twice in a row, but a player's movements have to vary in response to actions on the rest of the field."

"I was so young. I was still in tenth grade, and he was giving me more freedom than I wanted," Wayne says. "During the whole show, I was never stationary. Sometimes it was fun, but I got frustrated. I was like, 'Everybody else is getting basic blocking, so why can't I get blocking?' I was begging him for more direction, but that's not what he does. He turns that back on you every time."

Over time, Wayne came to realize that his conversations with his teacher were only partly about theater. "Find your character," Volpe tells his actors, by which he means they must fully understand and inhabit the roles of the people they are playing. Wayne tries to look into his characters from every possible angle: up close, from a distance, how others see him, whether he sees himself realistically or believes his own lies. He looks at the character's background, what motivates him in the present, what future he imagines for himself.

"The big thing you learn is there's not an endpoint," Wayne says. "It's a creative process, and it keeps evolving. Mr. Volpe might say, 'You're on the right track,' or even, 'You've found your character.' But then right away he says, 'Okay, now go somewhere else with it. Make your character better. Make him more believable.'"

When Wayne struggled with the role in *Blood Brothers*, Volpe said to him, "I know you can do this because last year you played one of the most difficult roles I've ever seen a ninth-grader do, and you were magnificent."

That role was Tom Collins in *Rent*. "I was glad when he gave me the part, but then I was like, *Whoa! How do I connect with this character?* This character is an MIT professor who just lost his job, and I don't think I ever heard of MIT before that—and he's a great guy who falls in love with a drag queen. I did know what a drag queen was, but I had never encountered one.

"I read the script and I watched the movie of *Rent*, and I looked at stuff on the Internet where people were talking about the play. Mr. Volpe talked a lot about it with us, about the whole context of this being something where AIDS was out in the open for one of the first times. It was awkward at first, but then I just had to say to myself, *All right, you're going to be a homosexual in this play, and you're going to be with a guy who dresses like a girl, and you have to be okay with that. People are counting on you to fulfill this part, so you've just gotta open your mind and figure out what that's all about.*"

W hat I liked is you were listening to each other, you weren't just saying lines," Volpe tells the *Good Boys and True* cast after rehearsal one afternoon. "This is not a half-ass-commitment play, it's a full-commitment play, and I think you're all understanding that. Each of these characters has to keep evolving."

He has watched from his usual spot—center of the theater, about eight rows back, next to Tracey Krause. He walks forward and takes a seat in the front row to talk to the cast, which is gathered at the edge of the stage. His writing journal, the "Book of Tears," as everyone calls it, rests on his lap. When he gives notes to the cast in the order in which he has written them into the journal, they come out in a kind of stream of consciousness.

"Zach, do you like pears? Would you eat a pear?" he asks, just a beat after his opening riff.

"Yeah, I'd eat a pear."

Volpe is thinking about a scene in Act 1 when Zach's character, Brandon Hardy, comes home from school and finds his mother waiting to confront him. As the young master of the universe, still believing (or hoping) that he is in control, he leans back on the couch, puts his feet up on a coffee table, and grabs an apple from a fruit bowl. Except that Volpe has decided he prefers a pear; visually, he likes the shape better, and a pear seems like something the wealthy Hardy family would eat. Also, once the actors are miked, he doesn't want Zach biting into an apple and having an audible crunch bounce off the auditorium walls.

"Okay, we're going to put pears in that bowl," he says.

Volpe is wearing a charcoal-gray sweater-vest (one of the couple of hundred sweaters he owns), a blue dress shirt, and a maroon patterned tie. He often wears a tie to school, almost never a jacket. (He has been known to give ties, sweaters, even expensive shoes away to students who have a family wedding or some other dress-up event to attend.) The half-glasses that he uses for reading are secured by a string around his neck. He has dozens of these strings, in every conceivable color, which his students know came from the Dollar Store. He is a sophisticate, a weekend denizen of New York's theater district, a clotheshorse. But he likes his students to know he is not too proud to shop at the Dollar Store. All teachers, he likes to say, *love* the Dollar Store. They *haunt* the Dollar Store.

And Volpe's tastes, in fact, are not uniformly highbrow. He is hooked on *Top Chef, Project Runway,* and *The Real Housewives of New Jersey.* He loves Joan Rivers and never misses her annual red-carpet narrations leading up to the Academy Awards telecasts. When we go to lunch or dinner together, a T.G.I. Friday's is at the upper end of places he proposes. One day he suggests we go to Friendly's, a chain I had not realized was even still in existence. "Oh, yes," he says, "and it's still as good as it ever was."

After settling the issue of the pear with Zach, he turns to Britney Harron, who fully inhabits her role as Truman Drama's designated diva. She is a trained singer and gifted dancer who radiates energy onstage. In musicals, it doesn't matter how many performers are in a number—all eyes turn to Britney. Her extended family and friends fill up whole sections of the auditorium at shows and account for thousands of dollars in ticket sales. "We all love Britney," Courtney Meyer says, "but she can be in her own little world. Britney World."

Britney had wanted the role of Elizabeth Hardy, the mother. But Volpe cast Mariela as Elizabeth and gave Britney the role of Elizabeth's younger sister, Maddy, who serves the story mainly as a sounding board, someone for Elizabeth to talk to about what's going on with her son. The role has some intriguing elements—Maddy is kind of hippie-chick bohemian set against her sister's two-doctor bourgeois household—but as written, it is the weakest in the play. "Britney, I want to stress to you the importance of finding something in this character," Volpe says. "I know, it's unfortunate. She's not part of the plotline. It makes it difficult, but you still have to find her."

If not the deepest thinker among Volpe's actors, Britney is probably the most comfortable onstage, a performer who loves the lights. "I'm sure you'll eventually get this," Volpe continues. "You never give me what I want in rehearsals, just in performance. But you can't wait. You have to start building this character."

He does not tell her how. He never does. It is the essential aspect of his genius as an educator. The world is full of people who cannot wait to tell you what they know. What animates Volpe is creating moments for his kids to figure it out for themselves. His ego, though not small, allows for great patience. Very few high school directors could be more versed in theater, more knowing about what the finished product should look like. But he lets his kids find their own way there.

His notes are often about the context of the material. The character Britney plays serves as a mirror for everyone else. She had attended the same exclusive high school as her sister (the female equivalent of St. Joseph's Prep), but hated it. "Why does she detest this world of theirs so much?" Volpe asks Britney. "As you think about that, you'll find the essence of this character."

Volpe moves on to a question for the whole cast. The scene in which Brandon first meets Cheryl Moody at the mall food court is written as a flashback near the end of the play. You see it already knowing about the scandal that ensued. Volpe has been musing about moving it forward, into Act 1, and wants to know what they think. Britney and Wayne immediately say they don't like it. Bobby adds, "I think that scene loses all its power if you move it."

It doesn't seem to bother Volpe that nobody likes his idea. He had been considering it; now he's not. "You're absolutely right," he says. "We'll do it as it's written."

BRITNEY HARRON (LEFT) AND
MARIELA CASTILLO
IN *GOOD BOYS AND TRUE.*

HERE'S SOMETHING
I DO WELL

His patience is not endless. In the middle of a rehearsal a few days later, Volpe hisses at Krause in a loud whisper: "Mariela has absolutely lost it. What's wrong with her? She's wooden. She sounds like she's on daytime TV. She's just lost it. This is a mess."

Of the six students in the *Good Boys* cast, Mariela Castillo has by far the most difficult part, that of a forty-five-year-old upper-middle-class doctor and mother. Volpe gave it to her because "at her best, she is remarkable. There are few high school girls who I can even imagine in this role, but she is fully capable of pulling it off."

Mariela is unlike her peers in several regards. She has plenty of friends at Truman, but her interests, relationships, and loyalties are mainly outside the school. She sings in a salsa duo with her sister, Thaimi, who is fourteen years older, and spends a great deal of time with family and friends across the Delaware River in New Jersey. She travels each summer to see her grandmother in Luquillo, Puerto Rico, a beach resort town east of San Juan. She is extremely close with her mother, a teacher in the Trenton public schools, and her father, a social worker and published poet.

Volpe considers Mariela to be "light-years" beyond the rest of the kids in her maturity. He doesn't relate to her as a teenager; he has more success if he regards her as a young actress. "That, to me, is what she is. There's something very adult about her." But on this day, he is frustrated because, after a strong audition and weeks of good rehearsals, Mariela has stopped growing into the role. With just one week left before opening night, she is headed in the other direction: backward. Volpe can be unsparing when he needs to be. Brutally honest.

As soon as the rehearsal ends, he turns to Mariela. The rest of the cast, sitting with her on the edge of the stage, seems braced. It was obvious how bad she had been. "Mariela, I'm not going to get real down on you," he says. "You're already down on yourself. When you're on, nobody's better. When you're off, everybody's better. You already know that about yourself. And right now, you're not good. Everybody's better."

Mariela's declining performance has affected the rest of the cast. Zach is blowing lines for the first time in weeks. Everyone in scenes with her is off because she is either skipping chunks of dialogue or speaking them without conviction.

Volpe is not done. "Some actors can show up at seven P.M., dress, walk up onstage, and pull it off. And some have to get here at five-thirty and sit quietly and think and close everything out. Mariela, you're in that second category. So whatever's going on in your life—

your boyfriend, your fight with your mom, your senior project, the book you're reading—you've got to put that aside for now, all of it."

Mariela looks straight ahead, right at Volpe. She does not argue or offer a defense. She looks upset, but doesn't cry. No one cries at Truman rehearsals.

"I know how good you can be," Volpe says. "I just need you to get there."

Mariela nods. She has heard him, every word. "I'll try, Mr. Volpe," she says quietly.

Mariela is different from the other cast members in another significant way: academically. When I embarked on this book, I naively assumed that Volpe's actors would probably be among the top students at their not-so-great high school, high achievers across the board. They are thespians! Immersed in theater. They could hold forth on Edward Albee and Adam Rapp. They knew the difference between August Wilson and Lanford Wilson. So I just figured that of course they would excel in the classroom.

But what I have learned is that they are not, on the whole, terrific students. Volpe's program is like a laboratory for the concept of multiple intelligences, the idea that people learn in different ways, that a person's ability in one sphere does not always predict or preclude performance in another. His students' engagement in theater taps into their souls and spirits. It excites the parts of their brains that relate to language, movement, and musicality.

But of the six in the *Good Boys* cast, only Bobby is a truly gifted student. Courtney, perhaps, could be with a bit more effort. Wayne reads haltingly and with great difficulty, but true to his steadfast nature, he works around it—he is always the first one to memorize his lines and be off book, because it is far easier for him than having to read them. Britney's grades are solid, not stellar. Zach is up and down, and true to *his* nature, he has a tendency to overvalue his achievements. This is part of what makes him a confident, happy person. When I ask him how he has done on his SATs, he says, "Pretty good, a little above average," but when he tells me the actual numbers, they are not pretty good, even by the standards of Truman, where students do not, in general, produce high SAT scores.

Among the six, Mariela is in a category all her own: special education. She could not even take theater classes until her senior year because her schedule was loaded up with remedial math and English and courses in study and life skills.

Her learning issues have a known cause: chemotherapy, administered in high doses, to treat childhood leukemia. She was diagnosed at three years old. The drug regimen diminished her ability to retain and sort large batches of information. It is a common consequence, written about in the medical literature under such titles as "Cognitive Effects of Childhood Leukemia Therapy" and "Disruption of Learning Processes by Chemotherapeutic Agents." One such study, in the *Journal of Cancer*, states: "Childhood survivors [of acute lymphoblastic leukemia] exhibit academic difficulties and are more likely to be placed in a special education program. Behavioral evidence has highlighted impairments in the areas of attention, working memory, and processing speed, leading to a decrease in full scale IQ."

Mariela is a perfectly fluid reader, but numbers trip her up. She has been taught what is sometimes called tic-tac-toe math, a different way of figuring algebra and other higher-level math for learning-disabled students. "I can get the right answers," she explains. "But what takes other people an hour takes me three or four hours."

Theater is where Mariela feels capable. "I'm not supposed to be able to remember things, but I found out that when I'm doing a play, I can memorize dialogue," she says. All the stages of a production come clear to her in a way nothing else ever has. "In theater, everything is staged and organized. It goes in order and fits together. I've seen how Mr. Volpe is so brilliant at that, and it's helped me organize my life in the same way."

As with anyone who has acted successfully, the experience gives Mariela both a thrill and a jolt of confidence—but for her, it confers an additional meaning and benefit. "Being onstage makes you feel like you have so much power, because you're persuading the audience you're someone you're not. You have them in the palm of your hand. I really needed that. It makes me be able to look at myself and say, 'Here's something I do well.' I never felt that way before."

A rtists and others involved in the humanities are sometimes the first to declare that the value of what they do cannot be measured. They know it is intrinsic to what makes us human— who are we without our greatest paintings, poems, music, and literature?—but are sure that none of it can easily be put through the filter of economists, social scientists, and educational theorists.

"Everything now has to be fully accountable," Peter Plagens, a New York painter and art critic, told the online magazine *Salon* in a 2012 story on the declining status of the artistic classes in America. "An English department has to show it brings in enough money, that it holds its own with the business side. Public schools are held accountable in various bean-counting ways. The senator can point to the 'pointy-headed professor' teaching poetry and ask, 'Is this doing any good? Can we measure this?' It's a culture now measured by quantities rather than qualities."

Jonathan Lethem, the novelist, lamented in the same story, "These days everything has to have a clear market value, a proven use for mercantile culture. Well, art doesn't pass that test very naturally. You can make the art gesture into something the marketplace values. But it's always distorting and grotesque."

In April 2012, *The New York Times* published a heart-wrenching essay by Claire Needell Hollander, a middle school English teacher in the New York City public schools. Under the headline "Teach the Books, Touch the Heart," she began with an anecdote about teaching John Steinbeck's *Of Mice and Men*. As her class read the end together out loud in class, her "toughest boy," she wrote, "wept a little, and so did I." A girl in the class edged out of her chair to get a closer look and asked Hollander if she was crying. "I am," she said, "and the funny thing is I've read it many times."

Hollander, a reading enrichment teacher, shaped her lessons around robust literature—her classes met in small groups and talked informally about what they had read. Her students did not "read from the expected perspective," as she described it. They concluded (not unreasonably) that Holden Caulfield "was a punk, unfairly dismissive of parents who had given him every advantage." One student read Lady Macbeth's soliloquies as raps. Another, having been inspired by *Of Mice and Men*, went on to read *The Grapes of Wrath* on his own and told Hollander how amazed he was that "all these people hate each other, and they're all white."

She knew that these classes were enhancing her students' reading levels, their understanding of the world, their souls. But she had to stop offering them to all but her highest-achieving eighth-graders. Everyone else had to take instruction specifically targeted to boost their standardized test scores.

Hollander felt she had no choice. Reading scores on standardized tests in her school had gone up in the years she maintained her reading group, but not consistently enough. "Until recently, given the students' enthusiasm for the reading groups, I was able to play down that data," she wrote. "But last year, for the first time since I can remember, our test scores declined in relation to comparable schools in the city. Because I play a leadership role in the English department, I felt increased pressure to bring this year's scores up. All the teachers are increasing their number of test-preparation sessions and practice tests, so I have done the same, cutting two of my three classic book groups and replacing them with a test preparation tutorial program."

Instead of Steinbeck and Shakespeare, her students read "watered-down news articles or biographies, bastardized novels, memos or brochures." They studied vocabulary words, drilled on how to write sentences, and practiced taking multiple-choice tests. The overall impact of such instruction, Hollander said, is to "bleed our English classes dry."

So far, forty-six states and the District of Columbia have signed on to what is called the Common Core set of standards. Under its guidelines, by fourth grade, students will devote half their reading time to nonfiction, including historical documents, maps, and other "informational texts"—even such materials as train schedules and recipes. By twelfth grade, 70 percent of reading is to consist of nonfiction. The intent is to reflect "the knowledge and skills that our young people need for success in college and careers."

In defending these new standards, David Coleman, president of the College Board and one of the architects of the Common Core, seemed to equate reading and writing that is not purely fact-based with self-indulgence. Speaking to education administrators in New York state in 2011, he said, "It is rare in a working environment that someone says, 'Johnson, I need a market analysis by Friday, but before that, I need a compelling account of your childhood.'" In the same speech, he said, "As you grow up in this world, you realize people really don't give a shit about what you feel or what you think."

Coleman is a classicist who studied at Oxford and a former consultant for McKinsey & Company who clearly enjoys his role as a provocateur. There is plenty of truth in what he says—people often *don't* give a shit about what you think—though I'd argue that a young person might first encounter that bit of wisdom by reading fiction.

Defenders of Coleman and the Common Core argue that nonfiction reading need not be dry and that high school students might, for example, read Michael Pollan's *The Omnivore's Dilemma*, narrative histories by authors like Doris Kearns Goodwin, or nonfiction stories in *The New Yorker* by, say, Malcolm Gladwell. But our education system is two-tiered in unintended and damaging ways, and the new standards and emphasis on accountability often make it more so. Where students are most in need of help is where the most stripped-down, deadening material is put in front of them. Under the Common Core rubric, students in, say, Chicago's tony northern suburbs might read *New Yorker* pieces—on the South Side, they'll get train schedules.

I witnessed perhaps the ultimate in bloodless curriculum while researching a magazine story several years ago—a robotic teaching method known as Direct Instruction. I. M. Terrell Elementary

School in Fort Worth, Texas, is perched on a hillside and surrounded by interstate highways. The area is called the Island. The only other thing on the Island is a housing project of more than fifty two-story apartment buildings, from which Terrell draws its entire student body. Using thick "presentation books" that scripted each word, teachers at the school signaled commands by snapping their fingers, clapping, or pounding on a book or desk, so the lessons were fast-paced and rhythmic. In a fifth-grade "reading for comprehension" lesson, students read a short passage and then were prompted to mine facts and define vocabulary words. In one of the lessons I watched, the word *drain* occurred in a chunk of text.

"The part of a sink that the water goes down is called a drain," the teacher said, reading from her script.

Her students then repeated, "The part of a sink that the water goes down is called a drain."

She then asked, "What is the part of a sink that the water goes down?"

"A drain!" the students shouted.

Few middle-class parents would stand for their children's being subjected to this method of teaching. Thomas Tocco, who was then the superintendent of schools in the city of Fort Worth, told me he was persuaded to try Direct Instruction because research showed that it worked—i.e., it acted like rocket fuel on test scores—and, basically, because he was desperate. "We had too many kids who were just nowhere in terms of reading," he said. The state of Texas was soon to toughen its test requirements, and Fort Worth was in danger of having as many as seventy schools classified as failing. "If that were the case," Tocco said, "you wouldn't have been able to sell a cemetery plot in this town, let alone a house or a business."

Near the end of my visit to Terrell, a sign in a third-floor corridor caught my eye. It said WRITER'S GALLERY. I wandered over to see what the children of Terrell Elementary had written. Would I learn what it was like to live on the Island, to strap your backpack on every morning and walk up the hill to this place? But there were no stories on the wall. Instead, in neat rows, were the certificates of students who had passed the Fourth Grade Spring Benchmark Writing Test, a section of the Texas state exams.

Hollander's essay and the comments of Lethem and Plagens cede ground and seem to grant that art and literature are too soft to withstand scientific examination. That if put to the test, the humanities fail. Certainly, the current system can seem rigged to produce that result. An effective test-prep class—one that drills students repeatedly on the kinds of questions they will encounter on a specific test—can, in a given year, send test scores skyrocketing. No music, theater, visual arts, or literature class will ever be able to compete with that.

There is nothing, however, soft about Volpe's theater classes and drama program. Even though theater is part of the "arts," an airy term, the time students spend with him is actually the *least* abstract part of their day—certainly less theoretical than a math, science, or history class. With each production, they set an incredibly high goal and go about building something. The process is more like work than play, and at the end, they are left with a tangible thing, as close to perfection as they could make it.

Much of what I observe in Volpe's theater program fits comfortably within the muscular language of education reform, with its emphasis on problem solving, high standards, "reaching for the top," and accountability. More broadly, scientific research does exist that supports the value of teaching the arts and humanities—and the perils of de-emphasizing them.

Children who get sustained musical education have long been assumed to reap educational benefits in areas other than music. For years, the notion was unproven, somewhere in the realm of received wisdom or suburban myth. ("Put them in music and they'll ace algebra!") But an expanding body of research—social science that looks at the performance of cohorts of students and brain science that uses imaging to look at the firing of neurons in response to stimuli—supports music's benefits. Instruction and practice in music can "fundamentally shape" brain circuitry and enhance performance on a wide range of tasks, including reading comprehension, Nina Kraus, a Northwestern University neurobiologist, said in a presentation at the 2010 annual meeting of the American Association for the Advancement of Science.

Much of the research on cognitive benefits of arts education focuses on a concept known as "transfer"—the brain's ability to map information acquired for one task or set of tasks and put it to use for some different purpose. Creative thinking is high-order reasoning that requires memory storage and the ability to understand context. Theater training—as well as music and the visual arts—takes place in what educators call "language-rich environments." The theory is that the whole multistep process required to create art expands the brain's capabilities.

A major study from 1999, backed by the MacArthur Foundation, tracked outcomes for large cohorts of high school students, divided between children who received extensive arts education and those who did not. One part of the study looked specifically at the impact on students involved in theater. Between ninth and twelfth grades, their reading levels increased at a rate of 20 percent more than a cohort of similar students—as measured by academic ability and socioeconomics—who were not getting arts education. The authors theorized that the theater students benefited by spending time "reading and learning lines as actors, and possibly reading to carry out research about characters and their settings."

In 2011, the President's Committee on the Arts and the Humanities, first established in the Reagan administration, highlighted current scientific research and issued a call for greater emphasis on arts education. "The brain prioritizes emotionally tinged information for conversion to long-term memory," the authors wrote, citing music and theater education as examples of disciplines with the potential to "cause an actual change in the physical structure of neurons."

But the presidential panel's report, "Reinvesting in Arts Education: Winning America's Future Through Creative Schools," gingerly stepped around some policy issues. Even some of President Obama's most ardent supporters in Hollywood and New York's creative corridors would not be able to read it without stumbling over language that is couched in politics, if not outright hypocrisy. "In this climate of heightened accountability, some believe that schools will give instructional time only to subjects that are included in high-stakes testing," it states.

Some believe that? Does anyone seriously believe otherwise? Drawing on a range of research studies and surveys, the report does go on to delineate the sorry state of arts education in America: Schools identified as "needing improvement" and those with the highest percentage of minority students are the ones most likely to eliminate arts education. According to the authors, arts instruction has declined by 49 percent since the 1980s for black children and

40 percent for Latinos. In New York City, public schools in the bottom third in graduation rates (less than 50 percent) offered the least access to arts education—"fewer certified arts teachers per student, fewer dedicated arts spaces, [and] fewer arts and culture partnerships."

The source for the New York statistic was a 2009 report by the Center for Arts Education, which stated: "In New York City, the cultural capital of the world, public school students do not enjoy equal access to an arts education . . . Where the arts could have the greatest impact, students have the least opportunity to participate in arts learning."

California's Education Code, the set of laws and regulations that govern K–12 education in the nation's most populous state, calls on all schools to offer courses in four arts disciplines: music, visual, theater, and dance. But a study funded by the Ford Foundation and other private donors found that nearly 30 percent of California public schools provide no courses at all in the arts. Sixty-one percent had no full-time certified arts teacher.

School administrators in California reported two barriers to teaching art, neither of them surprising: inadequate funding and high-stakes testing that requires them to focus on mathematics and reading to the near exclusion of all other subjects. The presidential commission noted that the research in California and New York was conducted in 2010. "The situation is undoubtedly bleaker now," they wrote.

Nowhere in the No Child Left Behind Act, passed by Congress in the first term of President George W. Bush, does it say to slash arts education. Nor does President Obama's Race to the Top program—a competition for $4.35 billion in federal grants to states that meet various educational benchmarks—make any such recommendation. But the federal initiatives are centerpieces of a decade-long trend of increased emphasis on high-stakes testing—meaning tests with consequences that fall on educators.

In almost all cases, the tests measure strictly math and reading skills, so even science and history have been de-emphasized. Study after study shows that the leanest curriculums are being offered in the highest-poverty areas, despite ample evidence that this is exactly the wrong thing to do. Many educators believe that the Race to the Top, with its strictly defined inducements and penalties, will do even more to constrict curriculums than No Child Left Behind.

In more than a dozen states, student performance on standardized tests accounts for 50 percent of a teacher's rating. Across the nation, test scores figure into educators' compensation. So when school administrators pare down curriculums and teachers teach to the test, it is usually not out of ignorance—but is a matter of professional and financial survival. They have been, as it is said in business, "incentivized" to do so. "If their very livelihood depends on it, what do you think they're going to do?" says Mariale Hardiman, a longtime principal and now an assistant dean for interdisciplinary studies at Johns Hopkins University. "Everything they put in front of the kids is going to look like the next standardized test they've got coming up."

I f we want to build a future in which the middle class can succeed," Chicago mayor Rahm Emanuel wrote in a 2012 opinion article, changes must occur that have the effect of "bringing responsibility and accountability to our teachers and principals." Think about that statement for a moment. The implication is that unless they are closely watched, educators would otherwise be like the children they teach—irresponsible and unaccountable.

As the father of three children who are now all the way through high school—thirty-nine years of combined K–12 schooling—I've gotten to know lots of teachers. Hundreds of them, in addition to the ones I had as a kid. Some good ones, some bad, most of them in the middle. But I have encountered very few teachers who seemed not to care.

No doubt there are some who become hopeless about their students' abilities to learn. It's possible that high-stakes testing and its consequences might shake them from lethargy or despair. But the collateral damage of this era of narrowed learning is far harder to measure and will be recognized, if at all, only years into the future. Our society may be less creative, and not just in the arts. To give just one example, the aesthetic appeal of Apple products—what sets them apart from the offerings of other technology manufacturers and has made Apple the highest-valued company in the world—has its roots in one man's music training and another's interest in calligraphy and typography.

In 2008, *School Band and Orchestra* magazine, a niche publication read by music educators and virtually no one else, published an essay by Jef Raskin. It was a piece of writing that had gathered some dust, as Raskin had died a few years earlier, at age sixty-one, from pancreatic cancer—the same disease that would kill Steve Jobs, his onetime boss and collaborator at Apple. The first Macintosh computer was Raskin's brainchild, though Jobs ultimately got much of the credit for it. (Raskin was its "true father," author Owen Linzmayer wrote in *Apple Confidential 2.0: The Definitive History of the World's Most Colorful Company*.)

Raskin played in his high school band—clarinet, trombone,

and drums "with equal ineptitude," he wrote. As he became more serious about music, he took up the piano, organ, and recorder. He studied music as a graduate student, performed professionally with orchestras and ensembles, composed music, and conducted. "Conducting opera, in particular," he wrote, "was a fine introduction to the problems of managing creative and independent-minded employees."

Raskin did not consider his later work in computer design at Apple to be a departure from music. It was, rather, a progression, a logical extension of his creativity and aesthetic sense. He was a visual artist, as well, and his work was exhibited in museums, including the Museum of Modern Art in New York. Was Raskin unusually brilliant? A genius? Yes, without a doubt. But if the public schools he attended had not offered arts instruction, he believed, he would not have fulfilled his potential. "If I did not study music," he wrote, "there would be no Macintosh computers."

Steve Jobs, too, gave credit to his arts training, which was just about the sum total of his higher education. He spent only six months around a college, not all of it actually enrolled—at Reed College in Oregon. He took a course in calligraphy, where he also learned about typefaces, and he talked about its impact on him and his company for the rest of his life. "I learned about serif and sans-serif typefaces, about varying the amount of space between different letter combinations, about what makes great typography great," he wrote. "It was beautiful, historical, artistically subtle in a way that science can't capture, and I found it fascinating."

What gets taught in America's public schools has always been a mixture of state and local preferences influenced by various passing trends. Global forces figure in. The Soviet Union's launch of the Sputnik satellite into space in 1957 led to an overhaul of out-dated science curriculums, funded in part by $1 billion from the federal government—big money at the time and one of the first major expenditures made by Washington for education, which had traditionally been almost solely a local concern. These days, our education system is more often compared with schooling in Asia—unfavorably. Children in those countries *outperform* our children, as nearly every story says. (When I used the search words *Asian students outperforming U.S. students*, I got a kind message from the ever-helpful folks at Google: *In order to show you the most relevant results*, it said, *we have omitted some entries very similar to the 782 already displayed.* Without the culling, Google produced a large number of hits: 6,900,000 of them.)

In 2010, high school students in Shanghai, China's largest city, finished first in an international standardized test of math, sci-ence, and reading proficiency given to students in sixty-five nations. The United States finished between fifteenth and thirty-first in the three categories tested by the Organisation for Economic Co-operation and Development. The world's most populous nation, increasingly seen as America's major world rival, had surprisingly outperformed South Korea, Singapore, and Hong Kong (the former British protectorate, now under Chinese control), the traditional powers in these comparisons of academic aptitude.

Not everyone in China, however, viewed this result as an un-mitigated triumph. Some expressed concern that an emphasis on rote learning was smothering creative thinking and intellectual risk-taking. "These are two sides of the same coin: Chinese schools are very good at preparing their students for standardized tests," Jiang Xueqin, a deputy principal at Peking University High School in Beijing, wrote in an essay in *The Wall Street Journal* shortly after the test results were announced. "For that reason, they fail to prepare them for higher education and the knowledge economy."

A principal at a school in Shanghai that figured into the international testing was concerned enough about the stifling atmosphere that he instituted reforms to foster more creativity. One of his innovations: a weekly talent show.

It is complexity, not simplicity, that engages Mariela Castillo. She can hook into information, remember it, and manipulate it for artistic purposes when it has context and interest. Human beings, it is often said, are hardwired for narrative, and theater taps into Mariela's brain circuitry in a way nothing else ever has.

Some students at Truman who were her classmates in the early grades of elementary school, when she was still in treatment, know of her childhood cancer. Few others do. She told me about it, but it's not something she often talks about.

Volpe tends to deal with what is right in front of him: his classes, his upcoming production, writing the check to the catering hall to cover the deposit for the prom, planning the senior trip, proofreading the certificates of National Honor Society inductees. He keeps himself extraordinarily busy. He is close with his students, some more than others, but he does not probe them with questions. If they want to share, he listens. If they ask for advice, he gives it. He does not go to the guidance office and pore over their files to learn more about them. The starting point for Volpe is when you become his student. Sometimes I'm surprised at what he does not know. Then again, I'm a journalist and I ask questions for a living. (One of our children once said to my wife and me, "You know it's not normal, right, how many questions you guys ask?")

Volpe knew nothing about Mariela's leukemia until I told him about it. He was aware, of course, that she was in special ed. "But I don't pay any attention to the special education side of her because I don't ever see it," he said. "It doesn't color my relationship with her in any way. Maybe I could be faulted for that. But I have never given her any accommodations or expected less of her, even in class, and I don't think I should. With me, she is absolutely brilliant. She is one of the best actresses we've ever had here."

So, to Volpe, in the week before the curtain goes up, Mariela's struggles in *Good Boys and True* are strictly those of an actress who is not fully finding her character, and he is frustrated about that. She has one aspect of the part down cold: the coiled anger of a mother who finds out her son has been involved in something awful. In some ways, this is the most difficult aspect of the role; it demands that Mariela portray a wealthy, professional, and mature woman, accustomed to control and decorous behavior, whose world has just been upended by her own child.

One of Volpe's favorite things to tell his young actors is that "less is more." Embrace the silences. Calibrate. Understand that restrained is usually better than expansive and that unhinged almost never works. But now Mariela seems to have learned that lesson too well. At a certain moment, her part calls for seething, spitting rage. He wants her to simmer, then boil over—to "build up to an explosion." On an emotional scale of one to ten, she needs to reach a ten. "Maybe you even need to go beyond that," he says, "if that's possible."

The range of this part is exactly why he chose her. "But she just can't get there," he laments. "She's underplaying the anger. There's not going to be enough arc to it. I think she's going to give a good solid performance, nothing to be ashamed of, but it's not going to be a hundred percent complete development of the character."

Along with Zach, Mariela has the most lines. Her character is the conscience of the drama, the voice of the playwright. "It's such a central part," Volpe says. "She'll be okay, but if that's all she is, our overall performance is going to be just okay, nothing more."

Mariela knows she is struggling, so when Volpe calls her out in front of the cast it is not a surprise, nor does it anger or embarrass her. "He's the teacher, I'm the learner," she says. "I have to consume everything he says and try to do what he's asking."

It's nothing more than constructive criticism, she tells herself. She knows how to take that very well. Her parents are demanding. She's heard a lot worse at home. She is in the habit of writing notes in her own journal after Volpe reads from his Book of Tears. After he talks to her that afternoon, she writes: "More emotion. Try to get to a 10." That night and for several nights afterward, she will spend hours in her room at home practicing lines and trying to hit what seems to her the right pitch. She is much too sophisticated to think it is just a matter of screaming—anyone can do that. Her voice has to tremble. It has to build. Her body has to be held a certain way. Like everything that takes place onstage, it has to be believable.

She tries it all kinds of ways. Different rhythms. Loud to soft. Soft to loud. How, in this situation, would a mother talk to her son?

"Mariela, are you all right?" her own mother calls out more than once.

"Yes, fine," she shouts through a closed door.

TRACEY KRAUSE, VOLPE'S ASSISTANT
DIRECTOR AND FORMER STUDENT.

VOLP, WE'RE GONNA BRING THE HEAT!

A dress rehearsal looms, to be followed by two evening performances in the Truman auditorium and then, finally, a performance at the Pennsylvania State Thespian Conference—where judges will assess whether Truman's *Good Boys and True* is worthy of being one of five selections, nationwide, for the Main Stage in Nebraska. As showtimes grow near, anxiety levels increase. Volpe keeps losing things. "Where are my keys? What did I do with them?" he demands during a break in one of the final rehearsals.

"Here," Bobby says, handing them over. "You just asked me to move your car, remember?"

He loses his pen. He misplaces his reading glasses, the ones attached to the Dollar Store string. The school's audiovisual coordinator, Tony Bucci, another former Volpe student, walks up behind him one day in the auditorium and sweetly attaches a little reading light to his Book of Tears so he can see it when the lights go down. Volpe somehow promptly loses it.

Courtney keeps flashing her middle finger at various cast members. It has become her primary mode of communication. Bobby becomes more manic. Solid, dependable Wayne tries his best to keep everyone in line. He is the coach in the play, and of the cast.

Volpe brings up Nebraska. He is still going back and forth, sometimes pretending it doesn't matter and at other times letting the cast know what it will take to get there. "I don't care if we go or not," he tells them. "It's political to some extent. You have to understand that. And who knows if they'll like the content of this play? We can't control that. It's really out of our hands."

If they are not selected, he says, they could all go to New York together, which he had done many times with groups of students— take the train, stay a night, see a couple of shows. It would be fun and a lot cheaper. "We'll have a great time. But if you want to go to Nebraska, keep in mind we are going to be judged on everything, and I mean *everything*. Blocking, lights, scenery, wardrobe, props, sounds you may make backstage. They are very, very picky."

Volpe and Krause spend much of the dress rehearsal focused on the play's nonverbal aspects. It's a reminder that theater is the original visual medium, elaborate playtime with costumes, makeup, and scenery—an exercise in tricking an audience, as much as possible, into believing that what they are seeing is real. Archaeologists have traced the beginnings of theater back as far as 2500 BCE, to the ancient Egyptians and sacred plays involving the myth of the god Osiris and his wife Isis. (The themes of those early Egyptian dramas are not unfamiliar even now—immaculate conception, resurrection, and a whole lot of violence.)

Tracey Krause, Volpe's assistant director, becomes even more profane, if that is possible. "Where's the fucking remote?" she whispers as a scene opens and Mariela, in her living room, sits down with Britney in front of a television screen to watch a copy of the tape to see if the male in it does, indeed, seem to be her son. She is supposed to pick up the remote off a coffee table, but it's not there. (There's no TV on the set—she's just supposed to point the remote in the direction of the audience, which will get what's going on: *She's looking at a screen!*—so the absence of a remote sort of wrecks the effect.)

In another scene, the issue is Courtney's hair, which is all wrong, according to Krause. "It should be in a braid. She works in a fucking food court."

Also, Mariela needs a handbag of some sort. Without it, she doesn't look fully dressed. Krause has something at home; she'll give it to Mariela before opening night. Britney's outfit seems just right: a long skirt and loose-fitting blouse that make her look appropriately bohemian. But *her* hair is a problem, too. Volpe makes a note to get her a headband to keep her bangs out of her eyes. He also decides that he doesn't like the big trophy on the desk of Coach Shea, the character played by Wayne.

"Whose idea was that?" he says.

"Yours," says Krause.

"Whatever. It's totally distracting. We need to lose it."

Volpe talks a lot about "stage pictures," the way actors arrange themselves in scenes. He hates when they stand in a straight line across the stage, because nobody does that in real life. Even when this cast gathers to listen to Volpe's notes, I am always struck by how naturally they compose a picture you would want to look at. It seems an indication of how bonded they are, onstage and off.

On this night, while Volpe reads from the Book of Tears, Bobby, Mariela, and Zach sit on chairs they have pulled forward, Courtney sits cross-legged on the hardwood stage in front of them, and Britney and Wayne stand in the back, not directly behind the chairs, but on the flanks. They look like a publicity poster for the play.

It has been far from a flawless dress rehearsal. The most notable flub was Zach skipping a line of dialogue; not a big deal, and Bobby smartly covered for him—except that as Zach walked offstage, with his microphone still live, he uttered, "Fuck! My line."

"Zach, there's nothing I need to say about that," Volpe says. "You know it can't happen again. Ever."

Mariela had made a wrong turn exiting the stage in one scene, then sort of U-turned and scampered off in half-light. "Sorry," she says when Volpe brings it up. Overall, her performance was much better, and she seems headed again in the right direction. But the play felt a little flat. That was not unusual for a dress rehearsal, in Volpe's experience, but also no cause for great optimism. At a low moment in the first act, he leaned over and said to Krause, "We can forget about Nebraska. If we're no better than this, we'll get hooted off the stage at the state festival."

He is not occasionally without his own drama. When has Truman Drama ever been hooted off a stage? Never. To the cast, he is more encouraging. "Was that great?" he says. "No. Was it even as good as some of our rehearsals? I'm not going to lie to you. It wasn't. But am I worried? No, I'm not worried."

. . .

On opening night at Truman, the cast gathers three hours before curtain. Zach has his game face on from the moment he walks into the auditorium, like he is first man up in the order and about to dig his spikes into the batter's box. He shouts, "Volp, we're gonna bring the heat!"

Sandwiches are ordered and consumed. Robby Edmondson's tenth-grade sister and heir apparent, Lindsay, puts microphones on the cast and does sound checks. Mariela sits by herself, earbuds in, looking intense but not nervous. Volpe told her she is someone who needs to find a quiet space, one within herself, and she has taken it to heart. Bobby, as usual, is noisy and a little scattered. Krause looks at him backstage, still in his street clothes as others are already dressing.

"We've got plenty of time," he says.

"No, we don't. Put your fucking clothes on."

About twenty minutes before curtain, Wayne gathers the cast and crew in a small room across a corridor from backstage. Robby Edmondson says a short prayer, then everyone locks arms and moves together in a circle as they chant, "Love you. Love you. Love you." Wayne has imported the tradition of this "love-you circle," as they call it, back from his summer drama camp.

Volpe comes in right afterward. "My job is done," he says. "*Good Boys* is a piece of art that you have created. It is a living, breathing thing, and you will remake it every time you do it. There are going to be mistakes. You have to know that. It's theater. When they occur, you just have to keep on going and know that later, you'll laugh about them."

He closes as he always does in these pre-performance talks. "I want you to go out there and have a wonderful time. I love all of you, and God bless you."

The set is uncomplicated, just one piece that rotates on casters. In its various positions, and with the stage crew carrying elements on and off stage, it sets off the locker room at St. Joseph's, Coach Shea's office, Justin's bedroom, and the sitting area at the food court where Brandon meets Cheryl Moody.

A young math teacher at Truman helped select music—a melancholy, indie-rock sound track to play during transitions between scenes. The house lights dim at seven-forty, and Robby Edmondson queues up "Dare You to Move," by the group Switchfoot. Zach walks to the front of the stage, alone in the spotlight, in khakis and a blue blazer with a St. Joseph's Prep coat of arms affixed to the left pocket. At the very least, he looks convincing. He has a long monologue to speak—twenty lines of type in the script, delivered as he walks the stage and leads a tour of first-year students. If Zach were a less confident person, he might have been terrified, and in fact, the part did scare him in the beginning. He felt, he said, "pressure on my shoulders. I'm a lead. If I don't do well, the show doesn't do well."

He is the least experienced in the cast, a more recent project of Volpe's. When he speaks casually, it's in a strong Philadelphia dialect, like just about everybody else in Levittown. He muddles his vowel sounds, drops some consonants and even whole syllables. The word *water* comes out as *wuhder*. (I still say it that way myself.) The name of the city is *Fluffya*. In everyday life, you would not mistake him for a private school lad.

He waits for the music to fade out, then begins: "We'll start the tour here, and I'll tell you a little bit about the school, and if anyone has any questions, I can maybe answer them, okay?" He points out the "quad" and the "field house" and refers to the "Ivies" and the "public Ivies," where all these newbies will ultimately matriculate. He calls attention to the campus golf course off in the distance.

The monologue sets the arc of the story. St. Joseph's Prep holds itself in high moral regard and self-consciously grooms America's future elites. Its graduates are monied, but believe in the concept of noblesse oblige. Brandon's father, referenced in the play but never seen, is off somewhere in the Third World, volunteering for Doctors Without Borders. Part of the way though the monologue, Brandon Hardy explains that everybody at the school must play a sport. *"Mens sana in corpore sano,"* he says. "A sound mind in a sound body."

Volpe nudges me with his elbow. "Zach is on fire!" he says. And he is. As promised, he has brought the heat. His diction is perfect, his pacing not rushed in the least. Latin hasn't been taught at Truman for nearly two decades, but he even pulls that off. As Zach gets to the end, Volpe says, "Wow. *Wow.*"

Zach's next scene does not go off without a hitch, and what occurs will repeat itself in each successive performance. He and Bobby are in the locker room at St. Joe's, getting ready for gym class. As they talk, they take their shirts off. They are nicely built boys, lean and strong. The auditorium is not quite filled to capacity—as at most high schools, only the musicals at Truman fully sell out—but when the shirts come off, the noise level in the auditorium makes it seem like the theater is packed. The high school girls in the seats hoot and giggle. A few boys whistle. They keep it up for a good thirty seconds.

Zach and Bobby handle it like total pros. They don't smile or react in any way. They just freeze until the noise subsides—what else are you going to do when your audience acts boorish?—then pick back up with the dialogue. Bobby would recall thinking, *They have to know that the rest of our clothes aren't coming off, right? Even at Truman we can't do that.*

O pening night includes not one poor performance by any of the six cast members. Britney, as Volpe said would happen, fully finds her character only once the houselights dim and she is under the stage lights.

What she injects into the role is tart, pungent humor. She manages to both gently mock and support her sister at the same time— playing it in a way that would ring true to anyone familiar with sibling dynamics. When her sister suggests that maybe Brandon isn't even having sex yet, and therefore can't be the boy in the tape, Britney throws her head back in laughter. Of *course* he is, she says. He has a steady girlfriend. What does she *think* they're doing?

Mariela, on opening night, is simply towering—"a different actress," Volpe says, from the one who had struggled in recent weeks. She has held little meetings with herself. Pep talks. She needed to perform at a level that would satisfy her director's high expectations—and her own. Theater is what she does well, and she has no intention of doing it poorly.

In one scene, a confrontation with Brandon, she must puncture his smug façade and shake the truth from him. It is an interrogation. "Who is she? The girl, the flesh-and-blood person you did this to?" she asks.

Each word comes out like a little grenade. Fully and slowly enunciated. As the scene builds, the character played by Zach begins to backpedal and tries to explain. *"Pardon?"* Mariela says. I had never before heard that word—*pardon*—said so aggressively.

Mariela's whole body is rigid with anger. Though the script did not call for it and it had never occurred in rehearsals, it looks like she is poised to haul off and smack him—and not a stage slap, but one straight from her boiling inner core. "I don't know what happened," Volpe says later of Mariela's transformation. "The part is so difficult, there were times I thought, I've just asked too much of her. It's an unfair expectation. And then this. You saw it. Stunning, just stunning."

To say that Courtney seemed perfect from the very beginning of rehearsals unfairly implies that she never got better. But she played the role of Cheryl Moody with such pitch-perfect subtlety that it was sometimes hard to discern improvements.

There is a scene in which Elizabeth Hardy (Mariela) seeks her out at work, at the same food court where she had been picked up by Brandon. Elizabeth says she hates that Cheryl was "dragged into this" and asks what she can do. "You know, people say that—'Is there anything I can do?'" Courtney responds. "But do they mean it?" She asks what Elizabeth has in mind. "Like reparations? For damages inflicted upon me by your son?"

If there is such a thing as righteous sarcasm, that's the note that Courtney hits. She has the smallest part as measured by lines of dialogue. But I found myself anticipating her scenes. As good as everyone else was, she sometimes seemed to achieve a superior level of intelligence and sophistication as an actor. As Volpe said from the very beginning, she *was* Cheryl Moody.

There were mistakes, of course, and one near mishap. Krause gave Mariela a handbag suited for a wealthy woman doctor, which she was supposed to have over her shoulder in one scene when she enters the living room after returning from work. She walked on without it. Wayne's hair had to have some gray in it to help make him look like an adult teacher, but the process went way overboard, and he looked like he had dipped his head in cake flour.

Bobby believed deeply in the notion that a play renews itself every day, in rehearsal or performance. He was always open to new gestures, new ways to use the stage. On opening night, he jumps up on the bed in his room while making a point to Brandon. It was a very good idea. Justin is wired; it seems like something he would do. But the bed, built by Tony Bucci, is not exactly a bed; it's just wood hammered together in the shape of a bed, with a plank where the box spring and mattress would be. A comforter is thrown over the thing. When Bobby makes his jump, the wood groans—but miraculously, Bucci's contraption does not come apart.

Volpe and Krause edited some of the worst profanities out of the dialogue. All but a couple of the *fuck*s. The word *cocksucker* is said with just a hard *c*, the rest of it unspoken, so I don't think most of the audience could have intuited what was meant. Some of the dialogue as written is so harsh as to be almost violent, so the editing makes a difference. It softens the play, and not in a good way. But after four decades, Volpe knows how to stay on the acceptable side of the line—even while presenting material that almost anywhere else would be received as offensive.

The principal, Jim Moore, and the district's superintendent,

Sam Lee, are in the audience on opening night, and both come up to him afterward to offer praise and congratulations. As they walk away, Volpe exhales. "Okay," he says, "that's over with."

Zach's mom sat halfway back in the auditorium with his dad, Tom Philippi, the "manly man," as she described him. Tom had gotten to know Volpe after Zach began in theater. He talked to him sometimes at Zach's baseball games, which Volpe regularly attended, along with the athletic events of his other theater kids who were on teams. Zach came home from school one day, and his father asked him if he had read about all the problems plaguing the Broadway production of *Spider-Man*. Zach looked at him and said, "You read about musicals now, Dad?"

In the end, it was Zach's mother who was most deeply uncomfortable with his role in *Good Boys*, enough so that Volpe and Krause heard about it. (Zach and Krause are related—second cousins.) They even feared she might try to pull him from the play. "At first both of them were like, 'You're gay now?'" Zach says. "Especially my mom, she didn't want me to play a gay role. It made her pretty uncomfortable, but she got over it."

On opening night, his mother says she thought the play was very good, though she preferred the last Truman production Zach was in—*High School Musical 2*. His father says Zach was outstanding, with one caveat. "I thought he was a little bit too convincing, but I guess that's a good thing."

The 2010 Pennsylvania Thespian Festival takes place clear on the other side of the state, six hours away. A bus carrying Volpe, Krause, the Truman cast, and a couple of dozen other theater students leaves Levittown just after dawn on the Thursday after Thanksgiving, rolls west three hundred miles on the Pennsylvania Turnpike, and pulls into the town of Connellsville, southeast of Pittsburgh. Over the next ten hours, they will watch performances by two other high school drama troupes, have dinner, sit through a two-hour musical, and attend a dance. I'm exhausted just being around it all. On the bus ride back to the motel, after eleven P.M., Volpe says, "We need our rest. I'm concerned about all of you getting the sleep you need."

Truman's performance of *Good Boys and True*, which will determine if they continue on to Nebraska, is to take place at eight-fifteen the following night after another packed day of workshops, scholarship auditions, and performances by other schools. "If you're in the play, get your sleep. If you are in a room with someone performing, be respectful and let them sleep."

My room is on the same floor with the kids. I've been around high school students on out-of-town trips where you can hear their revelry in the hallways and from adjoining rooms, but on this night, all I hear is silence—as if the guest rooms are populated by senior citizens who have turned in before the local news.

The next morning, Zach, Britney, and Wayne perform monologues for a panel of judges awarding college scholarship money. They earned the opportunity by first winning an in-house competition at Truman. As I watch the scholarship auditions that morning, it seems to me they are at a level entirely different from that of most of the competitors from the other high schools. Their choices of material are more ambitious. And they perform them with a greater sense of control. In general, they do not seem as *young*—do not present at all like kids you often see on school stages, in grown-up clothes, who have dressed for the part but cannot quite inhabit it.

I'm relieved when the scholarship decisions are announced later in the festival, and they are in accord with my observations. Zach and Britney are among a handful of students awarded small scholarships, just $100. Wayne, who performed a monologue from August Wilson's *Fences*, wins the top honor and a grant of $500.

One of the judges, a faculty member at the New York Conservatory for Dramatic Arts, later approaches Krause to ask if Wayne is planning to pursue acting. "He'll get work if he wants it," he says. "Especially with his look"—by which he means that casting directors do not have a big field of young, athletic-looking black males to choose from. He does suggest that Wayne could have had stronger "tactics" in his monologue—a more defined sense of his character's objective.

"Do you know what I mean by *tactics*?" he asks Krause.

"Yes," she replies, with a withering look.

There is no such thing as an old Levittown family, with the town having sprung up in the 1950s, but Krause's family was there from the beginning. Her maiden name is Gatte, from her father's side and the Italian part of the family. Her maternal grandfather, David Lloyd III, served on the school board. Both her parents are Truman graduates.

A student of Volpe's in the mid-1990s and a cast member in his first Main Stage (*Telemachus Clay*) at the theater festival, Krause often seems like a woman in search of her own sitcom. Willfully inappropriate, she plays the tough-talking Levittown chick, a teacher too wise to the ways of teen misbehavior to take any shit or give much sympathy. She is so out there that it takes me a while to realize how versed she is in theater, how effective a teacher and director she is, and how deeply Volpe relies on her. I go one night with her to Cesare's Ristorante, a white-tablecloth restaurant that attracts a crowd of regulars—politicians, police brass, merchants, and just longtime residents. Her parents dine here religiously on Friday nights, and she informs me that our dinner must be put on their tab. "It's the way it has to work," she says. She's not even sure the staff here would *let* her pay.

Krause had the typical Levittown childhood. She spent time with her friends, rode around in cars, hung out at the mall. In the summers she went to the beach at the Jersey Shore. She says she was caught up in the swirl of high school life, "gossipy" and unfocused. As a high school sophomore, she traveled with Volpe and other students on a theater trip to New York. She had never been to a Broadway show, or even to New York, which is but seventy miles north, an hour by train from Levittown. "It changed my life, just opened my eyes in so many ways," she says. "Just the spectacle of it. The excitement. The show itself. My eyes were like saucers."

Now she chaperones those same kinds of trips with Volpe. "Nothing's changed," she says. "Only very rarely do we take a kid up there who's been to New York before, unless it was with us. They react just like I did—those saucer eyes. It's my favorite thing, watching them have that experience."

The show she saw on that first trip was *Falsettos*. She keeps the playbill in a binder at home, with the programs from the sixty-plus New York shows she has seen since. The programs from shows in Chicago and London are in a separate binder. Krause being Krause, she has another totem from *Falsettos*—a tattoo on her right ankle that is a replica of the cover art on the playbill from Broadway. The original illustration, a line drawing of five dancing men, was done by the late artist Keith Haring. When Krause went to college in Kutztown, Pennsylvania, she discovered it was Haring's hometown. It seemed like karma. So she got the tattoo.

A hell-raiser as a Truman student and a rebel as a member of its faculty, Krause sometimes refers to herself as "Miss Bitchy," which is sort of a joke and sort of not. Even students who become close to her are sure that in the beginning she hated them. That is not strictly true, but you do have to earn her affection. She keeps the cell phone numbers of dozens of students in her own phone, a practice discouraged by the administration. "They don't like that I do that," she says. "But when a kid's in trouble or some kind of crisis and they need to reach him, then they like it a lot. They come to me and say, 'Tracey, can you help?'"

She tells me about education courses in college in which professors advised future teachers that they had to win respect from students before they showed much of their own humanity. "They said, 'Don't smile till Christmas.' How stupid is that? I'll smile the first day if I want to—or if I don't like my class, they might not see me smile the whole year."

A divorced mother of two, Krause dresses stylishly, though her skirts are sometimes on the short side and her blouses a little snug. I love being around her because I can never be sure what she might say. One day, she clues me in on some school gossip that involves her and makes reference to her surgery. I ask what kind of surgery, already suspecting the answer, and she says, "You know, the breast augmentation." Well, I know now.

Her energy level is staggering. She teaches all day, spends countless hours with the theater program, coaches her kids' soccer teams (she used to coach the sport at Truman), runs half marathons, has an active dating life, makes frequent visits to the tanning salon, and finds time to jet off to Las Vegas for occasional weekends to visit her best friend.

"I hate crazy girls," I hear her say more than once, even though there is always plenty of drama swirling around Krause herself. Sometimes it has to do with her romances, but more often, with some beef she is in with the administration or some colleague. Her passion and heightened sense of justice do not make it easy for her to keep opinions buttoned up. She tells me that many people assume that what bonds her and Volpe is their shared love of theater, which is true—but only to a point. "The main thing we have in common is that right is right and wrong is wrong," she says. "I'm telling you, Lou and I have more balls than anybody in the building."

Krause wrote Volpe a letter from college in her freshman year. She thanked him for helping her find focus and discipline for the first time in her life and for showing her a world outside Levittown and her social set. She added that she was studying education and planned to return to Truman to teach. She wanted to be his assistant director of Truman Drama. If he ever left, she planned to take his place. She started at Truman right after college, but it took her seven years to get the position of Volpe's assistant director. Someone else had it, and when he left, another teacher with more seniority was awarded the job.

Most of what she believes about teaching, she learned from Volpe. One of the lessons: Be bluntly honest with students. Tell them their strengths, their weaknesses, what they need to do to get what they want. Volpe always gives much more praise than criticism. It sometimes seems to me there is a formula—about three compliments to one reproach—except that I know Volpe's methods to be too instinctive for that. The praise is never phony, and the criticism never gratuitous. "The main thing is, Lou never lies to a kid, and I'm not ever going to lie to a kid," Krause says. "I've seen him lie to adults, but never students."

Krause also learned to close out the noise from other teachers who might sometimes question her methods. Volpe told her some might sincerely believe there needs to be a higher wall, more delineation of adult-child authority. "Lou made me understand that closeness and respect are not mutually exclusive. That's one of the biggest things I learned from him. I can joke around with my students, I can have fun with them, but I know there's respect. I never worry about that."

Krause serves a multitude of roles in Truman Drama. One of them is enforcer of decorum. In Connellsville, students from some of the other high schools wear sweatpants and sweatshirts to the workshops and performances—or even pajama bottoms. A Truman student in such attire would be sent back to the hotel to change. They wear neat jeans or slacks. Some of the girls wear skirts. The boys cannot let their pants droop and their boxer shorts show. "The theater is the theater," Krause explains. "You dress a certain way."

The festival is in some ways like any other kind of conference, in that awards presentations, schedule changes, and various other routine business matters are transacted at a lectern on the stage. Students hoot and holler when one of their own—their drama teacher or a fellow student—is called forward or even just when the name of their school is mentioned. This is another no-no for the Truman kids. "We do those little golf claps," Zach says, demonstrating with his hands stretched far out in front of him and his wrists pressed together. (Only the hands move.) "Very classy. We get mocked by some of the other kids for it."

In a showcase of shorter performances that afternoon, another high school performs a production number from *Pippin*. It's racy, with the student playing Pippin reclining onstage, his legs splayed, as girls shimmy and slither around him. Volpe and Krause are taken aback. They sound like prudes, which, considering their oeuvre at Truman, strikes me as more than a little ironic.

The director from the school doing this *Pippin* number is a friend of Volpe's. "She told me it was a little edgy," he says from his seat in the auditorium. "A little edgy? Mother of God!"

Krause swivels around to address a row of Truman boys behind her. "I just want you to know that you are *not* allowed to have anything to do with those girls."

"Really, Krause?" Bobby says. "You're going to trail us night and day to make sure?"

"If I have to."

At five P.M., Wayne, Britney, Courtney, Mariela, Bobby, and Zach find a corner of the library at Connellsville High to run their lines one more time. They sit on the floor in two rows, facing in opposite directions, using each other as backrests. They make a game of it. If anyone flubs a line, the whole scene has to be started again from the top. It happens just twice. The first time is Courtney's fault, and Bobby responds by punching her lightly on the arm.

"Hey!" Courtney says. "What was that?" She punches him back, but harder.

Bobby would remember that moment, and others like it, in the coming weeks and months. High school casts always get to know each other well—if they don't start out as friends, they become close over the course of the production. But this was more than that. How many actors ever get to do a play with people they absolutely love, who are as close as family?

W e've got, like, ten problems right now," Robby Edmondson says. Truman's cast and crew have been given two hours to set up in an unfamiliar theater, after which the doors will open again and nearly a thousand people will pour in. Robby has to learn the sound-and-light board, then program it for the play. He keeps shooing away Tony Bucci, the faculty audiovisual advisor, because he figures he can master it more quickly himself.

Everyone else at the conference is eating dinner in the Connellsville High cafeteria. The Truman kids gobble down takeout pizza as they haul in their set from the rental truck Bucci had driven behind their bus. A prop—a lamp that is to sit on an end table in the Hardy family living room—breaks backstage. Tyler Kelch, the stagehand who dropped it, looks like one of those cartoon characters with sweat shooting off his brow. "I can't believe I did that," he keeps saying. "Shit. Shit!" No one tells Volpe; these are the types of things he does not handle well at the last moment. Wayne finds some glue and puts the lamp back together.

The most critical problem is the size of the stage, which is much bigger than Truman's. The traveler, the curtain nearest the front, comes down right in the middle of where Volpe figured they should stage the play. There is not enough room to play it in front of the curtain. All other options, it seems to him, would have this intimate play taking place in an ocean of space.

With no obvious solution at hand, Volpe looks like he is about to hyperventilate. One of the kids is sent to find Mark Zortman, director of the theater program at York High School and a well-regarded practitioner in all aspects of technical theater. His arrival a few minutes later has the approximate impact on Volpe of a generous dose of Xanax. Zortman stands onstage, hands behind his back, as Volpe explains the problem. He walks around a bit, deep in thought. He consults with Robby. There is something both commanding and soothing about Zortman. He's a first responder with an artistic eye.

Zortman figures out where to put the set and how to light the stage to make it work. It is his idea to flood the whole area beyond the set in a blue light, which is a masterstroke—it will both make the stage look less vast and lend the production a foreboding moodiness.

With fifteen minutes to go, Volpe calls the cast together. He says he doesn't want anyone to be nervous or undone by the unfamiliarity of the theater. A stage is a stage. "I want you to support each other and love each other. Whether we get a chance to ever do *Good Boys and True* again, it doesn't matter to me. What you've done is what I'm so proud of.

"A director opens a door. That's all I did, nothing more. You walked through it. I want you to know that at ten-thirty tonight, when we're done, their jaws are going to be dropping in the audience. They are going to be stunned, because that's how good you are. So be proud of our tradition. They're out there, and they're excited that Truman is about to do a play. Think about that. It's special to them that we're doing this play. God bless all of you. I love you all."

As he walks away, I hear two voices call to him, "We love you, too."

. . .

Zach is what in sports is called a "red-light player"—the bigger the stage and higher the stakes, the better he is. He once again knocks his opening monologue straight out of the park. Just farther this time.

A few minutes later, his first scene with Bobby, when the shirts come off, causes the same reaction it had back at Truman, only louder—with perhaps six hundred high school girls shrieking. (High school theater attracts many more girls than boys.) The two boys again let it subside, then pick back up with their dialogue.

Toward the end of rehearsals, Volpe did something uncharacteristic. He told Zach and Bobby to stop acting in their scenes together. Just say the lines. He felt they were locked in and polished and did not want them to keep working it. Anything new they added, he wanted it to occur onstage, in performance. Spontaneously. There is a scene in Act 2 that is the most emotional in the drama. It occurs after it has become clear that Brandon has ruined everything—brought shame to his family and school and sullied the reputation of a girl he doesn't even know. He has a final falling-out with his friend Justin, whom he has lied to throughout. It's a breakup.

In the script, the dialogue is written with some exclamation points, but Bobby has stopped playing it with bombast. He speaks his lines slowly and softly. "Never talk to me again," he says. "Never call me. Never seek me out. If we see each other—anywhere—on the street—in passing—don't stop. Don't say hi. Don't wave. Don't anything."

Volpe would say of Bobby, "He is fearless. One of the smartest actors I've ever worked with. He came to see how powerful that character was in his quietness. Whenever I think of how far he took that performance, it gives me the chills."

In previous performances, Bobby stood face-to-face with Zach. In Connellsville, he walks behind him, puts his arms around him, and strokes his chest. He leans forward and whispers the words with his lips right up against his left ear. He has not told Zach he will do that. He had not known himself. "We could feel the effect we were having the whole play," Bobby would recall. "You can, or at least I can, get a read on the audience. We were bringing something they hadn't seen before. When I did that, I heard some gasps, then it was dead silence."

Onstage, as the scene plays out, Zach has tears in his eyes. He is no longer conscious of acting. "That's the ultimate," he says later. "I'm that person. I'm Brandon Hardy. I totally fucked everything up, and I just lost the best friend I ever had."

There is so much talk of "risk taking" in theater that it can lose its meaning. But the courage displayed by Zach and Bobby is palpable. They kept adding layers of intimacy and vulnerability to the already charged interaction between their characters.

Mariela is, again, remarkable. Wayne's big voice and presence are especially welcome in the bigger auditorium. As Coach Shea, he blows a whistle early in Act 1 to call his class together for calisthenics. "Two lines, gentlemen!" he says in his booming baritone. Anyone not paying attention before that was called to order.

Volpe wanted the transitions between scenes to be seamless and fast so that audience members never had a moment to squirm or shift in their seats as they waited for actors to arrive at their spots. The material is not light; he didn't think it could withstand being weighted down by a too-slow pace. In Connellsville, right from the start, the play clips along at the tempo Volpe wanted. He thinks to himself, *They just keep making this better.*

The very last scene is also a flashback—Brandon and Justin, as high school freshmen, meeting for the first time. Their dialogue is light and silly, just two boys testing each other, seeing if they might one day be friends. Justin teases Brandon about his last name—Hardy—and it turns out both are fans of the Hardy Boys.

The moment the play ends, the audience in Connellsville bursts into a thunderous roar, then a sustained standing ovation. The cast members take their bows. They clap back at the audience. They bow again. The ovation just keeps rolling. They stay out there and bask in the glory—too long for Volpe's liking. Remember: Truman Drama stands for many things. And not least, a crisp professionalism. Volpe motions with both arms over his head to them, a waving motion to signal them to get backstage. They don't get the message. Finally, they see him mouth the words—*Get. Off. The. Stage*—and finally exit.

Volpe has a difficult time himself making his way out of the theater and backstage to the kids. Other high school directors, many of them good friends, keep stopping him to lavish praise on the show. One teacher, someone he does not know well, asks how he had managed to get a professional actress to play the role of the mother, Elizabeth Hardy. Volpe pauses for a moment before he answers, thinking the question might be in jest, but it clearly is not. "No," he says. "That is Mariela Castillo. She's one of my students." Volpe asks the teacher if she had liked Mariela's performance.

"Oh my God, yes," she replies.

. . .

The cast and crew squeeze into a small room backstage, still caught up in the post-performance adrenaline rush. They know their performance has packed an enormous emotional wallop. They are hugging, high-fiving, finally letting loose and whooping it up in a way they are never allowed to do in the theater. When Volpe and Krause walk in, Zach shouts, "We brought it! We brought it again!"

The way the festival is set up, each school performing a full-length play is to be critiqued afterward by drama directors from other Pennsylvania high schools. The comments are considered a bit of constructive feedback from the outside, and the teachers who are asked to give them take it seriously. (The adjudicator from the International Thespian Festival, sponsor of the festival in Nebraska, was also in the house, but her verdict will arrive at Truman by mail, several weeks later.)

The three directors who come backstage to talk to the Truman cast clutch the forms on which they were supposed to formulate comments on the various aspects of the production from both a dramatic and technical perspective—blocking, diction, set, lighting, sound, wardrobe, props, and so on. As Volpe introduces them, the kids quiet down, waiting to hear what they have done well, where they can improve.

Two of the directors immediately apologize. Their forms are mostly blank. Some marks on the very top, then nothing. "I'm sorry, I started to write a few things down, but it just seemed so stupid to continue," Andrea Roney, the drama director at North Penn High School, outside Philadelphia, says. "You *know* what you did. You know how remarkable it was. There were nine hundred kids out there who just grew up a little bit. All I can say is thank you."

She continues on for a moment more, but looks on the verge of tears herself. "There is a need for this kind of theater in high schools, a deep need," she says. "You are so lucky to have a director who has this vision, who has taken you on this journey. This is a journey that will be with you the rest of your lives."

Debbie Thompson, the drama director at Upper Dublin High School, also outside Philadelphia, says, "This is the essence of theater, what you just did. Grappling, thinking, pushing up against limits. Most of us do not have administrators courageous or insightful enough to let us do a show like this. My kids are so excited to have seen it. They will talk about it forever." She adds, "I can tell how much work went into it, because it didn't seem like work at all."

The third woman says she has made written comments on her form, but, perhaps inspired by the first two, does not read from them. Jill Campbell, of State College Area High School, says she had been impressed by the Truman cast's adeptness at listening to one another. "You made every word count," she says. "And the silences, too. I heard the silences."

The next morning, the cast is scheduled for a "talkback" session to answer questions about their performance and the process that led up to it. The sign-up sheet had room for twenty attendees. Someone tacked another sheet of paper next to it, and more than a hundred kids put their names down. It is moved from a classroom to a lecture hall.

Bobby and Zach answer questions about whether it's hard to play gay characters. (No.) The cast is asked about how they were possibly allowed to do a play with such edgy content. The Truman kids respond that Volpe's status—and theater's high status at Truman—allow them to do things that might be impossible elsewhere. Some of the questions aren't questions at all, but just kids gushing about what they had seen the previous night. "So amazing . . ." "Oh my God, I was overwhelmed . . ." "Do you have any idea how powerful that was?"

The adulation seems to have an intoxicating effect on the usually grounded Wayne, sending him on an uncharacteristic flight of rhetorical fancy. "It was like we planted a beautiful flower," he says. "And last night, it bloomed."

He pauses, as if to let this soak in. Bobby looks at him and smirks. The expressions of his other four castmates read: *Really, Wayne?* He catches himself and smiles. "Uh, sorry," he says. "I didn't mean to lay it on so thick."

Afterward, a girl from another high school takes Bobby aside and asks if he's gay. "No, I'm not," he says. He thinks later that his answer disappointed her. "It was just sort of weird. It seemed like she was hoping I was, so maybe I should've said yes to make her happy."

That night is the awards ceremony, which includes the naming of an all-state cast. No school could have more than one of its actors named. Volpe, because he does the calligraphy for the certificates, traditionally calls out the names from the stage at the front of the big theater. The last name he calls is one of his own: Mariela Castillo. The audience rises to its feet and gives her another sustained standing ovation. She had willed and worked her way to her performance by reminding herself that theater was what she did not fail at—it was where she excelled. As she ascends the stage to accept her award, she feels "like a movie star getting her Academy Award."

Mariela was one of the first of Volpe's actors I had met. I have tears in my eyes watching her get that award, and a part of me wants to run up onstage and say, "Do you know that this young woman's performance was even more amazing than you can imagine? The obstacles she had to overcome?"

Volpe promised the kids he wouldn't open the letter from the organizers of the Nebraska festival without them present. They would find out when he did. Three days before the start of Christmas break, he just has a feeling as he walks to the main office after lunch to check his mailbox. Sure enough, the envelope from the Educational Theatre Association is in his slot, mailed from its Cincinnati headquarters. Volpe texts the cast and crew, including Robby Edmondson, knowing that they are not allowed to check their cell phones during class but they all do. (He just hopes none of them will get caught.) He asks them to meet him at the end of the period.

When the bell rings, they all come running. Volpe's classroom is filling up with a musical theater section, so they adjourn to a nearby empty classroom. He shows them the envelope, unseals it with a letter opener, and pulls out five typewritten pages. The last four pages are a detailed critique of the performance. The first page is a letter, which he begins to read out loud, but he doesn't get far. It begins "Dear Louis," and is followed by a one-word sentence: "Congratulations!"

They scream and shout, hug one another; they throw their arms around Volpe and Krause. Zach, the most openly emotional among them, keeps dabbing at his eyes, but he can't keep tears from rolling down his cheeks. He thinks of how fearful he was when he first got involved in theater and how quickly he was put at ease. "From the first day, everyone was like, 'You're one of us.'" Now he feels he has helped put his mark on Truman Drama.

They text their parents and friends. Texts go out to recent alumni of the theater program, mentors to many in the current cast. Volpe's current students want his former ones to know that the tradition has been upheld.

"That's another thing that makes Truman Drama different," Robby observes. "It's understood by everyone that it's not just about us. There's a standard that the kids the year before set, and the year before that, going all the way back more than forty years. That sounds like what everyone would say, but it's not just words. You feel it. It's pressure, but in a good way."

Volpe knew how deeply they had all wanted to go to Nebraska. But even more than that, he believed, "They are not ready to give up this play. They're just not. They have such a deep connection to it."

This time, the critique was fully completed. Aspects of the performance were rated as either superior, excellent, good, or fair—they got mostly *superiors*—and the grades were supplemented with comments. The adjudicator was Liz Hansen, a veteran high school drama director in Iowa and officer with the theater association. "The director did a brilliant job of crafting the arc of the play," she wrote. Of the cast, she said, "I did not see any weak links, only six totally committed teammates working together in each and every scene. There was genuine love and trust visible onstage—producing a powerful series of moments." Even in rare moments when the drama lagged, she stated, "I believe this was a script issue—not an actor issue."

The adjudicator's only real pointed criticism was of the set. The Hardys' living room, staged by Volpe as a modern, minimalist space, consisted of a sofa, a chair, a couple of tables, and, as Volpe said, "those straw-looking things that we put in a vase on the floor." He also arranged flowers in a vase on one of the tables, and the fruit bowl. The furniture purchase at IKEA came to less than $500. But the living room did not convince Hansen that it belonged to "two accomplished and wealthy doctors," nor did it reflect the "opulent lifestyle that produced the conflict within this family."

I didn't disagree at all. It would have been better if the living room conjured on Truman's ancient stage were composed of pieces from Stickley or Herman Miller, but where was Volpe going to find those? He certainly had no budget to buy them, and the parent population of Truman had no such furniture to lend.

A STREET IN LEVITTOWN.

THE THREE-BEDROOM HOMES ARE THE MODELS

THE DEVELOPER CALLED JUBILEES.

NO CHILD REMAINS
LOST IN LEVITTOWN

On the eve of *Good Boys'* world premiere at Chicago's Steppenwolf Theatre in 2007, the company's artistic director, Martha Lavey, commented on the play's focus on class. "To be born into privilege," she said, "is to be given the tools to replicate that privilege."

Joseph Stiglitz, the Nobel Prize–winning economist, wrote in 2012, "There are amazing stories of people who made it from the bottom to the top. But what happens on average? What is the chance of somebody from the bottom making it to the middle or somebody from the top who doesn't work going down? In terms of basic statistics, the U.S. has become less a land of opportunity than other advanced industrial countries . . . All markets are shaped by laws and regulations, and unfortunately, our laws and regulations are shaped in order to create more inequality and less opportunity."

What I found most heartbreaking at Truman was how far removed the students were from the parts of America where success replicates success, how little they seemed to know that, and how much wider the gap had grown in the decades since I was a student at their school. We didn't just think we were part of the middle class, the great engine of America powering us forward; we *were* part of it. Fully. In my era at Truman, many graduates did go on to achieve high levels of success—they became doctors, lawyers, college professors, engineers, business owners, high-ranking military officers. It was well within the realm of possibility because the climb was not as high. Our education in the Bristol Township school district was not terrific, but neither was it so far removed from what a student in a wealthier public school district would have received.

Now, though, children in America's privileged zip codes live at a higher altitude, their own airspace—a life of private lessons, tutoring, expensive SAT prep, summer internships rather than paid work, individual sports coaches to polish skills, college "coaches" to burnish résumés. These perks act as multipliers, a doubling or tripling down on an already overflowing basket of advantages: the parents' good genes, the family's wealth and status, the leafy neighborhood within the excellent school district. Children in Levittown did not benefit from these things when I was growing up. The difference is, they didn't exist in great measure elsewhere, either.

The Harvard professor and cultural historian Niall Ferguson, generally considered a political conservative, has written of a "cognitive elite" in America: "The problem is that this cognitive elite has become self-perpetuating: they marry one another, live in close proximity to one another, and use every means, fair or foul, to ensure that their kids follow in their academic footsteps (even when Junior is innately less smart than Mom and Dad)."

He has also observed that "the financial returns on brainpower have risen steeply"—as distinct from the fruits of factory work and manual labor—and that upper-middle-class parents now produce a disproportionate number of the smartest children because "smart people tend to marry other smart people and produce smart children." This is true to an extent, but if it were entirely so, Junior would rarely be less innately smart than his parents and they would not have to try so avidly to gain advantage for him.

At a scholarship audition, I watch as Bobby Ryan is asked to talk about the breadth of his community service. He looks genuinely bewildered by the concept. He says something at first about helping out in his neighborhood as younger kids went trick-or-treating on Halloween, but senses the answer is not satisfactory. "I'm sorry," he finally says, "I'm not really sure how to answer. I go to school and I do theater and I have a job."

In fact, I had seen Bobby step off Truman's stage mid-rehearsal, pull on his Chick-fil-A uniform, and walk out the auditorium door. And he wasn't the only one. If you had a shift about to start, you left. No questions asked. If a student paused or uttered an apology, Volpe would say, "Go. You've got to get to work." That is still a bedrock value in Levittown—work—even as teens in higher-end zip codes have moved on to unpaid endeavors to further augment their credentials.

Levittown, Pennsylvania, was one of the great wonders of its day. Before the backhoes and work crews descended in 1952, there were no sewers across its 5,500 acres, no running water, little electric service, and no police or fire departments. The landscape was a tableau of farm fields, barns, horses, cows, chickens, and the occasional house. William Levitt regarded the land he had acquired as frozen in time, belonging to a previous century, and marveled that such a backwater existed in the corridor between New York and Philadelphia. He set out not merely to build houses on this primitive territory, but to plant the seeds of a new civilization. Without a hint of irony or self-consciousness, Levitt marketed his sprawling development as a utopia: "the most perfectly planned community in America."

A camera crew from the documentary series *The March of Time* visited Levittown in 1953. In a grandiloquent, newsreel-style voice, the show's narrator, Westbrook Van Voorhis, began his report: "Today, at the eastern extremity of the state of Pennsylvania, a remarkable construction project is transforming the face of the countryside."

The transformation occurred with breathtaking speed. The Levitt construction crews needed just one day to put up an entire house. They worked as an assembly line, with each man assigned to specific tasks that he applied to one identical house after another. The houses were built on concrete slabs, so no digging was required. Precut lumber and nails came from a Levitt factory in California. "Another day, another forty houses," Van Voorhis intoned as one thirty-six-man crew, a fraction of Levitt's massive army, posed in front of a finished house. "The complete price is $10,500, for two bedrooms, a large living room, kitchen, bath, and dining space, and five closets."

The show notes other Levitt innovations, inspired by the builder's own vision of what constituted a childhood of privilege. He built grammar schools into the neighborhoods because he did not believe young children should have to ride buses to school. Five massive swimming pools—longer than fifty-meter Olympic pools, and wider—were dug so the children would have a place to cool off in the summer. On the periphery of each swimming pool were ball fields, also Levitt-built.

The documentary shows happy young couples picking out their home sites. One woman looks into the camera and says that she absolutely *must* live on Butterfly Lane. A police officer is interviewed after he has just returned a lost child to his mother. "That's the way it goes in Levittown," he says. "Lost kids, lost dogs, a few motor vehicle violations, but no crime." The narrator adds, in his sonorous tone, "No child remains lost in Levittown for very long."

William Levitt presided over Levitt and Sons with his brother, Alfred, but he was the public face of the partnership. *Time* magazine put him on its cover and declared that Levittown was "as much an achievement of its cultural moment as Venice or Jerusalem."

My parents were typical Levittown home buyers in that they came from nothing, had built no financial resources of their own, and in no previous era could have even dreamed of purchasing their own home. My father grew up in the Kensington section of Philadelphia, part of the city's hardscrabble "river wards" that consisted of blocks and blocks of narrow row houses. His father, who had emigrated at the turn of the century from the city of Odessa in the Ukraine, worked mainly as a trucking clerk, dispatching drivers on their routes. For many years during the Depression, he had no work, and my father and his older brother were sent to live with relatives. (A port city on the Black Sea, Odessa was a notorious underworld haven, so it is not surprising that the uncle who had the money to take my father in was one who had found his way into the gambling business in Philadelphia.) When my father was reunited with his parents, it was in claustrophobic conditions amid a multigenerational clot of extended family, all crammed into just a few bedrooms.

My mother's parents owned a corner grocery and were somewhat better off, though the store struggled because many customers could not pay or had to buy on credit, with debts recorded in a book kept behind the counter. Her father supplemented the store's receipts by delivering milk in a horse-drawn buggy.

My father began college in 1943, in an ROTC program, but lasted just one semester before he was called to active duty and shipped to Europe. He was wounded, not badly, in the waning days of the Battle of the Bulge. When he returned home, he resumed college at Temple University and then went through its law school, with every penny of his higher education paid by that great entitlement program called the GI Bill.

He was clerking for a Philadelphia lawyer, making less than $100 a week, when he drove out to Levittown for the first time to represent a home buyer. The freshly built town reminded him of a huge Army camp. Houses sprawled in every direction over bare terrain, with newly strung electrical wires crisscrossing overhead. The baby trees planted by William Levitt's workers were not yet much taller than the Fords, Chevys, and Studebakers parked in the driveways. He didn't love it at first, but it looked like a chance to get out of the one-bedroom city apartment he shared with his wife and my older brother and to have, for the first time in his life, an expanse of living space.

In 1955, my parents bought their Levittown home—a two-story, three-bedroom model called a Jubilee—for $12,500. The down payment was $100, which they had to borrow from my mother's father.

There were no closing costs or other fees. The monthly mortgage was $65. The house came with a driveway, a garage, and a washing machine (no more laundromat).

A newspaper account described typical Levittown home buyers as "young persons of moderate financial circumstances who had small children and might expect others." They not only expected them, but also produced them. In the early years, 30 percent of Levittown's population was under five years old. I was born in 1956, and my sister, the last addition to our family, came along in 1961. We slept upstairs in small rooms with dormer ceilings. My parents had a bedroom on the first floor, their own bathroom, and a big window that looked into the backyard—probably more personal space than anyone in their families had ever known. It is not hard to imagine that this felt like paradise to them.

If Levittown was the epicenter of postwar suburban optimism, my parents were exemplars and beneficiaries of its spirit. They raised us, built a life, and prospered—not extravagantly, but enough to definitively move up in class. I would say they moved up in both economic and social class, though on that later count, they sort of had a foot in both worlds. They stayed devoted to their Sunday night mixed doubles bowling league and were deeply involved in local politics—which were no less grubby than the politics they left behind in the city. But they also had subscriptions to the Philadelphia Orchestra and its Sunday chamber concert series, as well as season tickets to the Phillies.

The sense of upward mobility was central to the ideal of Levittown. The house plots were modest, typically about six thousand square feet, but they were footholds on the dream. For those who moved on, they were steps on a ladder. The early homeowners had come mainly from one of two places: Philadelphia's teeming neighborhoods, as my parents did, or from coal country in upstate Pennsylvania. There was a palpable sense of gratitude among many in Levittown, of celebration, for having landed in a better place.

My parents traveled a great deal later in their lives—to Europe numerous times, to Israel and South America. Wherever they found themselves, at some point during their journey—in a café in Paris, in some museum elsewhere in Europe, at the Metropolitan Opera in New York—my mother could always be counted on to turn to my father and say, "Do you think our parents would ever believe where we are right now?"

U.S. Steel's massive Fairless Works plant, on the banks of the Delaware River at Levittown's eastern fringe, employed more than ten thousand men at its peak in the mid-1960s. Thousands more found good-paying work at manufacturing plants with names redolent of an era of sweat and muscle—Vulcanized Rubber and Plastics, Minnesota Mining and Manufacturing, Rohm and Haas, General Motors. A defense contractor, Thiokol, occupied a big industrial parcel right between two of Levittown's residential sections. These were mostly union jobs. Overtime was plentiful, and men jumped at the chance to work holidays, which paid double time. Not all of these men were brilliant, and some distinctly were not. But they showed up on time and worked hard, and the union did the rest.

Even as a kid I would hear stories about how much money they made, which seemed like astronomical hourly rates. I never considered it bragging—I just think a lot of people were amazed to be more flush with cash than they ever imagined they would be. There were years in my childhood that it seemed like every other house had a huge Winnebago or some other kind of RV docked in its driveway.

One of my earliest memories is of sitting atop my father's shoulders in a gigantic crowd as then presidential candidate John F. Kennedy spoke at a rally in the fall of 1960 at the Levittown Shop-a-Rama. (Levitt built that, too, with six thousand spaces for cars. Public transportation was not a part of his utopian vision.) Somewhere around that same time, my parents had a meeting or perhaps a small fund-raiser at our home in support of Kennedy's campaign. It was probably called a coffee klatch. I must have been preternaturally politically aware, because I have a dim memory of this, too. Or maybe it was just that I had never before seen so many people congregated in our small living room. The author James Michener, a local Bucks County celebrity and big Kennedy booster, was among them. He left us with a signed copy of the novel he had published the previous year, *Hawaii*, one of those doorstop opuses (937 pages) that were his specialty. It stayed on our bookshelf forever. I couldn't have read it even if I wanted to. It was in German.

I suppose my parents were part of Levittown's elite, though I smile even as I write that because the words—*Levittown* and *elite*— do not much go together. My father loved being a lawyer and was a well-regarded practitioner, but the fact is he never liked the business aspect of the law or figured out how to make gobs of money at it. He was probably the rare lawyer who got a pay raise when he was appointed to the bench. When times were good at "the mill," as everyone called it, I'm pretty sure that many of the men who drew their paychecks from U.S. Steel made more than he did.

Like every boy I knew in Levittown, I knew how to do manual

labor. During my high school summers, I cut grass in parks and on the medians of highways, unloaded trucks, and walked beside road-paving equipment with a rake to smooth the hot asphalt along the curbs. During a long strike by the schoolteachers when I was a high school senior, I found a job in one of the area's small steel plants. Even for kids, there was good money to be made. College cost a great deal less back then, and we were able to earn a substantial portion of the money for tuition ourselves, an impossibility now. My best friend took a year off from college to mix big vats of chemicals at the 3M plant, where an old-timer told him, "Remember, don't take all your money and buy a boat with it—buy property."

I look back on that now and just marvel at the idea behind that admonition—that a person could earn so much cash from un-skilled labor that he just might go blow it all on something stupid rather than put it down on a solid investment like a house.

But for all the rich wages earned and the middle-class lives built, any claim that Levittown had to being some kind of utopia was discredited by its glaring defect: a persistent racism. The condi-tion was congenital, present from the moment of conception. And the racism was not benign; it was virulent. Part of being the "most perfectly planned community in America," an essential part, was for Levittown to be whites only. Levitt and Sons would not sell any of the 17,311 mass-produced houses to black families. The deeds signed by early home buyers expressly prohibited them from resell-ing to blacks. When questioned on the policy, William Levitt weakly insisted that he would love to sell houses to black families, but had "come to know that if we sell one house to a Negro family, then ninety to ninety-five percent of our white customers will not buy into the community. That is their attitude, not ours."

In 1957, Bill and Daisy Myers and their three young children moved into a little pink house in a section called Dogwood Hollow, one mile from the home my parents had purchased two years before. The Myerses were black and far better educated than most Levittowners. Both were graduates of Hampton Institute in Virginia. Bill was an engineer, and Daisy a stay-at-home mom who would later enter the workforce and earn master's degrees in education and psychology. The home was sold to them by a white couple next door—Lew and Bea Wechsler, left-wing Jews, former Communists, and civil rights activists—who purchased it with the specific intent of integrating Levittown by reselling it to a black family.

Beginning with the night they moved in, the Myers family was subjected to terror, organized by an ad hoc group calling itself the Levittown Betterment Committee. Rocks were hurled through their windows, a cross burned on the lawn. A stick of dynamite was discovered on their driveway. Daisy Myers answered her phone one night, and the caller asked, "Do you want to die in that house?"

My father belonged to the NAACP and the ACLU, and years later he would hire into his small firm the first black lawyer in Bucks County, Clyde W. Waite, a graduate of Yale Law School who had been turned away by numerous other firms and went on to be the county's first African-American judge. I saw my father take stands that were not always in his personal interest, and although he didn't talk about it much, I knew the Bronze Star he kept in a little plastic case came to him for breaking cover and risking artillery fire to go to the aid of a wounded fellow soldier. But when I talked to him about the Myers episode, I found out he had not been among the small group of Levittowners who went to the family's home to support them and oppose the angry mob. He regrets it still.

"I think it represented a show of cowardice on my part," he says. He was running for township commissioner, the equivalent of city council. "My political friends very easily talked me out of going over to that house. They said it would be a disaster for my prospects to be elected. They were probably right. But I took the easy way out and sat back."

The siege was covered on the networks' nightly news programs. A state court issued an injunction, and the mob eventually dissipated. The Myerses moved from Levittown four years later, but the episode was far from the community's last chapter of racial tension. There were several small black neighborhoods on the fringes of town, non-Levitt-built homes. In the schools, periodic brawls broke out between white and black students, and I spent parts of my high school years with police and police dogs stationed in the corridors to keep the races apart. In my recollection, the cause of every one of these blowups was the same: Word went out that a black boy had touched a white girl, or talked to one in an inappropriate way, or just looked at her in a way that suggested his intentions. It was primal. The girl was usually a blond cheerleader type, the boy an athlete.

Carl Grecco, the debate coach and a longtime history teacher, told me that he was assigned to be part of a team of teachers who were expected to run into the lunchroom to break up these imbroglios. He described ducking cafeteria chairs as he tried to fulfill his duty. Carol Gross, a retired gym teacher, said that she had her lip split open by Earl Williams, a black six-foot-eight basketball star who went on to play in the NBA and then had a long professional career in Israel. "Earl didn't mean to," she said. "He was put in the middle of it—he was always in the middle of it—and I waded in there to try to pull people away."

Levittown did not begin to integrate after the siege at the Myers home, and really still has not. Census figures put the black population, among Levittown's fifty-four thousand residents, at 2 percent. An equal number are Hispanic. These are much lower percentages than in nearby Philadelphia, or in Trenton, right across the river.

There is a Bruce Springsteen song, not one of his best known, called "Youngstown." It tells the story of a place that was working iron and steel so far back that it made cannonballs for the Union army. The mill is shut down and the owners have moved on. In the voice of the worker, Springsteen sings, "Now, sir, you tell me the world's changed. Once I made you rich enough, rich enough to forget my name."

They started making steel in Levittown only as far back as 1952, but the reality and sentiment of Springsteen's haunting requiem applies just the same. I play it sometimes when I drive around my hometown, looking for familiar sights and memories. Once the wellspring of hope, Levittown is now ground zero in America's new narratives: income inequality, the fraying of the working class, suburban poverty.

The giant swimming pools, operated by the LPRA (the Levittown Public Recreation Association), were once the pride of the community. They cost $20 to join for a whole summer of swimming, and I knew of no family that didn't belong. I used to get excited just when the envelope arrived in late May with the pool tags—one for each family member, a different color each year, with pins on the back that attached to our bathing suits. I may have had only one swimsuit each season, because I never remember transferring the tag.

Indian Creek was our pool, named for the Levittown section it adjoined. I pedaled there nearly every summer day on my black Schwinn bicycle. The pool was so big that if the wind was right, a waft of chlorine hit you from a couple of blocks away, along with the din from the massive number of kids in the pool. My Little League field was right outside the fence, so if I had a game in the afternoon, I brought my uniform and changed into it.

Eager to see what Indian Creek looked like now, I drove over there on a summer day and parked in the lot. There were no other cars there, no bicycles locked to the fence, and no swimming pool—not even a trace of a pool. It had been filled in and planted over. I learned that the whole property had fallen into terrible disrepair. The pool itself was cracked and unsafe, the pool house crumbling, and the fencing rusted and falling down. Filling the pool had cost $100,000, but it would have cost a lot more to fix it, and there was no money for that. The LPRA didn't have it, and Bristol Township had more pressing priorities than saving a swimming pool. Four of the five Levittown pools have met the same fate, with their grounds converted to "passive recreation areas." Whatever that means, it doesn't sound like any child's idea of fun.

The Levittown Shop-a-Rama, site of the Kennedy campaign rally and touted as "the largest shopping mall east of the Mississippi," was anchored by a Sears and another department store called Pomeroy's. We used to eat hot dogs from the counter at W. T. Grant, then play on the escalators at Pomeroy's until we got kicked out. The Shop-a-Rama had ninety stores at its peak, many of them locally owned, and was Levittown's best approximation of a downtown. When I drive by to look at it now, I see that the whole thing has been leveled. A Walmart occupies the site.

On another of my trips, I drove in from Bethesda with my daughter Sofia, our middle child. We crossed into Levittown from New Jersey, and on the bridge over the Delaware, I slowed down and pointed out the manufacturing plants up and down the river where the jobs used to be. The defunct 3M plant was right under the bridge. The steel mill was off to our right, just a couple of miles north. A Spanish-owned company called Gamesa has taken over and is manufacturing wind turbines, green energy for the future.

I had been to the mill not long before and received a tour from a Gamesa PR man. "This was the hub of the mill, the heartbeat," he said as we stood on a factory floor that was longer than two football fields. We were within sight of where the two blast furnaces and the nine open hearths had been—where the "pig iron," a product of iron ore, was melted into steel. It was a hot, noisy, nasty process. But the Gamesa site is clean and quiet. A ghost mill. Where more than ten thousand men once worked, there are two hundred. Some of them make no more than the steelworkers pulled down in the 1970s—in real dollars, not dollars adjusted for inflation.

A fter a rehearsal one day, I give a ride home to Tyler Kelch, who had worked on the *Good Boys and True* stage crew and would land a lead part in Volpe's next two productions. He is one of the brightest and most perceptive of Volpe's students, a technophile who spends a lot of time taking apart and putting back together gadgets of all kinds—computers, sound equipment, phones, cam-

eras. He was upset because he had just broken a video camera trying to give it night-vision capabilities. "Being the electronics geek
that I am," he says, "I knew how to do it. I really did. But I pulled
away a piece of glass near the lens, and when I put it back, I hit a
capacitor, which caused a little shock, and there went the camera."

We talk about Truman, its students, and their families. I mention that I recently looked at a study out of Stanford University
that explored the relatively new syndrome of suburban poverty.
Because of income inequality—the widening gap between rich
and poor—large swaths of America that had once been solidly
middle class no longer were. "I get that," Tyler says. "And it's not
like the people who used to live around here left and a bunch of
poor people moved in. It's the exact same people. They just got
poorer."

He's right about that. Pennsylvania ranks fourth in the nation
in its percentage of residents who were born in the state and still
live within its borders, often right on top of where they were born.
Many students I meet at Truman are second-, third-, and even
fourth-generation Levittowners. If I ask enough questions, I usually
learn that I know their families—their moms, dads, aunts, uncles,
or even their grandparents. We went to school together or played
on the same teams. It makes for some funny conversations. I was
talking one day with one of Volpe's students whose name sounded
familiar. She told me the name of her father. "Yeah, I remember
him!" I said. "First baseman, left-handed." (A remnant of the boy
who saw life through stadium lights, not stage lights.)

Tyler has one sibling, an older brother studying music at
Bloomsburg University, one of the Pennsylvania state colleges that
attract Truman students. His parents had grown up in neighbor-

hoods less than five miles from their current home. His mother works at the *Bucks County Courier Times*, feeding advertising supplements into a "big giant machine" that inserts them into the newspapers that get delivered to homes. His father, immersed in rock music, had built a recording studio in their home. "My dad, growing up in the sixties, he thinks he's a rock star, or he wanted to be," Tyler says. "He sang for friends' bands, and he was a roadie for my uncle's band. This dream never died in him. Even in his forties, he kept it alive, but maybe he's living a little through me, now."

His father works as a carpenter for a company that makes kiosks for trade shows. "It's not union. Right now he's technically a freelancer. He's been a freelancer for quite some time now. And we keep praying that they are going to hire him eventually, because he's worked for this company for so long. He went somewhere else for a while, and now he's back, so we're hoping that he's got enough time built up now."

Tyler is one of those kids cursed with an acute awareness of his parents' circumstances and struggles. Even when he was little, if his mother wanted to buy him something in a store, he would sometimes ask her not to because he feared the family couldn't afford it. "I wish I wouldn't have been like that," he says. "Some of it was cool stuff I'd probably still like to have."

His family's finances have been stressed in recent years, and both his parents quit smoking in order to save money. He hasn't seen that it's made much of a difference, "but they're trying everything they can." We pull up to his house. In the front of the driveway is an old van. Nearby is a boat. They both look marooned.

"That's the van that hasn't run since, like, the year 2000," he says. "And that's the boat we never put in the water anymore."

. . .

One evening, I stop in at a college and career fair in the Truman cafeteria. Students are taking brochures off tables, watching short videos, talking to recruiters from various schools and local businesses. A representative for the steamfitters and pipefitters union offers information about apprenticeships leading to work that pays between $17 and $29 an hour. The caveat is that such work has to exist, and in the current economy, it doesn't. And candidates have to take a math exam. "It's difficult," the union man says. "It might be easier to get into college than pass it."

Technical academies are well represented, most of them from the for-profit sector that has been under scrutiny in recent years because students too often emerge with tens of thousands of dollars of debt—but not jobs. Of course, the same criticism could be leveled against America's fully accredited four-year colleges. The technical schools offer training in a wide range of fields—pharmacy technicians, medical technologists, business accountants, cosmeticians, massage therapists, court reporters, and so on.

A U.S. Marine recruiter tells me that three Truman seniors have already enlisted, but he hopes to attract a couple more from the 2010 senior class. A young boy, perhaps ten, wanders over to ask questions about the meaning of the insignias on his uniform. "Hit the floor and give me a hundred push-ups," the recruiter says. The boy does thirty-seven. "That's pretty good," the Marine says. "Better than a lot of the high school kids."

Frank Zuccarini, an admissions officer, is standing in front of a table displaying literature for Rider University. "Truman is an interesting school," he says. "There's what we call the Bucks County effect, but it falls outside of that." He explains that he views Truman as distinctly different from the wealthier high schools in the county. Here, the students are not as aspirational. Their parents definitely do not have the same money. I ask if he has ever seen steamfitters and pipefitters recruiting at those other schools. If they were there, he hasn't noticed them.

Truman students are not terribly competitive with one another. Unlike where I live now, they do not apply for the same few spots in competitive colleges. They don't approach life as a zero-sum contest (where your loss is my gain). It doesn't make them the best candidates to be competitive out in the wider world. They live in their own kind of bubble, and I'm not sure they realize how hard many American children—for better or worse—push themselves.

But striving is not cost-free. For most Truman students, even the main campus of Penn State is a stretch. Many of them end up at its satellite campuses, or at West Chester, Bloomsburg, Slippery Rock, or other institutions in Pennsylvania's network of publicly supported colleges. And the Truman students who enroll at more expensive colleges—even solid but not exclusive institutions like Temple University in Philadelphia—often must take out tens of thousands of dollars in loans. They are the generation of working-class kids entering adulthood with heavy encumbrances.

A youngish guy with short-cropped black hair, Zuccarini has the affable, upbeat manner common to salesmen in any field. The school he represents, Rider, is a middling institution in Lawrenceville, New Jersey, with a hefty price tag—about $45,000 for tuition, room, and board. It began as Trenton Business College and is not well-known outside the region. I assumed that a big part of his mission was to attract higher-quality students to Rider in order to elevate its profile and reputation, but his attitude toward Truman actually angered me. He seemed to be there purely out of duty, with no expectation of finding a student. "We just don't see the test scores here matching up with the grade point averages," he says. "You get lots of 3.5 GPAs, but SATs in the 920 to 950 range. It makes you wonder about the course work."

He offers a kind of backhanded compliment: There's a "snob factor" at Truman's neighboring high schools that does not exist here. He finds that refreshing. What I should have asked Zuccarini was the following: *On the off chance a Truman student did qualify for your school, why would he or she want to pay $45,000 to go there?*

The whole evening feels sad. Truman's accomplishments are muted, its strengths not in great demand. I'm sure the school could still produce some good blue-collar union men, but that ship sailed a long time ago, right down the Delaware River and out to sea.

I ask Zuccarini if he ever recruits students from Truman's acclaimed drama program, but he doesn't know anything about it. A representative from Penn State's Abington campus tells me about their musical theater program, which she says rivals Juilliard's. But she doesn't know about Truman Drama, either. How is that possible? Her campus is thirty minutes away. Volpe has been written up numerous times in *The Philadelphia Inquirer*—big feature stories when he piloted *Les Mis* and Cameron Mackintosh came to Levittown, and again when he was the first to do *Rent*. If you were a recruiter at a nearby college with some kind of fancy musical theater program, wouldn't you know about that?

It seems a confirmation of what Volpe's kids have told me so many times: that no one pays much attention to them close to home because they assume nothing good could come out of Truman. They're invisible to their neighbors. Zuccarini says he thinks Truman kids could benefit from Rider's small classes and intense level of faculty engagement, and some could qualify for admission. But their credentials are not at the level that would bring them enough scholarship aid for them to afford it. "It's unfair," he says, "but it's the way it is."

Palmer Toto joined Truman's English department in 1969, the same year as Volpe, coached the basketball team, and now directs the school's guidance office. The two have been close friends for forty years.

Toto was gone from Truman for two decades. When his father died, he left teaching to take over his dad's Shell station, which was off an exit of I–95 in North Philadelphia in the same river-ward neighborhood where my father was raised. He bought other service stations and at one point owned six of them. He became a partner in an architectural finishing business (exterior finishes on buildings) and supervised employees on job sites. He climbed scaffolding and worked outdoors in extreme conditions. "I went to work in coveralls for twenty-one years," he says as we sit in his office on the morning after the college and career night. "It provided for my family. My mother was widowed at forty-six. Every month, I was able to send her a good check."

Ten years ago, Toto was walking with his wife on a beach in Ocean City, New Jersey. He turned to her and said, "You know what? I'm a teacher. That's who I am, and I'm going back to it."

He told her he planned to sell his business, return to Truman, and buy back into the retirement plan. He set it all in motion. He had not taken weekends off in years—part of the plan was to spend more time with his wife and family. He drove off to Truman one day late that summer to supervise an academic enrichment program. While he was gone, his wife choked on food and died. "As an adult, you know these things occur, horrible tragedies," he says. "You know friends who have gone through hell. You read books. You know about it. It's life. But you're never prepared. She died on a Wednesday afternoon. I walked out of my house on a Wednesday and my life changed."

Toto was in his mid-fifties and still had children at home. He cooked the same five meals on school nights, week after week, in the same order. Weekends were pizza and sandwiches, then the rotation began again. "You know what? You keep going," he says. "It's all you can do. My mother-in-law said to me, 'You were the perfect son-in-law. You were a great husband. You're doing all the right things.' It meant a lot for her to say that. I never did bad things. I didn't have any guilt."

What Toto was left with, besides his family, was the job at Truman. He taught English for a year, then was asked to lead the guidance office. "I have a gift in life," he says. "This job is my gift. I'm sixty-five years old. I waited twenty-one years to get back here."

Toto's time away gave him a singular perspective. He had been doing something entirely different. When he started back at Truman, he felt the full force of what had changed. It was bracing, like opening a door in a warm room in the dead of winter and getting a blast of arctic air. "Everything here was disturbed," he says. "Dad wasn't coming home with his lunch pail anymore. That job wasn't there. Maybe Dad wasn't even there anymore, either. The economics disturbed family life. We have a higher divorce rate, youngsters living with Mom and Mom's husband-to-be, and Mom is working two jobs, because they're not good jobs. They're low-level jobs, so just one of them doesn't do it."

About 6,200 students attend Bristol Township's public schools, either at Truman High, the district's lone high school, or one of its two middle schools or nine elementaries. More than three thousand of those children qualify for free or reduced-price lunch, a common measure of poverty within a school system. When schools were first assessed under the state's guidelines, the district scored near the bottom of state rankings. Through smaller class sizes and more intense attention given to lagging students, it managed to claw its way into the middle. In 2012, the district was awarded a place in the College Board's honor roll for increasing access to Advanced Placement courses and having a greater percentage of students with a three or higher on the exams. (A five is the highest possible score; many colleges grant credit for threes and above.) It was a significant honor. Truman was the only school in Pennsylvania on the list with more than 30 percent of its students in the free lunch program.

Samuel Lee is the district's superintendent. He was making an annual salary of $137,500, not a lot to lead a school district. He is a little guy, affable, who still spends weekends coaching youth soccer. He looks nothing like the superintendents from the fancy districts, alpha educators who dress like senior partners in law firms. Lee's suits look like they may have come from Today's Man. I'm afraid that I may have underestimated him at first and thought him some kind of discount superintendent.

I was there one night when Lee had to tell a meeting of about three hundred teachers and parents which programs and innovations had to be cut—including precisely some of the "extras" that had helped the district make its gains. What impressed me about Lee was the total absence of bullshit in his remarks. He made no attempt to suggest that if everyone just pitched in and worked harder, the kids would still get the same great education. Worthy programs were going to be dismantled, good young teachers put on the street. "Everything that is going to be presented tonight is not good for our kids," he said. "We are heartbroken."

Lee is a traditionalist, like many in Levittown, and no fan of charter schools or anything else that scrapes money away from school systems. In an open letter to township residents and policy makers, he criticized "idiosyncratic alternatives" to public districts, many of them "owned and operated by large national corporations whose number one mission is to enrich shareholders." You can agree or disagree. I admire Lee for knowing exactly where he stands and stating it clearly, without jargon.

The whole district tends to be that way. Meat and potatoes. Light on lyricism and lofty credentials. The website for the Bristol Township schools features a group picture of the members of the school board. One of the men is wearing a black T-shirt, another a short-sleeve yellow shirt with a brown tie. The caption under the picture says: *Elected by the people, unpaid for their services, and open to public criticism, board members must make the tough decisions. The qualifications for their positions are leadership, vision, and mental toughness.*

The discussions over the school budget sounded much like a couple talking around their kitchen table with a stack of bills, no hope of paying them and nothing but bad options. Lee called the situation "catastrophic." Some people in the township had been out of work entirely, including Earl Bruck, the school board president.

The unemployment caused home foreclosures, leading to shortfalls in property tax receipts, and therefore holes in the school budget.

Additionally, the state's new Republican governor had drastically cut education funds going to local districts—as well as money for state colleges. One remedy proposed by the governor seemed like it could have been satire from *The Onion*, but it was reported by the Associated Press. It said that Governor Thomas Corbett had proposed that the state's institutions of higher learning should consider closing their budget shortfalls by drilling for natural gas on their campuses.

The deficit in the Bristol Township schools came to a whopping $603 per student. Taxes could not be raised, so the quality of education would be cut. A ninth-grade academy in a separate building, which had been successful in acclimating students to high school, was to be shut down. Pre-kindergarten was in danger. Fifty-nine teachers would be laid off. The district once offered instruction in five foreign languages. Then four. Now it was going to be just two— Italian and Spanish. The foreign languages would be taught almost exclusively at the high school level, not in middle school, when many students in wealthier districts begin to learn a language, if they have not already started at the elementary level.

The arts curriculum had long been in decline. There was no instruction for string instruments at Truman anymore, and therefore no orchestra. For musicals, Volpe had to hire professional musicians. This latest shortfall would involve more cuts in the arts. In the high school, electives of all kinds were eliminated, and some seniors who were on course to meet graduation requirements were encouraged to just leave school at midday after taking their core courses.

Jim Moore, the school's principal, said it was not "lack of effort" that caused Truman to be poorly ranked in previous years, but a matter of resources. "There's been an investment in education here, above and beyond bare bones, and it paid off," he said. "Now it's going to be scaled back. There will be fewer opportunities for kids to do things that are not math, science, or English."

At the meeting when the cuts were announced, a mother of a Truman student asked if the cuts wouldn't just dig the community into a deeper hole. Who would want to buy the empty houses in a district that did not offer a full-bodied curriculum? "By cutting education," she asked, "aren't we subjecting our kids to the same fate that we're all living right now?"

School board president Earl Bruck was just as blunt as Sam Lee. "Absolutely," he said. "We are."

But the drama courses that Volpe and Krause teach—Theater 1, 2, and 3 and musical theater—were spared. Truman is holding on to that. Moore said the determining factor was not Volpe's status but, in a sense, his popularity. "You can't have a high school without any electives," he said. "You try to keep the ones that are highly popular, and Lou's classes are what kids in this school want to take."

THE CAST OF *GOOD BOYS AND TRUE*.
FROM LEFT: COURTNEY MEYER, BOBBY RYAN,
MARIELA CASTILLO, ZACH PHILIPPI,
BRITNEY HARRON, AND WAYNE MILETTO.

I WOULD KILL
FOR YOU

I n mid-June 2011, the cast members of *Good Boys and True* receive their high school diplomas at the traditional commencement on the football field. A week later, they board a morning flight at Philadelphia International Airport, change planes in Chicago, and land that afternoon in Nebraska. This is the post-graduation beach week they yearned for—on the Great Plains, about as far from an ocean as you can possibly get in America.

Zach keeps talking about experiencing what could be called the "Truman Drama effect": the sense of acclaim they feel only when they leave home. "They say we're known in the nation, which is insane, to think you're a part of that," he says. "Because in Bucks County, we're not known for anything good, just negative things."

Truman Drama will not perform for another three days. The kids attend workshops and scholarship auditions, watch the performances of other high schools, and go to dances at night. They are living on campus with a couple thousand other high school–aged kids, most of them eager to get to know one another. The festival is what is sometimes indelicately called a meat market.

Luke Robinson, a tenth-grader at Truman, is among the handful of non–cast members along on the trip. A skinny kid with braces, a member of the debate club as well as drama, he has a passion, bordering on obsession, for recycling. He constantly pesters students and teachers to properly dispose of their plastic water bottles. He meets a girl at one of the dances. "Yo, Luke," Zach teases him the next day, "you're the only one of us who has gotten any action. What's up with that?"

Just like he does every year, Volpe worries about the seniors who are about to go off on their own and away from his day-to-day reach—all but Wayne, who invites no worry. Five of the six are headed to college. Courtney, as yet, has no plans. "All that self-confidence you see in them, it's not as deep as they sometimes want you to think," Volpe says as we sit one morning at a coffee shop near the University of Nebraska campus. "They're not doormats, but they know they're up against kids who have had more resources. I've seen it. They feel intimidated sometimes, even by kids from Pennsbury." (Pennsbury is a neighboring high school whose students are drawn from the upper end of Levittown and also several wealthier communities to the north.)

Confidence is a funny thing in high school. Almost everyone has it in the wrong measure—either too little or too much. Volpe is in a ruminative mood, thinking out loud about some of the kids. He has given them his all and hopes it's enough. "Courtney at some point in her life is going to have to realize what a beautiful, brilliant, and perceptive young woman she is," he says. "She has to come to terms and honor those parts of herself. I'm sorry, but I can't do that for her. I've done what I can. It's up to her now. She's going to have to own it."

Zach's challenge, in some ways, is the opposite. "I worry that high school will be the best part of his life. I don't want that to be the case," Volpe says.

He sees Zach as "fawned over" at school and at home. His success in sports has filled him with self-regard, and when he comes up short, he has a tendency to be moody afterward and sometimes to shift blame—Volpe recalls Zach complaining to him after he pitched in a baseball game and got hit around that the coach should have known his arm was tired. But when he had recently given up a bunch of runs at an all-star game, he said to Volpe that sometimes "you just have to tip your cap" to the opposition—give them credit. "Zach hasn't failed a lot at Truman," Volpe says. "It's been such a wonderful environment for him in that way. But I worry what will happen when he struggles and no one is there to catch him. So when he gave credit to the other team, I was so happy to hear him say that. It's a good sign."

A well-intentioned activist working on issues of poverty in America's older, close-in (code for "falling apart") suburbs contacted me after a story I wrote about my hometown ran in *The New York Times*. Janis Risch, the executive director of Good Schools Pennsylvania, was starting to organize in Levittown. She had some business in the Washington, D.C., area, and we met for coffee. I passed along Tyler Kelch's insight—that Levittown was full of people who once felt a part of the middle class but had fallen down the ladder.

In a follow-up e-mail, she asked me, "What do people in Levittown need?" What do they need? Maybe they need United Steelworkers Local 4889, which used to throw its muscle around at the mill, to make profit machines like Walmart pay employees better wages. But, realistically (to use Courtney Meyer's favorite word), probably no one is going to empower America's globalized workforce, any more than anyone can turn the clock in Levittown back to 1964.

Truman students have a strong sense of being on the wrong side of a divide even without knowing the full dimensions of it. At my hotel in Nebraska, I finally get around to writing back to Risch. I still don't have a great answer, but I tell her a little about the theater festival. "I'm seeing these kids do this remarkable thing, and it fills in some of what's missing for them," I write. "What I'm thinking right now is that everyone in life needs to have had at least one brilliant, inspiring teacher."

That, I know, is far from a new idea. But then again, I have never known a single person who achieved a measure of success and could not look back and credit at least one treasured teacher. What Volpe's students gain from him is a passion and sense of self unrelated to anything having to do with money, power, or status. Nothing matters except what they do together. He never lets them feel defeated. When he tells them they could do theater with a bare stage and a lightbulb, they absolutely believe it. They believe it so deeply that if that ever really were the case—and he said here's the stage, here's the bare bulb—they wouldn't question it. They'd get to work, rehearse the play, and figure they were taking it to Nebraska.

"I'll be chasing this for the rest of my life," Bobby says of his experience in *Good Boys*. I asked if he meant success onstage or in some field of entertainment. "No, not that," he says. "I mean I'll be chasing how happy it makes me, how totally into it I am every single second. No matter what I'm doing in life, I want that. Now that I've experienced it, I'm not going to settle for less."

The real cost of the Nebraska trip, including airfare and fees for the festival, is about $1,500 per Truman student. With money from the theater department budget (mainly ticket receipts from productions) and a grant from the school board's charitable foundation, Volpe cut the cost that each of the kids had to pay to about $550, still a struggle for some of them. He and Krause contributed money of their own, as they have consistently over the years. I asked him how much of his own money he spent to get the production to Nebraska, and he would not say. Throughout the whole course of my working on this book, it is the only question I recall Volpe not wanting to answer.

Some of the other schools performing on the Main Stage arrive with thick, glossy playbills that look like what you get in a Broadway theater—with pictures and bios of the cast and crew, along with their tributes to all the important people in their lives. Truman's program is one eight-and-a-half-by-eleven-inch sheet of blue paper, folded in half. On the front is the name of the play, its author, and the date and place of the performance—Thursday, June 23, 2011, at the Lied Center for the Performing Arts, Lincoln, Nebraska. On the middle two pages are the order of the scenes and the names of the cast members. On the back page is an advisory that the play contains mature themes, as well as the following note:

> Truman Drama is proud and honored to be presenting its fifth
> Main Stage show at the International Thespian Festival.

Previous productions include *Telemachus Clay, Equus, Pageant,* and *The Rimers of Eldritch.* In addition, Truman has piloted productions of *Les Misérables* and *Rent* for Music Theatre International and in November will present a pilot for a school edition production of *Spring Awakening,* also for MTI.

I say something to Volpe about the elaborate playbills of some of the other schools. "Oh, I think this is all we need," he says. "Don't you think?"

Yes, it's all they need. Five Main Stages. First high school to do *Rent,* and they'll be getting to *Spring Awakening* when they get home. They don't need any glossy paper, thankyouverymuch.

The performance of *Good Boys* is at ten A.M. The theater is to open at precisely eight to give Truman two hours to mount the set, get in costume and makeup, and do sound checks. Robby Edmondson will have to get familiar with the lighting board. Tony Bucci has driven the rented U-Haul truck with the set from Levittown again, this time to Lincoln, about 1,300 miles and twenty-four hours on the road. On the morning of the play, he backs the truck up to the loading dock that leads backstage. The kids arrive at seven-thirty A.M. and sit in the rear of the truck as they wolf down a breakfast of bagels, pastries, and fruit.

It's cold, unseasonably so for Nebraska in late June. They pull hoodies up over their heads and drink hot chocolate. Courtney disappears for ten or fifteen minutes. "Where the hell is Courtney?" Krause says. She reappears looking like a dockworker, with a toothpick in her mouth, and explains that she has been on the phone. It's really early to be talking to anyone back home—everyone figures she found a bench where she could lie down and get a little more sleep.

Truman's contingent is not big enough for a division of labor. Luke Robinson, Tyler Kelch, and a few others are along to serve as a stage crew, but when the door leading from the loading dock into the backstage area lifts up, everyone, including Volpe, climbs into the U-Haul and begins hauling stuff inside. Bucci and Wayne take charge of fastening the set together on the stage.

A problem arises. There is *always* some kind of problem. Bucci turns a bolt on one of the casters—the wheels on which the main set piece turns—and it snaps. The rules of the festival are clear: The professionals backstage, permanent staff of this very large university theater, are not to lend a technical hand. It's theater, right? Problems come up, and the high schools are supposed to solve them.

With not a lot of time to spare, Volpe asks me to rush into downtown Lincoln, find a hardware store, and purchase a caster the same size as the one that broke. I'm not sure when I last felt this kind of pressure. If the main set piece does not rotate, it's useless. What happens if it can't be fixed isn't clear. They can't play a scene in what is meant to be a school locker room against a backdrop that looks like a living room. (Well, they *can*, and maybe they'll have to, but it would look really stupid.) As Volpe puts it, "There are no work-arounds here."

I come running back in with the caster in thirty minutes' time, thoroughly relieved and a little proud of myself, since I am not normally a handy guy in a hardware store. Alas, one of the pros backstage has taken pity and slipped Bucci a spare part, so my moment as a hero is brief.

The cast members are dressed, milling about onstage, looking out into the vastness of the 2,200-seat theater. They take pictures of themselves and text them back home to their parents and friends. "How many stages the size of Truman's would fit on this stage?"

Volpe asks Bucci, even though he has been here many times before. Bucci say he figures at least three.

Volpe looks into the empty balcony, a long way up. "If I ever had to perform in a place this big," he says, "I would throw up."

T he cast last performed *Good Boys* in December. Six months have passed, a not insignificant period of time for seventeen- and eighteen-year-olds. Volpe believes it has made a difference. When they began to rehearse again, "their added life experience, their love for each other, their rivalries, it all enriched it."

The performance in Nebraska is, without a doubt, even more powerful than those that came before. The tension and anger—the violent emotions suggested by the playwright's words—are played right on the knife's edge. The standing ovation at the end is as sustained as it was in Connellsville at the Pennsylvania festival, but with double the number of people on their feet.

When Volpe talks to the cast backstage before this performance, it is his last time with them. He has not written anything down. It works best for him at these moments if he just speaks the words as they come to him. In a cramped dressing room, he stands between Tracey Krause and Carol Gross, the retired gym teacher, a close friend who volunteers at the school and takes every trip with Truman Drama. Next to Gross is Bill Hallman, another friend and the president of Pennsylvania's Educational Theatre Association.

"This is our final talk," Volpe begins. "A few minutes ago, I looked at Tracey and I looked at Bill and Carol, and I wondered what I was going to say, and even then, I got emotional. I welled up. Because we will not be together, all of us, in this same way ever again. But I want you to know, when I see my students from the past, there is always that something. That memory I can pull out, and I know today is one of those memories."

Volpe is composed, but others are not. Bobby wipes away tears, then gives up and just lets them fall. Courtney says softly, "Stop. Please stop." Volpe continues on.

"You all came to this in your own way. Britney came right away. Wayne came right away. Zach was the last. But you all came at your own pace, and when you were ready. Is today the last time we're going to be together? Physically, yes. In my heart, no.

"I think that is the best payoff for being a teacher. You always have these memories. I can go back to *You're a Good Man, Charlie Brown*. I can go back to *Into the Woods*. And I pull out these beautiful pictures. I can go back to Tracey going out onstage the night of her Main Stage show at this festival. I can go back to her fighting with her boyfriend before the show started. I have all that in my heart.

"I just want to thank all of you, not only for this play, but for *Rent*, for *Dirty Rotten Scoundrels*, for *High School Musical*, *Blood Brothers*, for Theater 3 and for Musical Theater. I want to thank you for making me a better teacher. You did.

"And I want you to know that you have become part of my life these last four years. If I see you tomorrow, if I see you next year, or even if I *never* see you again, I will see you for the rest of my life. I will. I mean that. I will see you for the rest of my life. When you go out there onstage in a few minutes, I don't want it to be sad. I want it to be a celebration."

Nearly everyone now except for Volpe is crying. Courtney begs him again to stop, but he is not done. *Good Boys and True*, he says, was a "monumental accomplishment of art, of self-expression. You guys created it. You know what you've done. When I look back on my career, on my forty-three years of teaching, I will say this is the best work I have ever done. The very best work. You know me, all of you know me well, and you know I would never say that if I didn't mean it."

He finally, at this point, begins to choke up. "How many students can have this? How many teachers can have this? How many teachers last week packed their bags, picked them up, and drove home? And won't see their students again until September? How lucky are we? I say to God, why did you pick me? Why did you pick Ms. Krause? Why did you pick Ms. Gross? Why are we the lucky ones?

"Why did you pick us and make it so that our students are like our children? And you are. You're like our children. I would kill for you. I mean that. That's our blessing, and in a way it's our curse. Because we have to say good-bye."

It is ten minutes until the curtain will rise. "All I can say is, Have a wonderful time when you go out there. And think of me. I want you to think of me. I don't mean to be selfish when I say that. But I want you to know that you will always be in my heart, and I want to be in your hearts."

VOLPE AND HIS SON, TOMMY.

I JUST WISH I COULD HAVE
LOVED HER MORE

O ne day, as I sit with Volpe in his living room, he turns the conversation back to his father, Thomas Volpe, the ex-Marine who owned the Rex Café in South Philadelphia for all those years, and to his own son, Tommy, whom he and Marcy named for his father. "The three best years I had with my father were the three years before he died, after we had Tommy," he says. "After Tommy was born, it was like his world changed in one night."

He stops. "Wow, I don't know where that came from," he says. He jokes that he feels like he is on a psychiatrist's couch. "It's just that I regret not knowing him better. I didn't know him at all. But after Tommy was born, he didn't care about anything else. It was all about Tommy. He was a great fisherman, a deep-sea fisherman. Sometimes, first thing in the morning we would hear him pounding on the door, and he would say, 'I want to see my grandson. I'm going fishing and I want to see him before I leave.'

"We would say, 'It's six A.M.,' but he didn't care. He was almost obsessed with him. He talked about taking Tommy fishing. My father always had a garden. He got little tools for Tommy, and they went in the garden together. It was like Tommy was going to do all the things with my father that I was never interested in doing. And he would have, because he adored my father, and my father adored him."

Tommy was born in 1972, just a few months before I began in his father's classroom. He is a teacher now in Levittown at an elementary school about two miles from Truman. He has become a gardener, though not a fisherman. The first time I saw him, he was asleep in his crib during one of those dinners where Marcy cooked pasta and we all talked about books. It was a different time, when teachers felt comfortable having students around without fearing they could fall under suspicion. (Palmer Toto, the basketball coach, once piled a bunch of us into his car and drove us to his favorite cheesesteak joint in South Philly.) Volpe had other groups—acolytes, I suppose we were. There were girls who formed an orbit around him, bohemian and literary types who were looking for a voice and a spirit to speak to them from beyond Levittown. I was part of a distinct group—"the four boys," as Volpe still calls us. I don't know if he would have "killed" for us, as he told the *Good Boys* cast, but we cared for him deeply and we knew he cared for us.

One of the four, Bruce Martin, I met on the first day of seventh grade, at twelve years old. We found ourselves seated next to each other at a worktable in a metal shop class. The room smelled of metal shavings mixed with whatever grease was used in the lathes and other implements that I never learned to use. The teacher's name was Harry Shears, his real name as far as I know. Bruce and I discovered that our older siblings, his sister and my brother, were friends. We were both middle children. We played the same sports and the same positions in those sports—at times, a test of our friendship in a way that his superiority in shop class was not. (Forty-five years later, we talk every week or so by phone, and our families vacation in the summers together.)

Darryl Hart's background was not at all like mine. His parents were Southern Baptists and religious fundamentalists, unusual at the time in Levittown. He was forbidden to dance or attend movies. The fourth member of the group, Don Snedeker, was also, in his own way, an outlier. His father had died in an auto accident, and his one sister was considerably older, so it was just him and his mom at home in a town where two-parent families with lots of children were the norm. He sometimes took the train to Manhattan with a different set of friends to shop for music and clothes—an unheard of level of sophistication in our world.

Don would spend most of his adult life in Costa Rica. He taught English at a university, married, and had a son. He practiced yoga long before it was fashionable, and was probably in the best shape of us all. In 2009, he collapsed and died after a tennis game. He was fifty-three.

Bruce became an editor, first at *The Philadelphia Inquirer* and now in the financial industry. Darryl is a professor of social and religious history, an elder in the Orthodox Presbyterian Church, and still a religious conservative—though not always predictably so. The most recent of his more than twenty books (he publishes as D. G. Hart) is a denunciation of the evangelical movement's involvement in American politics. His blog, ostensibly about matters of theological thought, is peppered with references to the Philadelphia Phillies and *The Wire.*

When I take a step back and consider this group of friends and where we came from, I think we were unusual. We were more outwardly directed than the town we came from. More open-minded, more questing. The four of us gravitated to Volpe for a reason. We were restless, and there was never a question that we were getting out of Levittown. "Our senior prom song was 'We May Never Pass This Way Again,'" Darryl recalls. "Every time I heard it that night, I thought, *I sure as hell hope not.*"

What would we have been without Volpe? It's impossible to say. Different, for sure. He helped connect us to one another. However close we were, we became closer. To the extent that we developed in the same ways—became interested in the same things, have parallel sensibilities—he had a lot to do with that. He gave us a shot of intellectual courage, a love of words we could never shake. If I had never encountered Volpe, I suspect I would be a lawyer like my father—no tragedy, but not what I think I was meant to be.

Because of his background, Darryl may have been the most changed by Volpe, and maybe the most in need of him. We sat for hours one afternoon in 2011 in Philadelphia's Rittenhouse Square, the most time we had spent together in many years. "I oftentimes was intimidated in his class," Darryl says, which I never knew or would have imagined. "I think this is where my religious background was a factor—the idea that God's words come to us inerrant. That there are truths, and you don't interpret them. It was hard for me to accept that meanings could be variable or contested. It made me uncomfortable. I felt ham-fisted at times, unable to keep up with you and Bruce and Sned [Don Snedeker], because those discussions came more naturally to you. You weren't hung up on trying to find one right meaning."

Like so many of the Volpe students I talked to, Darryl could remember a specific moment of enlightenment. The stories are uncannily similar. Volpe bestowed praise—based on a particular thing a student had written, said, or acted onstage—and it resonated for life. His words were not just something a student *liked* hearing; he or she *needed* to hear them at that moment. They went right to a place that no other teacher, and no parent, had touched. In Darryl's case, he had written a paper on the novel *Deliverance* and social Darwinism, the kind of thing a high school boy would grasp on to. "I don't think I had a clue," he says. "But Lou found things in the paper to comment on that made me feel he was genuinely intrigued by my ideas."

He recalls Volpe telling him, "Darryl, you're really smart." From the perspective of four decades later, that may seem a self-evident and unnecessary thing to say to someone who had the brainpower to go on to Harvard Divinity School and then to Johns Hopkins for his Ph.D. "But no one had ever told me that before," he says. "I didn't get it at home. I remember in third grade, coming home with straight A's on my report card, and my parents, being fundamentalist Christians, said, 'Be careful. Don't be too proud. You've got to be humble.' So they didn't slap me down, but they made me remember where my world was. It was a good lesson, I think, but it limits you some."

None of us participated in Volpe's nascent drama program. Darryl and Bruce played on the basketball team; Don, the aesthete among us, played soccer and tennis. But we were boys who liked to think and talk about elements inside the literature he put in front of us—relationships, emotion, conflict, ideas. "I'm bookish," Darryl says. "That's who I am. Without stating it overtly, I felt Lou was saying to me, 'You can go somewhere with this. There's a part of the world where people care about this stuff, and you can fit into it.'"

As an academic, Darryl has the keenest memory of what Volpe actually had to say about books. He has kept some of the notes from classes. He remembers once telling Volpe that he was binging on Kurt Vonnegut novels, "going through a Vonnegut stage." He recalls that Volpe offered a note of caution, or perhaps even a mild reproach.

"Cynicism," he said, "is romanticism turned sour."

Volpe's favorite book, we all knew, was *The Great Gatsby*. So it became our favorite book. It's a cliché, yes. You love the book your favorite teacher loved. And it is *Gatsby*, which everyone loves. But even now when I reread it, I'm amazed at how current it feels, like it was written yesterday. Tom Buchanan could be a Duke lacrosse player, Gatsby a Wall Street derivatives dealer whose life story unravels at the same time his deals do. I have always identified most strongly with Nick Carraway, the keen observer and narrator, a man both detached from and immersed in the events of the book. Of course I would. Nick is the storyteller with incomparable access to his story.

I naively assumed my English teacher was also a Nick guy, that he, like me, saw himself in Nick. But he does not. Volpe reads *Gatsby* at the beginning of each summer because he loves the book's architecture—"There is no other novel that is so structurally perfect"—its word choices—"It is a poem, a long poem; every word fits"—and because every time he begins it again, he is swept up in Gatsby's dream.

James Gatz's reinvention of himself, from child of a failed North Dakota farm to New York aristocrat, begins when he is just the age of Volpe's students, and about the same age as Volpe when he first met Marcy Hargrove. Fitzgerald wrote, "So he invented just the sort of Jay Gatsby that a seventeen year old boy would be likely to invent, and to this conception he was faithful to the end." In nighttime "reveries," Gatsby embroidered his story, convincing himself "of the unreality of reality."

Gatsby is alone when the book begins, and he dies alone, with his life exposed as a sham and almost no one to come to his funeral. "But every time I read it," Volpe says, "I believe in Gatsby's crazy dream. I do. I'm a sucker for it. I want it to be true. I want him to have Daisy. I want him to have the love he wants."

Love, sex, trust, betrayal, pain, forgiveness—all were a mystery to me when Volpe was my teacher. I was sixteen when I started in his class, a week short of eighteen when I graduated from high school. My friends and I were open-minded, or at least we would have said we were. We were far from bullies or bigots. But we lived in Levittown. We used the *f*-word—*faggot*—though I'd say it was largely disconnected from any literal meaning. For me, at least, it was a universal insult, like calling someone a jerk. I didn't know what it meant when I started using it, and after I found out I probably didn't want to think about it.

By his mannerisms, by the rhythms of his speech, Volpe was different. He seemed like he could be gay, but no one I knew talked about it. There were no openly gay teachers at our school—I'm not even sure if that would have been professionally possible—and certainly no "out" students. And Volpe had a wife and a child. That a man could be a father and married to a woman (the only kind of marriage permissible at the time) *and* gay was utterly outside our frame of reference. Oddly, I do distinctly recall that we talked about his marriage. We thought Marcy might not be right for him. She didn't seem nearly as immersed in literature as he was, and we wondered if he might be happier with someone who shared his love of books. As I said, we didn't know much.

Fifteen years after I left high school, Lou and Marcy split up and divorced. I came to understand that he was gay, though I can't say exactly how I learned that. He never had a big formal coming-out to lots of people, and he certainly had no reason to call me up and tell me. When I would see him, his new status was just assumed and accepted. He had a more candid relationship with my classmate Hillar Kaplan, an artist in Los Angeles and one of the group of girls in high school who orbited around him. After his marriage ended, she might say, for example, "Lou, how's your love life? Do you have a partner?" But my relationship with him was still rooted in the mid-1970s, and we didn't have those discussions.

When I set out to write about him, Volpe made it clear right from the start that he wanted me to tell a complete story, that I should put in or leave out whatever I saw fit. When I asked him once if he wanted to see the proposal that was circulated to publishers, he declined. He didn't want me to be influenced by anything he might say about the proposal. Nor, I think, did he want to fit himself into some conception of himself he read in my writing. It was like I was one of his actors. He had trained me, and now he trusted that I would create something that was true and honest, unflinching but not gratuitous.

In the course of my research, people sometimes asked, "Are you going to write about Lou and Marcy?" By which they meant his sexuality. And I always replied that I thought he'd be pretty unhappy if I didn't. In time, I would visit with Marcy (for the first time since I was her husband's student) as well as with Tommy.

For a man who is gay, and knows that he is gay, to marry a woman may seem inexplicable now, especially to younger people. But it was far less so four decades ago. "When I began dating her, it was there," he says. "It was always there. We've talked about this over the years, because we've remained good friends. And Marcy has said to me, 'Did you love me? Did you ever really love me?' And you know what? I did. I did love her. I just wish I could have loved her more."

In many ways, Volpe has a younger person's sensibility. His tastes in music, movies, TV, and drama are as modern as can be. At times I found him almost childlike in the way he lived so relentlessly in the present. Each year brought a new group of students and possibilities, a new play and a new musical to produce. The picture kept changing, and that was the way he liked it. Generationally, though, he could seem older than his chronological age—more a child of the 1950s than the 1960s. He was never a rebellious youth, not a part of the counterculture, not forever young in some stereotypical Baby Boomer way. He was a compliant Catholic schoolboy who sold furniture at a department store to help pay for college before taking a job at a suburban high school.

He never imagined that he would be anything but a married man with a family. "I was conflicted, but my feeling was, This is what is expected of me," he says. "This is what a young, Catholic, educated boy from a good family does. The thought of going out on my own and having a life wasn't even in my consciousness. It wasn't there. And yet I had a very good friend who did exactly that.

"He was a friend from Father Judge. And after he graduated, he went to night school and he came out. *He came out!* At the time, this was unheard of. This was pre-Stonewall, pre–gay rights, pre-pride, pre-everything. It was like, *Oh my God, oh my God, what is he doing?* I thought it was totally suicidal. The funny part of it is we went to high school together for four years, and yet we never talked about homosexuality. How bizarre is that? That was the insular world I lived in."

It will never be easier to be gay than straight. But Volpe, born in 1948, may be part of the last generation of gay men and women in America who believed they absolutely had to conceal their sexuality to others—and, if possible, deny it to themselves. (It is worth recalling that for much of Volpe's life, sex between two men was technically illegal; sodomy laws prohibiting such behavior in some states were in force as recently as 2003, when the U.S. Supreme Court finally invalidated them in *Lawrence v. Texas*.) As a teacher, Volpe helped his students find some true self within—even as he was unable to do that for himself. He excelled at reading people perhaps because he spent so many years trying to make himself unreadable.

One night during his marriage, Volpe went to a bar in the town of New Hope, a gay mecca in Bucks County. He just lost himself in the crowd, alone, stayed for a short time, then drove home. Being with someone else, "man or woman, was something I did not want to ever happen." He did not want to cheat on Marcy and didn't want to violate his marriage vows or wreck his family. He was both gay and unrelentingly traditional.

When he became a father, he no longer even thought much about his predicament as a gay man living a life that was in part a pretense. "Once Tommy was born, that's all I cared about. You have this child who comes into the world and it changes everything. Gay is of nonimportance. Straight is of nonimportance. The only thing that matters is you have this child and love this child and do the best you can for him.

"The whole thing, the issue of my sexuality, became more and more buried. I didn't think about it as much. It just wasn't a priority in my life. Tommy fulfilled every dream a father could want. He was a wonderful student, a great kid, lovable, personable, a good athlete. I would have loved to have another child, at least one more. I always wanted to know what it would be like to have a daughter. It's a sorrow of mine, it really is, not to have experienced that."

As he was just about to turn forty, and with his son still in high school, Volpe spent time one night with a friend, a married man who was part of a couple he and Marcy socialized with. "I sort of suspected that he was gay, but he and I never talked about it," he begins. "But that night we did, and I talked to him about my gayness, too. We opened up about it. And it was like opening up a door. And then all the sudden there were all these other doors behind it.

"That's exactly what it was like. It was like one door opening and another door opening and another door, and I thought, *Do I start closing them all now? What do I do? Do I close these doors again, even as I'm so close to being who I am? Do I want to close them?* And I decided not to. I hid my life—no, I didn't hide my life, I hid who I am—for over forty years because of the way I was brought up. And I didn't want to do that any longer."

What followed, Volpe says, was "a night of reckoning between me and Marcy. I sat down in our bedroom and I told her what happened—*nothing* really happened between us, but certainly emotionally and psychologically it did. We never had a sexual relationship, we didn't, but we did kiss. He was much more experienced than I was. We had a few touchy-feely moments, but very chaste, clothes on. And that all came out. And for me that was a big deal. And I think she was surprised that it all came out.

"Marcy and I had never talked about my homosexuality, but she must have known. I can't imagine deep down inside of her that she didn't. But I told her that night that I was gay. And it crushed her. It totally crushed her. It was devastating for her.

"But once I said that, I knew it was something that you can't make go away again. I've seen it so many times in literature, where that moment happens and it can never be taken back. There's the novella by Philip Roth, *Goodbye, Columbus*, where the Jewish girl, very rich, is going with the very poor Jewish boy in the course of one summer. And she wants to end it. She needs to go on and live a rich life; it was very *Gatsby* in a way."

What happens in the Philip Roth story, published in 1959, is that the young female character, Brenda Patimkin, leaves her diaphragm in her clothes drawer, where her mother is certain to find it when she puts her daughter's laundry away. It seems not to be an oversight, but, rather, something intended to explode the relationship. It is an odd literary reference for Volpe to make, because the person who discovers this evidence of illicit, unmarried sex is someone outside the relationship, the mother. But I think I got the point. He had not explicitly told his wife that their marriage was over. But he had created an irrevocable moment—opened a door—that could only lead to one inevitable outcome.

Lou and Marcy agreed that until their son left home and went off to college, three years away, they would go on as if nothing had changed. "We decided that we would live a life—perfect—so you would never know what was wrong, and that is exactly what we did. In a way, it was very easy. We still had feelings for each other, and we had Tommy, who was the most important thing."

Tommy was at Holy Ghost Prep, a private Catholic high school. He was a baseball star, one of the top players in the area, a naturally strong and fast child who rode a two-wheeler before he was four years old. *The Philadelphia Inquirer* once named him its high school athlete of the week, and Holy Ghost would induct him into its sports hall of fame. Lou and Marcy, neither of them athletic, joked that they didn't know the source of his gift, but figured it must be from Marcy's birth parents, whom she never knew.

Volpe attended every one of his son's high school baseball games. His role was to keep the official scorebook and put down the code that marked every measurable moment of the contests: hits, runs, strikeouts, stolen bases, errors, wild pitches. He was dedicated to it. When he broke his right arm in an accident, he kept the score left-handed. He never felt comfortable sitting with the other fathers, so his scorekeeping duties gave him something to do. It was the same as when he socialized with Marcy and other couples. "When the husbands and wives would get together, I never fit in with the husbands. Ever. I've never felt like I fit in with any particular group, my whole life. The people I'm most comfortable with are my students."

There is nothing soft about Volpe. He is just under six feet tall, no gym rat, but he runs and is in shape. He is commanding in his own way, but he didn't feel that way in the presence of the baseball dads. It was one thing for him and Marcy to joke about how they ended up with such an athletic son, but altogether different to hear it from others. At the baseball games, some of the other men would ask Volpe how he ever produced a ballplayer like Tommy. "I think maybe they didn't mean to be insulting to me," he says, "but at that time, that's how it felt to me."

When Tommy left for college, Volpe left the bedroom he shared with Marcy. "I established myself in a guest bedroom," is how he put it. (For someone so deeply involved in theater, he can be surprisingly undramatic.) When Tommy came home that year for Thanksgiving break, his father told him they were splitting up and the reason. Tommy would recall his father being "very straightforward about it. He said, basically, 'I have something to tell you,' and he went from there."

Volpe's recollection is the same. "I sat him down and said, 'Here's the story.' I told him about me. Interestingly, Tommy's best friend is gay, a friend from Holy Ghost Prep. He was the best man at Tommy's wedding. I'm thankful for that. I think it made it easier in some ways—not that it was easy at all, because it wasn't."

E very profession has an 'old boys network,' but Broadway is one of the only professions in America where most of the 'old boys' are gay," the actor and comedian Jim David wrote in *The Advocate* in 2012. "Gay men have commandeered the business of creating theater for so long that being gay could actually be considered a career move."

There is no single answer to why so many gay men gravitate to the theater, but one of the best explanations is that their artistic contributions are essential to theater's success. It is a venue that welcomed them always. Theater is a collaborative exploration of the drama of the human condition, and those who are outsiders often are the best people to reflect on that. It is where a great many gay men have gone to find and form community, and where Volpe went. "You can be involved in theater as a gay man and feel completely safe," Volpe says. "It is not an issue, whether you are a director, costume designer, lighting designer, or an actor, you are part of the family. You can be as flamboyant or as private as you want to be. Where else is that true?

"No one is going to judge you. That's the biggest thing—that sense of trust. When you are in the theater, it's like being in church—the church of the theater. There is this unwritten rule: We all respect each other. And I think it has always been that way. When you think about French theater back in Molière's time, the Greeks, it isn't something that has just happened. It has always been there. The arts maybe draw in more gays than any other area because of that feeling of being able to have self-expression without being condemned or labeled or ridiculed or bashed."

Of course, all gay men do not love the theater, any more than all black men excel at basketball or all Asians work with computers. But in all these cases, there is a correlation that has to do with affinity, sensibility, and ability. The whole question is so fraught with stereotype that we often resist exploring difference so as not to be limited in interest or talent by ethnicity, gender, sexuality, or any other factor outside our control. And in doing so, we overlook how those same groupings confer advantage. In the theater, passion and perfectionism and insistence on aesthetic standards are prized qualities, not unruly and unwelcome traits.

The playwright Tony Kushner has described the attraction of gay men to the theater, and their influence on it, in one word:

fabulousness. "If you possess it, you don't need to ask what it is," he writes. "When you attempt to delineate it, you move away from it. *Fabulous* is one of those words that provide a measure of the degree to which a person or event manifests a particular oppressed subculture's most distinctive, invigorating features. What are the salient features of fabulousness? Irony. Tragic History. Defiance. Gender-fuck. Glitter. Drama. It is not butch. It is not hot. The cathexis surrounding fabulousness is not necessarily erotic. The fabulous is not delineated by age or beauty. It is raw materials reworked into illusion. To be truly fabulous, one must completely triumph over tragedy, age, and physical insufficiencies. The fabulous is the rapturous embrace of difference, the discovering of self not in that which has rejected you but in that which makes you unlike, the dislike, the other."

The theater for Volpe was where he felt alive and engaged and at home long before he had any idea why. "When my mother first took me, I would go see these beautiful girls in their beautiful costumes and the magical lights and handsome men and think, *That's such a great life*—never realizing, being young, that it's not real," he says. "I loved it right away. It was so much more interesting to me than seeing a building being constructed. Some people maybe think that as a gay man, you're only interested in handsome men, or whatever, in the theater. But that's not true at all. I am mesmerized by beautiful women, mesmerized by them. I look at them and think, *Oh my God.* They take your breath away. It is not just a sexual thing—it's sensual, it's visual."

Which is what the theater is for Volpe. Sensual, visual, rich in language. It is a more perfect world in the sense that he controls it. The drama and pain expressed onstage do not continue to ripple outward. One door opening does not lead to another and another. It all resolves when the curtain comes down.

As a director, Volpe conveys his love of this world to his students. He brings his sense of beauty and aesthetics and discernment of character to the staging of Truman shows. Are these specifically gay sensibilities? That wouldn't matter to him. It is who he is and what he loves.

I have not seen Marcy since high school, but when she greets me at the front door of her town house, I don't feel the distance of all the years that have passed. She gives me a long hug. She wants to see pictures of my family and to hear about my friends, the other boys who had come to her house for dinners. "Is Bruce still as handsome as he was?" she asks. She pulls out pictures of her own, taken during my high school years, and we try to remember the names of the people in them. She tells me about her recent medical travails, including, as she says, "my two fake hips and my fake knee."

She is just as warm as I remembered her. As funny and direct. If Lou is part of the last group of men who felt like they must stay closeted, Marcy is part of the last generation of crackerjack and competent working-class women who were directed into business or secretarial courses rather than college. (In that way, she reminds me of my own mother, who was still working as a legal secretary in her eighties. She could type documents and, if need be, sharpen up the legal reasoning.)

"I got my education through Lou," Marcy says. "Through typing all his papers and everything else. I didn't mind. I liked it. A dear friend of mine said, 'He used you. You would sit next to the principals at the proms. You would make chatter. You could always talk to anybody. You were the perfect wife.' I got angry when he said that, because it's not the way I feel. It wasn't playing a role to me. It's what I wanted to do, and I enjoyed it. I loved being a teacher's wife."

She made more money at first than he did—$6,500 as a secretary to a real estate attorney, compared to the $6,000 annual salary he made teaching. He went to graduate school two nights a week (the traditional way teachers increase their salaries is by getting advanced degrees) and taught adult education two other nights at a local college. On Saturday nights they went out to eat at one of the better local restaurants and felt rich and happy because they could order anything on the menu. On Sundays, he graded papers and watched football with Tommy while she went to T.J.Maxx and shopped for clothes. "It all just felt right," she says. "We agreed on everything, and I'd say it remained that way pretty much through our marriage. He still says to me sometimes, 'We were the best team ever.' It's just sad the way it turned out. It's a very tragic love story."

When she and Lou divorced, they sold their home and each of them moved into a town house—in the same development, across a road and about a three-minute walk from each other. He said to the sales agent, "We want to buy two of them."

She cooks holiday dinners. Birthday dinners. Anniversary dinners for Tommy and his wife. Lou is always at the table. They are a family, a modern family outside the norm, but not so unusual that plenty of others wouldn't recognize themselves in it. They make the best of imperfect love.

Marcy does make it clear that her relationship with her former husband is on his terms. He is the director. They can go weeks, even months, without seeing each other. "He runs hot and cold," she says. "You get an arm's length, and then he pulls it back and you don't hear from him for a long while."

Our conversation goes back and forth between past and present with an ease that is its own revelation to me. "Can I ask you something?" she says at one point. "Do you think Lou is swishy?"

I think for a moment. No, I finally say. I would never consider him that, and not just because the term itself is dated. The word signifies unmanliness to me, and I don't think of him that way. Just the opposite. He stands up for himself, for others.

"But if you just met him, would you think he was gay?"

Yes, I say, I would.

She recalls that in his early years of teaching, he came home from school one day "down in the dumps." She asked him what was wrong, and he answered that one of the kids suggested to him that he was "a fag." It had something to do with the way he carried his books. She comforted him by saying, "They're high school kids. What do they know?"

In retrospect, you might imagine he was trying to tell her something. Another time, they went to a gay bar in Philadelphia with a friend who was gay. A man offered Lou a seat, and he declined but said his wife would like to sit down. Marcy has replayed this scene numerous times in her mind and now sees it differently. She thinks that the man who offered the chair expressed surprise that Lou had a wife. "Strangers could see it," she says. "Kids could see it. I loved blindly. If I didn't love him so much, would I have seen it?"

We look at a picture of Lou with Tommy, who was about eighteen months at the time. Lou is twenty-five years old, dressed in a leather jacket, handsome, cradling Tommy in the crook of his arm in the bleachers at a high school football game. "Sometimes I don't even see it now," she says. "I know that to some people that makes me a fool."

Marcy and Lou are their own drama, a melancholy piece with

its roots in the pre–sexual revolution 1950s. I can imagine it as something he would want to put onstage at Truman. Or that he would see Off-Broadway and then have to go down the street for a cocktail as soon as he exited the theater, like he told his kids was the case after he saw Edward Albee's *The Goat*—the play about "certain things that can kill love even if you don't want it to."

"We didn't know anything, either of us," Marcy says. She would listen as "the girls in the lunchroom" at work talked about their marriages. "Maybe it was bragging, but some of them were like, 'He can't keep his hands off me. He chases me around the kitchen.' And all I could think was, *Why don't I have that?*"

When they told Tommy they were divorcing, he didn't understand at first. He said to his mother, "But I never hear you fight."

"But we don't touch, either," she answered. "We never touch."

To this day, Marcy is fiercely protective of her ex-husband. She tells me about a friend of his who, in her mind, is not truly loyal. He makes caustic remarks about Lou. Never offers real praise. It angers her. In some ways, she thinks he usurps what should be her role. "Let's be honest," she says. "If anybody's going to cut Lou down, it should be me. Because of my own things with him."

When her marriage ended, she had no guidebook to turn to, nothing that plotted a future course for a woman whose husband declared himself gay. He was still a teacher, a heralded one, but she was no longer a teacher's wife. "He was trying to find out who he was, but in the meantime, I had to figure it out, too, because all of the sudden I was a single woman in my forties."

Not long after I visited with her, a storm in the area knocked out power for a night. Lou walked over and asked if she wanted to stay in his guest room. "It's dark in my place, too," he said, "but you won't be by yourself." She declined, but appreciated the kindness.

They had a longer talk that night. Their time apart had just caught up to the time they had been married—twenty-one years. Neither of them has found anyone else. "Look at us," he said to her. "The years floated by, and here we are. We're both alone."

How long did it take my mom to cry?" Tommy Volpe asks me when we get together at a tavern near his home.

About five minutes, I say.

"That long? You sure?"

The mythology within the family is that Tommy is most like his mother in personality—straightforward, rarely diplomatic, occasionally quick to anger—but I found him a mix of both his parents. He certainly has his father's gift for irony and occasional sarcasm. "My question is this," he says. "If you're gay, don't you have to *do* something about it?" He is not questioning his father's sexual identity, whether he really *is* gay—just commenting on his lonely life in the years since his marriage ended.

Lou and Marcy are united in their belief that what happened in their marriage took a terrible toll on their son. Tommy was a "casualty of war," his father says. He got off track and fell behind in his studies. He stopped playing baseball. Knocked around for a while, tended bar, took the long route through college, got started late on a career. His first marriage ended quickly.

Tommy could not agree less that any of this was his parents' fault. "I never look at it that way," he says. "I know how they feel, but I did what I did and I did it because I wanted to. The consequences may not have been great, but for some of that period, I was having a good time. People say it's bad that I didn't get started teaching until I was thirty-three. I lost out on money or whatever. But I don't care about money. It's what happened. I'm better for it."

He says his father was there to guide him and offer support, "but he didn't intervene. There were no bailouts. My problems were mine to solve." Of what occurred in his family, he says, "I'm not sorry about any of it. It's what happened. I couldn't have two better people as parents."

I hear an echo of his father's worldview when I talk to Tommy, a measure of acceptance—knowledge that life cannot be meticulously plotted out through the acquisition of credentials and the avoidance of missteps. "He was meant to find the theater," he says of his father. "Or the theater found him."

It's a mind-set entirely different from the assumption that a steady glide forward is possible—perfect childhood, the best schools, straight ahead to marriage and career—or that it is even preferable. Only fools believe this. No one would want to watch a theater piece with that arc. It's not real. The Volpe outlook is distinctly working-class. It is not pessimistic, but it *is* pragmatic. As a parent or an educator, you hope to create conditions for success. But there are no guarantees. Stuff happens along the way.

Tommy teaches sixth grade, and has been at it long enough now that some of his students have become his father's students. He has had kids in his classes who live in Red Cross shelters. He knows about Levittown's boom times, but never experienced them. "What I learned from my dad is, set the expectations really high," he says. "Convince your kids they can meet them and help them achieve it. What you don't want for them to ever think is, *I come from a shit town, so my life is going to be shit.* That's the attitude that he gets in the way of. He puts a stop to that thinking, and I try to do the same."

Tommy Volpe never dreamed he would become a teacher in his

father's district. "It just sort of happened, but it feels right," he says. "Maybe it's corny, but I feel like I'm giving back. I didn't go to school in Bristol Township, but it gave me the life I've had."

A new group of Theater 1 students walks into Volpe's classroom. Most of them stop for a moment just inside the door and gaze at the couches, the mobiles, the posters, all the happy chaos of a space that looks nothing like any classroom they've known. They settle in, and he tells them, "I'm not here to make you a great actor. That's not my job. The reasons you should be taking this class are far more important than learning to act. I want you to gain confidence, learn something about life, grow up a little bit. I want to help you see who you are."

They start with a game, an icebreaker designed for the many students Volpe gets every year who have rarely if ever spoken up in a class. He passes out potato chips, tells everyone they are at a party. They must tell the class about a guest they have brought. Among the guests on this day: Lady Gaga, 50 Cent, Jesus. The guests are introduced around, wander off, get into other conversations. Soon everyone is laughing, eating the chips, and trying to keep track of where their initial guest has gone.

In a more advanced class several weeks later, Theater 3, students are studying *Red Light Winter*, a drama by the writer Adam Rapp. Volpe starts by regaling them about a documentary he watched the previous night about Joan Rivers (who ever knew there was continuous Joan Rivers fare on TV?) and a bit she did that he found hilarious. Something about Halloween and kids at her door who did not like that she was giving out apples instead of candy. So she told the children, "Then just eat the razor blades!" Volpe is cackling about this. Some of his students look at him like he is an insane old man.

A boy near the front of the class seems to have gone to sleep. Maybe he worked late the previous night or he was at a party, but Volpe just ignores him. Another is stitching up his lacrosse stick, but he's listening. "How's your sister?" Volpe asks another student. He is talking about her twin, who is at home and within days of giving birth.

These classes operate on Volpe time, which is different from the time a math teacher might keep. Here, interruptions and digressions are encouraged. They are an integral part of the program.

The class is reading the play aloud. A moment after they begin, Volpe says, "Let me just stop for a moment and say that this is one of the best parts I can imagine for a young American actor. It's breathtaking." He is talking about one of the two male characters, Adam. "It's a fine line the actor has to walk. His character can't be sentimental. It has to be honest and truthful and yet heartbreaking."

When I listen to the students read, they stumble over certain words they have not come across before—like *Copenhagen* and *Zurich*. (Where I live now, at least one kid in each class would have been to those cities.) The word *Aristotelian* comes up. Volpe tells them how to pronounce it. "We'll talk about its meaning tomorrow," he says.

His students do possess some advanced knowledge. There is a reference in the play to a lambskin condom. A girl in the class says that lambskin is not good at protecting against AIDs. It's too porous. A couple of others in the class agree.

They reach a scene where a character tells his whole sad life story to a prostitute. "Why would anyone ever do that?" Robby Edmondson, Truman theater's technical whiz, asks. "She's a complete stranger. Why wouldn't you talk to a friend as opposed to someone you just met?"

"That's a very good point, Robby," Volpe says. "But sometimes you might tell a stranger things you would never tell your best friend."

At the back of the room, a boy with a beard and hooded eyes raises his hand, and Volpe nods for him to go ahead. "Sometimes if you're sad about something, depressed, you feel better after you tell someone about it," he says. "It might not matter who they are."

The student is repeating twelfth grade and struggling with a chaotic home life and some legal issues of his own, but he is bright and tuned in to this class. Volpe is rooting hard for him to survive the year and get his diploma. He responds to the boy's comment by doing something rare for him: He tells a deeply personal story of his own. He does so, it seems to me, to support this young man who just spoke up. "When I got divorced from my wife, it was a good thing," he says. "I didn't want to be married. But it was sad. I went to a therapist. I guess you could say that she was a stranger, in a way. But I needed someone to talk to, and she was helpful. But I only saw her once a week, just an hour out of the whole week, and I was feeling so bad that an hour wasn't enough. So I wrote in a journal. I didn't even care about spelling or punctuation; I just wrote. And that was also like talking to someone."

Seamlessly, they resume discussing the play. Mariela Castillo, who can have a bit of a prudish side, objects to some of the language. "I feel like this is porn," she says.

"I understand where you're coming from, but I don't agree," Volpe says. "It would be easy to make it porn, just show it all, but that's not what's done here. The craft is making it theater. That's where the interest is. You can go on the Internet and see porn, and it's boring, or it very quickly gets boring. But this isn't boring."

Several other students offer opinions. The bell rings. No one gets up. They're still talking about the play. "You gotta go," Volpe tells them. He adds that he will not be there for a couple of days, that he and Krause are off to a conference of theater teachers.

"No!" somebody shouts.

"When are you coming back?" a voice calls out.

"When do we get to do the second act?" another student asks.

One of Volpe's students, a drama kid, had recently come to him privately and revealed he was gay. It is something that occurs probably at least once a year. Volpe is an obvious person to confide in—living proof that a person can be gay and also a respected and even revered member of the community. Volpe is always cautious in these situations. He first asks: Are you sure? Some of his students are still as young as fourteen. Not fully formed. He thinks some girls may find it "fashionable" to declare themselves gay, though he's yet to encounter that in a boy.

This particular student asks if he should tell his parents. Volpe does not automatically say yes. He does not always know the families well, so he can't anticipate the response. He tells this boy to take his time, and also suggests he talk to his guidance counselor. "Maybe it's a cop-out on my part," he says, "but I don't ever want to pretend I have every answer or that I have training in things I don't. I'm a teacher. I've lived the life I've lived. That doesn't make me an expert on every single one of these situations."

But he does always offer himself as a safe haven. He says to this student, "If someone is mean to you, if you get harassed or feel scared or uncomfortable, you come and see me right away. Don't worry about what period it is, or what class it is. I'll stop what I'm doing, whatever it is, and be there for you."

There is a GLAAD chapter at Truman—the Gay and Lesbian Alliance Against Defamation. Volpe considers it "an enormous step forward." If someone had told him thirty years ago that such a thing would exist, he never would have believed it. "It's still not easy," he says. "I know there are students I teach who have a charade they play. They're gay, I know that they are—my gaydar is pretty good— but they are not ready to reveal that, which is absolutely fine. They're very young and they can't yet make the switch over to that place. But they may have a sad life until they come to terms with who they are."

Volpe has spoken periodically at the GLAAD meetings, but it's not one of the groups he serves as faculty advisor. Whether he is "out" at Truman is a matter of interpretation. He has not "announced" it, he says, and does not talk about it any more than "straight teachers run around telling people they're straight. It should be an even playing field. It's not something I feel I have to do. But it's well understood. My students would have to be blind to not know I'm gay."

He thinks coming to terms with his sexuality made him a better teacher and theater director, though exactly how is not easy to say. "I know it did, but I really have to think about how to describe it. I guess once I acknowledged who I was—not only recognized it, but felt good about it—it influenced how I saw theater and it opened my eyes more to how I direct plays.

"If you are not hiding something about yourself and you have finally faced down a demon—not that being gay is a demon, but that is how it felt growing up and through much of my life—you are going to be a more open and more aware person. And those are very important things for a director to be. But you have to also understand that theater is removed—it is once removed from life. It can feel very real, but it's not life itself. It's not the same thing."

His students do, of course, understand that he is gay. "It's pretty obvious, but it's not up for discussion," Courtney Meyer says. "He's such a big figure in this school that if someone was ever hostile about that aspect of him, it wouldn't go over well at all.

"If you're in the theater program, you're changed," she continues. "You accept. You are exposed to people and ideas that, if you were a close-minded or bigoted person, you can't be anymore. You change without knowing it or even thinking about it necessarily."

It's not something that can be quantified, but I have the feeling that students at Truman are sometimes just plain *nicer* than what I'm used to seeing. The school feels like an unusually accepting place, especially in light of Levittown's aversion to difference of all kinds and its legacy of bigotry. In 2012, a special education student, a boy with disabilities from a stroke he suffered before birth, was voted prom king. It wasn't a joke or some post-modern ironic comment on the concept of proms and prom kings and queens. It was from the heart. He was beloved by the senior class, and it was an emotional moment when the honor was announced at prom.

Afterward, his mother wrote a letter of thanks that was published in the newspaper. Her son, she said, was not "the all-star jock, the class president, or the lead in the school play; he's just a nice guy who enjoys talking to people about sports, food, and what their plans are." She expressed her gratitude that he had been at Truman for the previous four years "with such wonderful, accepting, and thoughtful young men and women."

Zach Philippi believes the spirit of the theater program extends into the rest of the school. "I think it sets the tone. Maybe there's some cases where people get bullied at Truman, but I honestly don't see it. It's not considered cool, and people don't put up with it. To me, it starts with theater. It's open to everybody. Gay, straight, out, not out. I've only gone to one high school, so maybe it's that way everywhere, but that's not what I hear."

It's not surprising that the revered Zach, high school alpha male, would have a sunny view of social relations at Truman and perhaps even an idealized notion of how easy it might be for an outsider to fit in. I wondered what L. J. Carulli would tell me. He is the student who played the role of the street drummer and drag queen Angel Dumott Schunard in Truman's *Rent*, and was himself openly gay at Truman. "The most fearless boy I ever taught" is how Volpe describes him.

Carulli has played Angel again in a couple of professional productions of *Rent*—high points, so far, of his post-Truman years. Much of the rest of his life has not been easy. He is taking classes at the local community college while helping to care for his disabled mother, whose oxygen tanks I pass by on the front porch when I visit him. He says he might like to become a teacher. His father had been in the sign business—big neon displays, some of them hung in Atlantic City's gambling district—but with the decline in the economy, demand for those signs dwindled, and now he is working part-time at Walmart.

Carulli's education before Truman was chaotic because his family moved several times and he bounced between schools in

Philadelphia and its suburbs. The prospect of going to Truman terrified him at first. He had friends who were familiar with it, and they warned him that it might be a dangerous place for a boy who was shy, slightly built, and gay. "But it wasn't like that once I got there," he says. "Of course I was picked on every once in a while or somebody said something in the hall, but it never went beyond that. Mr. Volpe was like the biggest figure in the school. I don't know what it would be like without him.

"Then once I got involved with drama, it was like I was protected. Every kind of kid was in drama—the popular kids, the kids who played sports. You were their friend, and it wasn't like they even had to say anything to the rest of the school. People who were mean or bullies or whatever couldn't pick on you. They knew they had to leave you alone."

CAST MEMBERS OF *SPRING AWAKENING*.
FROM LEFT: COLIN LESTER, JUSTIN McGROGAN,
JONATHAN EARP-PITKINS, TYLER KELCH,
AND ADELBERT LALO.

SPRING AWAKENING

Music Theatre International is one of those businesses that seems to traverse two distinct time periods: the modern era of robust websites and instant communication and an earlier epoch of musty mail rooms, bad coffee, hand-selling, and sentiment. The company was founded by Frank Loesser, who wrote the music and lyrics to *Guys and Dolls* and *How to Succeed in Business Without Really Trying*. It owns the theatrical rights to hundreds of shows—standards like *Les Misérables, Fiddler on the Roof, The Music Man,* and *Damn Yankees*; just about the whole Sondheim canon; every Disney musical; and much of the newer work from London's West End, Broadway, and Off Broadway.

The current CEO and co-owner is Freddie Gershon, a classical musician in his younger days who studied for eight years at the Juilliard School. He became an entertainment lawyer with an all-star list of clients that included Eric Clapton, Van Morrison, and Bette

Midler, and a producer of concert tours and Broadway shows. Along the way, he published a novel about the music business with the title *Sweetie Baby Cookie Honey.*

His spacious office in Midtown Manhattan feels more like a drawing room than a work space. The floor is covered with a big Oriental carpet, the walls decorated with fine art. Gershon, in his early seventies, trim and natty-looking, shakes my hand, offers me a seat, and begins talking before I can ask a question. He had recently been awarded an honorary Tony Award for his long contributions to the world of theater and specifically for creating the Broadway Junior line of offerings—thirty- and sixty-minute versions of works that can be performed by elementary and middle school students. The program nurtures a love of musical theater in children and has the additional benefit of cultivating future Broadway ticket buyers.

"What they appreciated is that I'm putting tushies in the seats," Gershon says, giving a Yiddish twist to the old showbiz expression "asses in the seats." "That's why I was given the Tony. They don't give a fuck about the art, some of them, but they love that I'm building audiences from the ground up."

Current Broadway is not entirely to Gershon's taste. It's too overloaded with circus acrobatics and special effects. Ticket prices are through the roof. And the craft? Don't even ask. "People like David Merrick, Jerry Robbins, Hal Prince, if you showed them this stuff, they'd say, 'I'm impressed. Now lose it.' They understood that you need to strip it down. Trust the material. A good story, a great song, it's enough."

The money constraints of high school theater enforce a certain discipline and purity. Gershon read a newspaper story about an unusually prosperous high school that spent upward of $200,000 on a show, and it infuriated him. "To do what?" he says. "Impress people?"

Drama is deeply embedded in the culture of American high schools, perhaps not quite like football, but close. At MTI, it represents a steady business—year after year, teachers make selections from the company's catalog, send in their checks for the rights, and wait for the scripts and other materials to arrive in one giant box. For a show that runs over two weekends and five or six performances, a school like Truman pays as much as $5,000, mainly for the licensing fee. High schools with bigger auditoriums pay more.

Rates are set by the size of the theater and the popularity of the show, so a production of, say, *Beauty and the Beast*, which tends to sell lots of tickets, is the most pricey, but also gives a school the best chance to make its money back, or even turn a profit. MTI also sells various extras: T-shirts themed to the shows; licensed artwork; items from the "prop shop"; sound effects CDs; an OrchEXTRA music system, with the show music loaded, for schools that do not use a pit orchestra.

MTI licenses about fifteen thousand shows each year for professional, amateur, and school performances. Gershon says schools represent the core of the business, and the company could be successful if that was all it did. In bad economic times, the school trade drops off less than the rest. After the recession hit in 2007, the company heard from a handful of schools that could no longer mount productions. In most cases they were not killing their programs, but experiencing financial shortfalls peripheral to the drama program, which they hoped would be temporary—for example, no funds to pay janitors to stay after three P.M. or for buses to transport late-staying students.

Occasionally, a show is canceled for more idiosyncratic reasons.

Gershon tells me about some materials that were sent back to him from a high school in Texas that had paid to license *Annie*. The principal included a note with the boxed-up scripts explaining they could not do the show because they had discovered it was satanic. Gershon called him right up. "I'm the owner of the company," he said. "How can I address your problem?" The principal said that he was disturbed that Daddy Warbucks came from Hell's Kitchen.

"It's a neighborhood in New York," Gershon explained.

"See then, that's right," the principal said. "It *is* satanic."

The older Gershon gets, the more attached he is to the scholastic part of MTI. It is both a business for him and a kind of mission. "It means everything to me. Look at what's happening in the other parts of their lives. These kids, they text each other. They don't know how to read faces. They don't have antennae. Theater gives them what a computer takes away, what no classroom teacher can teach. They learn to work with other people. They learn patience and tolerance and how to be deferential to each other. They learn to be good citizens. It's unifying. It has an impact on kids that can't be quantified. Educators don't know how to measure it."

He notes the growing "pressure and resistance" to arts education during the school day (as opposed to after-school theater). "People say, What's all this froufrou singing and dancing and acting got to do with anything? How's it help them get better SAT scores? But in the arts, you learn a vast amount of information without even knowing you're learning it. It's the only way some people can learn."

I tell him about Mariela Castillo and how theater was the realm in which she finally realized she has the ability to process large amounts of information. "That's wonderful," he says. "But I'll tell you something—those things happen more than you think."

Gershon and Stephen Sondheim are friends—in fact, Sondheim was one of the first to agree to have some of his plays condensed into the short Broadway Junior versions for younger children. (When other authors resist, fearing their creations will be "chopped up," Gershon persuades them by "invoking the icon.") He and Sondheim help financially support a drama program at a school in Lower Manhattan for special needs children, including some with autism.

When Gershon learned that one of the students, in the midst of a rehearsal, spoke his first word ever, he said to Sondheim, "We have to see this." They took a car together to the school. "I said to him that the one thing we can't do is cry, because it could be disturbing to them if they see two old men cry."

Gershon rode in the limousine from Manhattan that day in 2001 to see Truman's version of *Les Misérables* along with Cameron Mackintosh, a co-owner at MTI. People at their level of theater can see straight into the soul of a production, beyond what can be dressed up with money, technology, lavish set design, or even beautiful voices. "Lou Volpe is as good as you get in high school," Gershon says. "He's better than some people in the professional business. There is a sense of collegiality and respect and awareness among everyone involved in his shows. You cannot fake that kind of thing. You feel that from them, and it comes from their teacher. It's the only place it can come from."

John Prignano, MTI's senior operations officer, also traveled to Levittown that evening. He had first seen a Truman show at a festival the previous year. "Every kid onstage had a character," he tells me. "They were all one hundred percent committed. That doesn't happen often. Acting is all about the choices that you make in the moment. I thought, *Someone is really teaching them to trust their choices, and whoever that is, I want to work with him.*"

The popularity of *Les Mis*—the staggering ten thousand–plus performances in London's West End since its 1985 opening, the long Broadway run—made it a natural for the school market. But its scale was an obstacle. Three and a half hours in its original form. Based on a complicated novel by Victor Hugo. Mackintosh's personal attachment to *Les Mis*, one of his first great successes, was another complicating factor. "That show was his baby," says Gershon. "He knew every nuance, every problem that needed to be solved."

When first offered the chance to do the pilot, Volpe declined. He didn't understand why he was chosen, and the challenge of it left him petrified. Why don't you ask some other high school that has better facilities? he said to Steve Spiegel, MTI's president at the time. He protested that his stage was just thirty-five feet across. Some high school stages were about *twice* that wide. His sound systems and acoustics were substandard; the seats were those awful wooden planks. Spiegel said that he didn't care about any of that and neither did anyone else at MTI. If they wanted a rich school with all the best facilities, they could easily have found one. "We think you can do this for us," Spiegel said.

That terrified Volpe even more. He felt like he had been tapped on the shoulder for a mission beyond his reach. He feared that if the show did not succeed, it would never be licensed for other high schools and he would be blamed. When he told his friends about the offer and his decision to decline it, he imagined they would understand his reasoning. They didn't. They all had pretty much the same reaction: *Have you lost your mind?*

Volpe thought of his late mother and what she so often said to him: "What's the worst thing that can happen?" When he had revealed to her that he was gay and asked if she was surprised, she said to him, "*Louis*, I watch *Oprah*, you know." She was unafraid, unflappable, fully modern. He liked to think he lived by her creed, but he could not honestly say he did in this case.

He called Spiegel back two days later to make sure the offer was still good. Told that it was, he agreed to take on *Les Mis*. "I still sometimes wonder why I backed off that," he says now. "There was no excuse. My mom was probably up there having a fit."

Another high school, Holy Trinity in Hicksville, Long Island, had staged a previous MTI-sanctioned pilot of *Les Mis*. Mackintosh was impressed, but not ready to give his approval afterward for a wider licensing. "Cameron wanted it redone," Gershon says. He gave notes on the performance, which were passed on to Volpe.

When the curtain closed on Truman's production, Mackintosh turned to Gershon and said, "Let's lock this," signaling that he had blessed Truman's version of his show. Volpe's choices—his rewrites and cuts, made in consultation with MTI—would be enshrined in *Les Misérables School Edition*. "Cameron will not ever lower his standards," Steve Spiegel says. "If they had not performed at this level, he would not have allowed it to be released. It was very much in the balance, and they pleased him."

Volpe usually produced Truman's musicals in the spring in order to build in more rehearsal time. But MTI liked the pilots to be produced in November so they could be marketed for the next school year, which meant Volpe and his students had to get started in the summer. Rehearsals for *Le Mis* and *Rent* began when students would normally be enjoying their time off, or working—to say nothing of Volpe's time off—as would rehearsals for the third pilot he took on for MTI.

On June 29, 2011, less than forty-eight hours after he returned from the triumph of *Good Boys and True* in Nebraska and two weeks after the previous school year ended, Volpe climbs into his Mercedes coupe and sets out on the twenty-minute drive to Truman. The car is an indulgence that he has made into self-parody. (Its color is *slate*, not gray, he likes to point out.) He parks in Truman's empty lot, walks through the school's quiet corridors, and slides his key into the lock of Room B8. He makes his clockwise circle of the room and fluffs the couches, then turns the air-conditioning up, takes a seat behind his desk, and waits for everyone to arrive.

Marcy had once said to him, "I know you love me. I know you love Tommy. But that school is where your pulse is. It's where your heart beats." She wasn't wrong.

The fatigue left over from the difficult trip back from Nebraska—multiple flight delays, another night in a hotel after they couldn't get all the way home—is magically gone. What he feels instead is the anticipation and excitement of another production lifting off. Auditions are soon to begin for the rock musical *Spring Awakening.* The collaborations with MTI came to him at different junctures of his career. After the success of *Le Mis*, he embraced the opportunity to do *Rent* as soon as he was asked. "It was totally different," he says. "*Les Mis* gave me a lot of confidence. I was a different director after that. It was beyond what I could have ever dreamed of. With *Rent*, they were not burning up the fax line as much, and they didn't come down to look in on rehearsals. I felt like they trusted me more. It may have also made a difference that it wasn't a Cameron Mackintosh show."

It was no less a triumph. Composer and lyricist Jonathan Larson, *Rent*'s creator, had died just months before *Rent*'s 1996 Broadway debut, from a tear in his aorta. The show's immense success would forever be linked to the sadness and shock of his sudden death. At Truman's opening night, Larson's father, Allan, sat in the fourth row of the theater, and when the curtain came down, Volpe invited him up onstage, just as he had Mackintosh five years before. Allan Larson accepted a handheld microphone and said that his son was with them in spirit, and that he would have loved the performance and been thrilled that *Rent* had reached a high school stage. He turned to the cast, which was gathered behind him, and said, "Thank you for honoring Jonathan's memory."

"It wasn't maudlin; it was celebratory," Volpe says. "But it was emotional—the most emotional moment we've ever had. People were weeping."

The process of how *Spring Awakening* came to Truman was different from either *Rent* or *Les Mis*. Volpe lobbied for it. Just about begged. He told John Prignano, "When you're ready for a pilot, I want it. Just let me know and we'll do whatever it takes to make it happen." His ardent pursuit was not necessary. *Spring Awakening* was going to be difficult to revise for a high school production, and the show's creators were not convinced it was even possible. MTI executives had already decided that if permission was granted for a pilot, they would ask Volpe to direct it at Truman.

Volpe and Tracey Krause had seen *Spring Awakening* on Broadway not long after it opened in 2006 and fell in love with it. It was experimental, alive, subversive, and right in Volpe's sweet spot—a coming-of-age story with characters the same age as his high school actors. The music was composed by Duncan Sheik, who had a separate career and a following as a singer-songwriter. Lea Michele, who a few years later would become a big star in *Glee*, played the role of Wendla, the most prominent female part.

One of the features of the Broadway production was that about twenty audience members were seated onstage. They didn't do anything, and in fact were instructed to be still and quiet, but they were integrated into the set. A couple of months after they saw it for the first time, Volpe and Krause took students to New York for the show and, through connections, scored the seats onstage. It was an exhilarating experience. The Truman kids and their teachers were on a Broadway stage—if not exactly in a cast. (It was also a huge bargain; the seats, which technically were "obstructed view," cost only $30 each.)

Volpe's advanced theater students studied the show and performed parts of it in class. The 2011 class of seniors who made up the *Good Boys* cast knew it would ultimately be piloted at Truman and were disappointed to miss it by just one year. "Maybe I could, like, screw up in a couple of classes and have to repeat twelfth grade," Bobby Ryan joked when he found out the show had been scheduled.

On the morning of auditions, Krause arrives a few minutes after Volpe, takes a seat next to him, and sets her coffee cup down on his desk. They are joined by Ryan Fleming, Truman Drama's vocal director. Fleming doesn't teach at the school; he is the choir director at a local church and an accomplished vocalist who sings with the Opera Company of Philadelphia and in a highly re-garded choral group called the Crossing, which performs in Phila-delphia, New York, and Europe. His role is to help select the cast and then to try to elevate nontrained voices to as high a level as possible in the time he has to work with them. "There's no longer a full-time vocal teacher at Truman," he says. "It's terrible, it really is. All we have here is what I can shove down their faces in a short pe-riod of time."

Communities and schools get poorer in all kinds of ways, be-yond what can be measured by income levels. Levittown has gotten musically poorer, which is related to other parts of the community that have frayed. Fleming only rarely encounters Truman students who attend church, traditionally one of the great incubators of vocal music in America. The mainline Protestant churches in town, built on land Levitt set aside, have hollowed out, and many are left with graying, older congregations. Some Levittown residents have migrated to megachurches elsewhere in the county, where Fleming considers the musical opportunities to be inferior. In 2012, even Levittown's Catholic grammar school, Saint Michael the Archangel, once so bursting at the seams that class sizes were in the fifties, was scheduled to be shuttered before winning a reprieve.

Truman students sometimes seek private lessons from Fleming, often in the weeks before an audition to give them a leg up to make the show. But most can afford only a handful of sessions, even though he doesn't charge them much.

Fleming's other role with Truman Drama is to be nervous. While Volpe and Krause certainly care deeply about the quality of voices in their shows, it is fair to say Fleming listens differently and cares more. Volpe *assumes* they will have the voices to go forward with a show; Fleming worries and doesn't assume anything.

"How many kids are out there in the hall?" Volpe asks before the nine A.M. start of auditions.

There are about seventy, far fewer than for *Rent*, but *Spring Awakening* has not been made into a movie and does not carry the same cachet. Beyond that, Volpe's program has become like an elite high school sports team, and therefore a little intimidating—if you're a student in the school, you don't just show up and try out unless you feel you have some game.

"I want to know how many boys," Fleming says.

The show has eleven lead parts—six of them boys—and a small ensemble. Fleming is confident about the girls, but concerned about having enough male voices that meet his standard.

"If we're not happy with the boys, then we just won't do it," Volpe says. "We'll do a different show." He may mean that at the moment he says it, but it's hard for me to imagine him telling MTI that he has changed his mind.

Spring Awakening is a big, risky proposition—a pilot and a show very much on the knife's edge—and he is undertaking it with young kids, some of them totally new to Truman Drama and one another. "There's a lot of talent out there," Volpe says the morning of auditions. "I have confidence in them or I'd never do this. But Ryan has a point. They're very much untested."

In a perfect world, one in which he controlled the timing of everything, Volpe would have liked *Spring Awakening* to come his way a year or two earlier, when he still had the core that performed *Good Boys and True*. They were an almost foolproof group—capable, mature, deeply committed to him and one another. They had voices, both the girls and the boys. "That group, you didn't have to wait for them to come together," he says. "But that's a luxury. Will I miss the leadership of Bobby and Wayne? Yes. But that's the way it is. You have to create new Bobbys and Waynes."

Volpe, Krause, and Fleming sit in a row of three chairs at the front of the audition room. It reminds me of *American Idol* or one of its many spin-offs, except that those shows are modeled after *these* scenes. High school auditions are cauldrons of tension broken up by moments of unintentional comedy. The stakes are high for the kids, but also for the directors—one wrong choice and they have set the show off course, perhaps irrevocably.

The first to audition is an incoming ninth-grader, one of several that morning who would not begin classes at Truman for another two months but is hoping to start high school with a place already secured in a Volpe show. She is a lovely girl, long black hair, a shy smile. Her hands tremble as she hands over her name and contact numbers on an index card. "Relax," Volpe says. "Take a nice deep breath."

She sings "Mama Who Bore Me," the opening song in the show, with a degree of competence but little presence—she seems just to want to reach the end without dissolving. "Thank you, that was beautiful," Volpe tells her. When she leaves, he says to Krause and Fleming, "I want to make sure not to lose some of these younger ones," meaning he wants to be encouraging enough for them to want to audition in the future.

Next comes another freshman girl, who sings the same song but in a faint whisper. "She was in tune," Fleming says. "I'll give her that."

Luke Robinson, the recycling maven who worked on the stage crew in Nebraska, steps forward with a big, goofy grin on his face. He is a charming kid who gives the impression of being entirely comfortable with himself, as if he knows that he fits the stereotype of a high school geek—braces, involvement in drama *and* debate— and just doesn't care. Luke had a lead part in *Dirty Rotten Scoundrels*, the previous year's musical, but is still considered an emerging talent. He auditions with a number called "Don't Do Sadness," which starts out like a moody indie-rock tune and then builds into hard-driving rock. He hits the notes. Makes the turn from soft to pulsating. Sells the whole thing.

"I have to tell you, I am in shock at what I just saw from you," Volpe says. "Are you the same Luke we had here last year?"

Krause offers her own version of praise: "I could just punch you right in the face. Where has *that* been?"

Robby Edmondson is less surprised. He graduated earlier in the month, but is in the room because Volpe is paying him to help out on the technical side of *Spring Awakening*. (Robby is also starting college and continuing his gig working the lights for the pro hockey and basketball teams in North Jersey.) "Truman Drama's a cycle," he says. "Wayne and Britney and Mariela and all of them, they defined it for a couple of years, just like Antonio [Addeo] and some other kids did before them. Now Luke feels like it's his time. You can see it. He's ready."

A few minutes later, one of Truman's out gay students (there are several) auditions. He is funny and popular with classmates, theatrically and often hilariously effeminate—he plays it that way—but cannot hold a tune. Volpe admires his audacity, but says, "I feel bad. I'd love to give him a part because I know he doesn't have that much else in his life and it would mean so much to him. He's such a nice kid and he'd give four thousand percent. But he only has one role—swishy gay boy—and there's not a part for that in this play."

It's a long morning—a mix of familiar faces and new blood, a range of voices from good to god-awful, a couple more revelations. Volpe and Krause keep up a constant patter, if for no other reason than to amuse themselves.

Britney Harron's little sister, Shannon, another incoming ninth-grader, gives a polished audition and clearly is in line for a role. "Let's give her a really big part, just to annoy Britney," Volpe says.

A hippie-looking girl with torn jeans, short blond hair, and multiple piercings hands in her card and says she will be in ninth grade, "but I should be in tenth. I have to do ninth over." She's pretty good, but Krause says, "Do you think she's too drama-y?"

The girl who follows her gives a promising audition and seems like a possibility. "She's one of my criminals," says Krause, who had her in class the previous year. Everyone laughs. "No, really. She's on probation for stealing a car."

Georjenna Gatto presents a different kind of problem. She is a stellar student from a solid-as-a-rock family, ranked fifth in the incoming senior class, beautiful and poised, a proven performer in past Truman productions—and also the captain of the field hockey team, an honor she had been accorded even as an eleventh-grader. Sometimes students can mix their sport and a show, but field hockey is a fall sport, and this is a fall musical *and* a pilot. Volpe has made it clear to her that if she wants to do both—be in the show and play field hockey—he can put her in the ensemble, but will not cast her as one of the five female leads.

"You can do both," Georjenna says. "Nobody at Truman thinks if you're an athlete, why would you have that theater side of your-self. But the timing has to work out, and it doesn't in this case."

She was racked for weeks with indecision and anxiety. "We won't hate you," her field hockey teammates assured her, but she knows they want her to play. Some have been her teammates since the seventh grade. Georjenna's parents keep saying it is her decision to make, a phrase she hears so much from everyone in her life that she thinks she might slap the next person who says it. She thinks her dad—a football coach and assistant principal at a high school in the neighboring town of Bristol Borough—wants her to stay with her sport, but he doesn't press it. She feels like screaming: *Somebody just tell me what to do!*

Field hockey is like most of the teams at Truman. It wins a few games, though not many. Georjenna knows that sports are yet another way outsiders judge her school. She remembers taking a drive with her mother when she was a little younger. They got about twenty minutes out of Levittown, into some posh-looking community, and her mother said, "Isn't it strange? It's like two different worlds."

When she competes in sports against those schools, Georjenna sometimes feels girls from the other teams don't respect Truman. "I'm sorry, but you can tell. They have their noses up, like they're so much better than us. It's frustrating. We're the same people. We want the same things. They don't know us, but you can feel that they're looking down on us."

No one looks down on Truman Drama, but Georjenna wants to make sure she doesn't make a decision based on the relative status of field hockey and theater. She has a specific part she wants, the role of Wendla, which Lea Michele played. Every time she thinks about maybe playing field hockey, her mind shifts to another thought: *I* really *want this part.*

She thinks *Spring Awakening* has a chance to be the biggest thing she'll ever do in high school. As much as she loves her sport, it cannot rise to that. And she definitely does not want to compro-mise and take a part in the ensemble. She tells herself, *It's my last year of high school. I want to do one thing and go all out.*

Casting decisions are made quickly, often the very day of audi-tions, or after callbacks if they are required. Georjenna auditions with "Mama Who Bore Me," a performance Volpe will later attach one of his favorite words to: *stunning.* When she is finished singing, he says, "Georjenna, you know what I'm about to ask you. I know it's a very difficult decision for you."

She stops him. "I'm going to do the show if I get a lead," she says. "I'll call up my coach right away and tell her."

"You're okay with that?"

"Yeah," she said. "I'm totally okay with it. I'm sure of it."

The big revelation is Carol Ann Vaserberg, a short, delicately built junior with a speaking voice so soft, sometimes you have to strain to hear her. Before her audition, she says to the panel of three who will be judging her, "If any of you know my family, please don't hold it against me."

I do know her family, which is populated by smart if somewhat eccentric people. I graduated high school with her uncle Ralph, who had been a baseball teammate of mine starting from about age ten. I know another of her uncles, Roger, who was a year behind me in high school and played the lead in Volpe's first musical, *You're a Good Man, Charlie Brown.* A gifted visual artist (Volpe considers him "an artistic genius"), he also designed and painted much of the set. I even know Carol Ann's grandmother, who was locally renowned as a former professional softball player. I do not know her father,

Robby, the youngest of the three Vaserberg boys, but he is apparently considered something of a character around town.

As soon as Carol Ann begins to sing, Fleming leans forward, wide-eyed. The song is "The Dark I Know Well," a chilling number from near the end of Act 1. Her voice does not match her tiny frame; it is massive, rich, and laced with feeling. When she hits the last note, Fleming says, "Can I ask you a question, Carol Ann? How is it possible you've been in this school two years and this is the first time we're seeing you?"

She replies that she is academically oriented and had not participated in many extracurricular activities. She spends much of her time studying and reading for pleasure. "But I know *Spring Awakening* and I wanted to be in it," she says. "I love it. I think it's really cool." (She will later tell me she had decided to get involved as an "homage" to a friend who introduced her to the music in the show.)

"Well, I'm a little bit pissed at you," Fleming says. "Do you know the experiences you missed? The productions you could have been in and the fun you could have had?" She nods. "Well, I'm glad you're here now."

When Carol Ann leaves the room, Volpe, Krause, and Fleming just sort of look at one another in amazement. When I ask Fleming later to sum her up, he says, "A true alto belter. Her voice had a very raw yet warm and vulnerable quality." He adds, "I'm just always shocked when a person like that shows up without even realizing what they have."

As much as they like new and unknown talent, Volpe and Krause are always concerned about the issue of dependability. A Truman show requires a huge commitment: rehearsals every day after school with all-day Saturday sessions added in as productions grow near. This one comes with the additional burden of summer rehearsals; once the cast is picked, they will reconvene in August to get started. And a production is a team effort. They can't have flakes, loose cannons, over-emoters—any of that.

Carol Ann is talented, composed, clearly smart and, in the little you can tell in a brief audition, seems very nice. But still, she raises a concern. How could someone with all that raw talent just now be showing up, two years after entering a high school known for its theater program?

Volpe asks Robby if he knows her. "Yeah, she's quiet, has a group of friends, good kid. I think she's just kind of shy."

"There's nothing we have to worry about?"

"No, I don't think so. If she makes a commitment, she'll follow through on it."

The boys, as Ryan Fleming had predicted, are a cause for concern. Luke Robinson had been terrific. Two other holdovers, Colin Lester and Justin McGrogan, are solid in their auditions and have already excelled in previous shows. Tyler Kelch is going to be in the show—he has serious musical and acting chops—but is dissatisfied with his audition. "Two weeks ago I could hit all those high notes," he says as soon as he finishes singing. "I don't know what happened. I lost, like, a whole octave. I guess my voice changed again."

"You were fine," Fleming says.

"No, I wasn't."

"Okay, enough, Tyler," Krause says. "Stop being such a drama queen."

Beyond this core of four boys, it's a crapshoot. It will all come down to who walks through the door and how they perform. Volpe's choices are often from the gut. "I love his face! It's so expressive," he says after the audition of Adelbert Lalo, a senior who has never even auditioned previously. "I can just see him in this show."

Adelbert is no Carol Ann, in terms of out-of-the-blue talent, so he raises no red flags. I ask Fleming if Adelbert can sing. "Not really, but I think I can probably get him there," he says. He gives the same verdict on another newcomer, Jonathan Earp-Pitkins, who is also destined to be cast.

The last boy chosen is Mike McGrogan, a senior and the older brother of Justin. He has not been in previous shows. Confident to the point of overconfident, he has already enlisted in the Marines and will report after graduation. He is on the wrestling team. His singing is mumbled and atonal. Everyone auditioning also reads lines, and Mike's acting is not much better than his voice. There is one nonsinging role in the show for a male (and another for a female), and Volpe wants to put him in it.

"I don't think he's castable," Fleming says.

"Not even in the nonsinging role?"

"Not really."

"I think he is," says Volpe, who always figures that, given several months, he can turn an athlete into a thespian.

Fleming just rolls his eyes.

The source material for *Spring Awakening* is a once-banned German play of the same name, written in 1891, about adolescents trying to escape the bonds of their abusive parents and oppressive religious authorities. The characters in the musical have names like Ilse, Gregor, and Hanschen. Their spoken dialogue is stilted—"What do you think, Wendla? Can our Sunday School deeds really make a difference?"—but we are just to assume this is how Bavarian teens talked back in the day. Their true feelings come out in the songs, a mix of melancholy folk/pop and hard-driving, punk-infused rock.

The play, by the long-forgotten German playwright Frank Wedekind, seems like an unlikely vehicle to be turned into a Broadway show, but then again, who would have ever imagined a big blockbuster being made out of the Book of Mormon? Or a beloved musical based on a barber who slits the throats of his customers and bakes them into pies? *Spring Awakening* did not match the commercial success of those hits, but it was a critical triumph, winning eight Tony Awards, including Best Musical. (It was nominated for eleven Tonys in all.)

The energy, raucousness, and pure weirdness of the show called out to Volpe. Newspaper headlines on reviews from some of its regional productions give a hint of its rebellious heart: "Teen Angst Runs Wild"; "Love, Sex, and Death: *Spring Awakening* Packs a Punch."

Reviewing the Off-Broadway opening in 2006, *New York Times* critic Charles Isherwood wrote that it is "disorienting to find nineteenth-century German schoolboys . . . yanking microphones from inside their little woolen jackets, fixing us with baleful gazes, and screaming amplified angst into our ears. It is also exhilarating. When was the last time you felt a frisson of surprise and excitement at something that happened in a new musical? For that matter, when was the last time something new happened in a new musical?"

Six months later, upon the show's Broadway opening, Isherwood's review focused more on the coming-of-age aspects of the story: "In exploring the tortured inner lives of a handful of adolescents in nineteenth-century Germany, this brave new musical, haunting and electrifying by turns, restores the mystery, the thrill, and quite a bit of the terror to that shattering transformation that stirs in all our souls sometime around the age of thirteen, well before most of us have the intellectual apparatus in place to analyze its impact. *Spring Awakening* makes sex strange again, no mean feat in our mechanically prurient age, in which celebrity sex videos are traded on the Internet like baseball cards."

The reviewer also notes the "almost insurmountable difficulty faced by the actors, adults mostly in their twenties meant to represent fourteen- and fifteen-year-olds in disturbed thrall to the transformations of impending adulthood."

But that is one challenge Volpe does not face. His actors *are* adolescents. He has a different hurdle, and one more daunting: How on earth will he put the words, songs, and themes of *Spring Awakening* on a high school stage? I had not previously seen the musical, but after I read it and listen to the music, I say to him, "What the hell, Lou? How are you going to pull this off?"

"I know," he says. "What am I doing, right?"

But I think he's just responding to my prompt. He's not worried at all.

Another one of those headlines on the reviews said, "*Spring Awakening*: Hell, Yeah." Which is pretty much Volpe's attitude. It's the kind of show he loves. Edgy, exuberant, a little dark. Most important of all, it speaks to his kids.

VOLPE WITH ALLAN LARSON, FATHER OF THE
LATE PLAYWRIGHT JONATHAN LARSON,
AFTER OPENING NIGHT OF TRUMAN'S *RENT*.

THE EDGE OF
THE KNIFE

D o I sometimes wonder about the appropriateness of the material Volpe brings to the Truman stage? Yes, but mainly in terms of how others will regard it. My wife, Ann Gerhart, is also a journalist—she writes and edits at *The Washington Post* and is the author of *The Perfect Wife*, a biography of Laura Bush. As parents of school-age children, we shared certain predispositions. One was to let our kids read or watch just about anything, at whatever age, as long as it had content and intelligence. We found violence more disturbing than sex. I used to joke that it was the Disney Channel I considered pornographic, because of its banality.

Ann's mother managed a theater in Lancaster, Pennsylvania, and her father was a sax player and the longtime post–Glenn Miller leader of the Glenn Miller Orchestra. From the time she was a little girl, her parents took her to the Village Vanguard, the Blue Note, and other New York clubs, where she would listen to the music and the road stories of her father's fellow jazzmen until closing time.

My parents didn't make much of a distinction, either, between art for children and adults. If we could understand it, we could see it. I was fifteen years old when I sat in a movie theater with my parents and caught a (too-brief) glimpse of Cybill Shepherd's bare breasts in *The Last Picture Show,* just before she plunges off a diving board and into the water. (When I recently looked back at this iconic scene on YouTube, I was surprised to see that it is actually more humorous than erotic; just before going off the board, Shepherd throws her panties and scores a direct hit onto the snorkel mask of a boy looking up at her from the pool.)

Ann and I once took our then thirteen-year-old son, Bill, to a live performance by the comedian Wanda Sykes, a favorite of his. It was profane in the extreme, but the political and social satire was smart and pungent, even more so than we had seen from Sykes on television. Other patrons shot us disapproving looks; I was half afraid that child welfare authorities were going to burst in and take him away. But he loved the show, and unless I have missed something along the way, it did him no damage.

Each year, *Dramatics* magazine, the publication of the Educational Theatre Association, sponsor of the big summer festival in Nebraska, publishes a list of the musicals and dramas that were most frequently performed in America's high schools over the previous year. It's a telling list, in part because it doesn't change all that much from year to year.

The musicals on the 2011 list, from one to ten, are: *Disney's Beauty and the Beast; Little Shop of Horrors; Seussical; Thoroughly Modern Millie; The Wizard of Oz; Hairspray; Guys and Dolls; The Music Man; Bye Bye Birdie;* and *You're a Good Man, Charlie Brown.*

And the straight plays on that list: *A Midsummer Night's Dream*; *Our Town*; *Almost, Maine*; *Alice in Wonderland*; *You Can't Take It with You*; *The Crucible*; *Twelve Angry Men*; *Twelfth Night*; *Romeo and Juliet*; and *Arsenic and Old Lace*.

These are for the most part great shows. Well-deserved classics. You can't go wrong doing Shakespeare, Arthur Miller, or even the brilliant John Waters, creator of *Hairspray* (first on film) and the midnight movie classics *Polyester* and *Pink Flamingos*. But the list, taken in total, is more than a little vanilla. *The Music Man* and *Guys and Dolls* date to the 1950s, *Our Town* and *Arsenic and Old Lace* to the late 1930s. *The Wizard of Oz* was first performed as a musical in 1902. To give an idea how static the list is, the George S. Kaufman–Moss Hart comedy *You Can't Take It with You* first appeared on it in 1939, not long after the play concluded its Broadway run. In the seventy-four years since then, it has never fallen off the list.

Students participating in these productions will sing and dance and reap the great joys of high school theater. They'll bond together and deepen friendships. But they will encounter none of the cross-currents of current social debate, and their shows will feel urgent only insofar as the students are personally involved in them. No one would tolerate a science curriculum that glossed over the discovery of DNA, or even a high school football team that ran the old single-wing offense and never threw a forward pass. But high school theater programs that draw material mostly from bygone eras are regarded as somehow quaint.

The most current work on either list, *Almost, Maine*, is a pleasant but innocuous mélange of stories about love and romance in a fictional New England town. Reviewing the Broadway production in 2006, *The New York Times* warned that the show could leave audience members with "the cloying aftertaste of an overly sweetened Sno-

Kone." Volpe directed *Almost, Maine* at Truman in 2009. Some of his kids hated it and wondered why he had inflicted it on them. "The worst thing we ever did," Bobby Ryan says. "I mean, what was it about?"

Volpe chooses to look back fondly on Truman's *Almost, Maine* because of the set, which involved lots of Christmas trees and snow. "When the lights came on, even I gasped," he says. And the show itself? "It was a little twee."

Volpe has done some Disney. And Shakespeare. And lots of Sondheim. "It's a balance," he says as we talk about his choices one day. "I don't always go looking for the most modern pieces. But what you cannot do is pretend that the history of theater goes from *Macbeth* to *Death of a Salesman* and then straight to *Beauty and the Beast*. That's such a disservice." *The Phantom of the Opera*, he notes, is still running on Broadway after twenty-two years. "And that's fine. It's entertained a lot of people. But I'm not in the entertainment business."

One day I spend some time by myself in Truman's auditorium, just looking at all the banners on the walls, which commemorate each of Volpe's productions since 1972. The plays from the very early years look like they are drawn from the *Dramatics* magazine list. After that, they diverge from typical high school fare. Looking at them, you get a sense of Volpe's evolving tastes and, over time, his greater sense of confidence and boldness. Up there from the 1970s and 1980s are *The Wizard of Oz, Bye Bye Birdie, Oklahoma!* and *Grease*. From the ensuing decades: *Pippin, Hair, The Who's Tommy,* and *Blood Brothers*. The banners from the early 2000s memorialize a couple of Sondheim shows—*Sunday in the Park with George* and *Sweeney Todd*, as well as *Parade* and *Pageant*—and the two previous pilots, *Rent* and *Les Mis*.

Many of the nonmusicals dwell on those edge-of-the-knife sub-jects that, as Courtney Meyer put it, made people uncomfortable, including *Equus, The Rimers of Eldritch, Telemachus Clay,* and *Grue-some Playground Injuries,* a two-person play that was chosen for Nebraska. Volpe is by no means the only high school director to do these musicals and dramas, but he is probably the only one to do all of them. Taken together, they demonstrate his quest to bring students the most demanding theater they can fathom.

Volpe spends a lot of weekends at the theater in New York. When he loves something, he immediately thinks, *Can I do this? Can my students handle it? Can my principal and my school board handle it?* "Honestly, I never ask permission," he says. "My mother taught me that it's always better to ask for forgiveness. The way I feel is that if I'm going to do a show, then everyone has to trust that I'm not going to embarrass the building or the school district. They have to know that it's going to be of the highest artistic quality, and it's going to help my kids grow up a little bit.

"I've had criticism, some of it pretty harsh, but I knew that was going to happen when I chose certain plays. But I've never done anything that is gratuitous, that's shocking just for the sake of being shocking, and I never would. That's not theater. It's pornography."

Volpe has built up a storehouse of trust over four decades. If he unintentionally offends, he *does* get forgiveness—or at least enough forbearance to keep on going. In 1997, when he staged *The Who's Tommy*—the phantasmagoric tale of a deaf, dumb, and blind pin-ball wizard—the school board president walked out after Act 1. Volpe, who watches his musicals from a folding chair set against the back wall of the auditorium, saw her grab her coat and pocketbook and charge right past him and out the door. "I thought to myself, *Oh my God, there goes my job.*"

A few days later, he got a letter from her saying she appreciated all his great work, but found it disgraceful that the show glorified drug use. Volpe wrote back and said that he only wished she had stayed for the second act, which he considers a condemnation of drug use. "I thought, *What a shame. She missed the whole point, but you have to stay for Act 2 to get it.* We wouldn't go out there and glorify drug use. It's wrong, and it would be such a cliché."

But part of the "brand" of Truman Drama is that it is daring. It's out there. "He has a reputation to uphold for trusting his students and challenging them," Tracey Krause says. "He can't start giving them *Guys and Dolls.*"

I ask Volpe if in choosing material, he enjoyed testing the limits. He laughs. "Oh, did I leave that part out? Of course! I love the idea of going as far as I can go and not going any further. I love to look in the faces of the kids when they are thinking, *Oh, we do this? We make art at this level? People write about us?*"

Students who come through the program feel sophisticated in relation to the rest of the high school universe, a rare thing for a Levittown kid. "I love it when they come back from college and tell me, 'We're doing *Angels in America* in class, and when I told the professor that I read that in high school, he said, "You read *Angels in America?*"' But why not? What is it about that play that shouldn't be read by a person who is sixteen or seventeen years old?"

One other factor, not inconsiderable, figures into Volpe's choices: He has to keep himself interested. (If forced to do *Arsenic and Old Lace,* he might himself want to take poison.) Maybe some other high school directors would choose not to do *Good Boys and True* because it has only six parts and therefore limits student participation. But Volpe had seen it Off-Broadway and wanted to direct it.

His favorite Sondheim musical, *Sunday in the Park with George*, is about the artistic obsession of the painter Georges Seurat and the price he paid for it. I ask him why he loves *Sunday in the Park* so much. "The short answer," he says, "is I am Georges." He quickly adds, "Not nearly possessing his genius, not at all."

Volpe identifies with the main character's tortured perfectionism, his anguish over details no one else would ever notice, his joy at creating art from a blank canvas. ("Look, I made a hat where there never was a hat," from the song "Finishing the Hat" in *Sunday in the Park* is one of Sondheim's most famous lyrics.) "The musical has this ability to open me up and make me take a good, hard look at myself," he says. "My joys, sorrows, failures, triumphs. It's brutally honest and yet painstakingly loving. I've seen it countless times, and it never changes or loses its power to move me."

The show was critically acclaimed, but didn't initially catch on with Broadway audiences. "If I could, I would do every Sondheim musical," he says. "And I've tried. I've done my best. We've done *West Side Story, A Funny Thing Happened on the Way to the Forum, Into the Woods, Sweeney Todd*. When we did *Sunday in the Park with George*, which is very rarely done, I don't know how many people totally loved or understood it. Maybe it was a selfish act, but I loved every second of it."

There are, of course, some plays he cannot produce at Truman. *Take Me Out*, which won the Tony Award for Best Play in 2003, is a favorite of Volpe's and bears some resemblance to *Good Boys and True* in the way it explores versions of masculinity. But some of the scenes include frontal nudity as the characters, professional baseball players, talk in a shower room, and even Volpe cannot put that on a high school stage.

Floyd Collins is a small musical that Volpe wanted to direct at

Truman. Based on a 1925 cave-in at a Kentucky coal mine that left a man trapped, the show is really about the media circus that ensues as rescuers try to reach the man and his fate becomes a national *cause célèbre*. "I saw it at the Harold Prince Theatre in Philadelphia and thought, *I have to do this show. The setting is the 1920s, but it's the O.J. trial.*"

Volpe scheduled the musical, but after he held auditions, his musical director told him they were headed for a debacle. The music was harder than Sondheim, and they didn't have enough kids with the voices and musicality to pull it off. "I had to let it go. But I was furious about it, just furious. I was like a child."

When Volpe announced that Truman would perform *Rent* in 2007, the musical was nearing the end of a twelve-year run on Broadway. A movie version had come out two years earlier. If not quite in the center lane of American culture, *Rent* was surprisingly close considering its content and characters—among them a drag queen, an ex-junkie, and a lesbian performance artist. Three hundred Truman students auditioned for parts, about one in every five at the school. Many had seen the movie without even realizing the story came from the New York stage rather than Hollywood. (And before that, from the Italian opera, as *La Bohème*.) Tickets for the five performances, over two weekends, sold out more than a month in advance. "The school just went bananas," Volpe says.

The play was double cast, as is often the case in high school productions, with actors performing on alternating nights. But only one student played the role of Angel: L. J. Carulli, the junior who was gay and "out" since the ninth grade. "He owned that part and he got the most applause every night," Volpe says.

I thought about this for a moment, about how an audience in Levittown rose to its feet after a show like *Rent* and saved its most rousing cheer for the gay boy who played a drag queen. In my day, something like that would have been received as a joke or a freak show. The people on their feet would have been laughing. But that had not been the case. "They appreciated how he played that role, his craft, just how amazing he was," Volpe says. "And the students knew L.J., they knew about him, and they respected his courage. It was overwhelming to me, and it was groundbreaking for this school and community."

In the six years after Volpe produced *Rent* at Truman, fewer than 150 high schools—out of the more than twenty-five thousand with theater programs—have performed it. It is a startlingly low number considering the show's immense popularity, especially with young audiences, who were so enamored of it that the term *Rent-head* came into being to refer to devotees of the show who saw it dozens of times.

The high schools near Truman in Philadelphia's northern suburbs, in Bucks and Montgomery Counties—many of them filled with high-achieving students born to wealthy, educated parents—have passed on *Rent*. As sharp and sarcastic as Volpe can sometimes be, he is rarely judgmental. When I ask him why none of the close-by schools has staged Jonathan Larson's musical, which won the Tony Award in 2006 for Best Musical and the Pulitzer Prize for Drama, he doesn't answer right away. Some of the directors at the local high schools are his close friends, and he seems to be trying to imagine their world. Finally, he says, "I think some of these other schools, they're wealthier, and the families have more sophistication, but they really value their comfort. They're almost *too* comfortable. They want that feeling of security and don't want anything to rock the boat. A show like *Rent* raises questions about the world we live in, and they're not interested in that.

"We are *not* comfortable at Truman," he continues. "Maybe that's a blessing, artistically. I don't want to say that the people in this community have nothing to lose—of course they do—but they don't live in these perfect little worlds. And I don't think they look to Truman Drama to do shows that reassure them that everything is beautiful in the world. Because it's really not, and they know that."

Volpe, of course, has conditioned his community. People who no longer even have children at the school, or never did, call at the beginning of the year to find out what plays he is staging. "They want to be challenged, and I think they're sometimes disappointed if we do something too predictable."

He has created theater fans in places you might not predict. Late one afternoon, I stop to talk to one of the janitors I have come to know, an older African-American man who is buffing the front hallway. "What's Mr. Volpe doing this year?" he asks me. I tell him a bit about *Good Boys and True.* He says he has seen most of Volpe's work, sometimes in performance, or just by looking in on rehearsals. *Rent* was his favorite. "I saw the movie, too," he tells me. "And the kid they had here, he was better than the one in the movie."

I was pretty sure I knew which character he was talking about, but asked just to be sure. "The one who did the homo part," he says, referring to Angel and L. J. Carulli. "I couldn't believe how good that boy was."

. . .

The public high schools in Bethesda, Maryland—Walt Whitman High and Bethesda-Chevy Chase—are academic hothouses that serve the cosseted classes inside the Capital Beltway: the children of government officials, diplomats, lawyers, scientists, and consultants. The schools are situated in Montgomery County, Maryland, a swath of suburbia that is both well-off and, in its politics, reliably liberal.

Our older daughter, Sara, attended Whitman starting in ninth grade, just after we had moved from a far more modest neighborhood in Philadelphia. It was a shock to all of us at first. Whitman would become the subject of a 2006 book called *The Overachievers: The Secret Lives of Driven Kids*, though what I had first noticed at Whitman was what these driven kids were *driving*. We had to get used to teenagers zipping around the parking lot in their Mercedes and BMWs as we lumbered along in our twelve-year-old Volvo wagon.

When Sara joined the choir, we were required to fork over a substantial sum of money for her winter competition trip, which was to take place on a cruise ship floating between Caribbean islands. She had gone to majority-black schools in Philadelphia. At Whitman, sometimes derisively called "White-Man," she noticed that among the few black students at the school, several spoke British-accented English; they were the children of some kind of African royalty.

I still had a Philadelphia sensibility—maybe even a Levittown sensibility, as much as I would not have wanted to own up to it—something in my DNA, some congenital chip on my shoulder that probably goes back to my parents' working-class roots. So, yes, on some gut level, much about this slice of America where I found myself annoyed the hell out of me. The community, just like the wealthy enclaves near Truman that Volpe talked about, seemed too invested in its own comfort. We had places that sold "gourmet" hot dogs and "gourmet" empanadas and even gourmet treats for dogs. I said to my wife once, "What the fuck is wrong with just a hot dog?"

People were at once worldly—they read *The New Yorker* and took family vacations in Europe—and also shockingly inward-looking. In Philadelphia, starting in seventh grade, Sara had taken public transportation to the magnet school she attended and walked five city blocks between the train station and the school. We didn't consider her commute on public transit to be heroic or extraordinary. It was what students in Philadelphia (and many other cities) had long done if they attended a school outside their neighborhoods.

In Bethesda, we encountered parents—*parents of high schoolers*—who would not allow their children to take the Metro (subway) with friends to visit the zoo or the Smithsonian museums. Another mother said to my wife, "You would let her do that?" These same types of parents might very well pay for their children to take a "service" trip to, say, Costa Rica, but those excursions were adult-supervised, so they gave some seeming assurance that children would not disembark at a wrong transit station, get lost, or encounter anyone that the trip planners did not intend for them to meet.

Neither of the Bethesda high schools has done *Rent*. Their upcoming shows for 2012—Neil Simon's *Brighton Beach Memoirs* (from 1983), *Anything Goes* (1934), and *The Music Man* (1957)—are pretty much guaranteed not to shake anyone out of their suburban comfort.

Matthew Boswell teaches theater at Bethesda-Chevy Chase High School as part of the International Baccalaureate progression of courses, a European-based equivalent of the Advanced Placement program. As taught by Boswell, it is a demanding course that many B-CC High students find to be among the most challenging they take over their four years at the school. He is no longer directing shows at the high school, and neither is his wife, who taught at the school and served as his assistant director. They stepped down when they started a family.

When I talked to him recently, he said that concerns about what would be tolerated by school administrators and the community explain only partly how high school directors choose material. "My take is, there aren't a lot of high school directors who last at the job more than five years or so," he says. "Remember, it's not their primary job—ninety-five percent of the time it's an extracurricular activity—and the stipend given breaks down to about two dollars an hour. So what do most time-strapped drama directors do with the limited time they have to stage a show? They put on shows that they themselves have been in and know very well. And most of them know the oldies but goodies, though of course some are just oldies."

Boswell did direct *The Who's Tommy*, which is as edgy as *Rent*, at B-CC High. Some of the more visceral scenes—for example, when Tommy is sexually abused by the pedophile Uncle Ernie—he staged in a way that was more stylized than literal. He knew that would "appease the community" and allow him to do the show. But a director has to be on the job for an extended period of years, he says, to understand how to bring a school along and introduce more modern shows, and most directors don't last long enough—let alone forty-plus years.

. . .

The decision to produce *Rent* at Truman did create opposition and a rare challenge to Volpe, though not from school administrators or parents. It came from J. D. Mullane, a columnist for the *Bucks County Courier Times*. Mullane praised Volpe as "a local legend" and noted the program's groundbreaking accomplishments, but expressed concern over the play's "heavy" topics. His main worry was about a couple of kisses that would take place. "Volpe has, oddly, left it up to student actors to engage in same-sex kissing—two boys and two girls—as the script calls for."

Mullane had it in his mind that in the digital age, these kisses would be captured by cell phone and other video equipment and posted on the Internet, where the images would stay forever and inflict lifelong embarrassment on the actors involved. He feared, as he wrote, "high-tech harassment." He also expressed concern that younger members of the audience would be adversely affected by the content of *Rent*. "What will an audience of suburban middle-aged parents with young kids in tow conclude?" he wrote. "Despite the tough content of *Rent*, there is no disclaimer for theater-goers, who may be expecting something along the lines of high school chestnuts like *Oklahoma!* or *Bye Bye Birdie*."

It was telling how Volpe responded: He didn't equivocate, apologize, or give even an inch. He went into the mode I imagine he was in when he confronted Tracey Krause's abusive boyfriend in the Truman corridor. About the issue of same-sex kissing, which onstage was pretty chaste, he said, "I have the same feeling about a same-sex kiss as I do about an athlete patting another athlete's ass during a game," he said. (The newspaper substituted the word "buttocks.")

Volpe also rejected the notion that he needed to issue any warnings about the content. "Parents know their children better than any high school theater director, and if they want to bring their children to this play, they will do that," the column quoted him. "There are seven- and eight-year-old children who could watch this play and be fine, and there are seven- and eight-year-old children who would watch this and not be okay. And [the parents know] their children. It's up to the parents."

Mullane went to the show and pronounced it "excellent," although he did not drop his objections. For those who would be attending the remaining performances, he wrote, "Don't forget to send someone you love a backstage Hershey kiss, available the night I saw the show. As an announcer said, 'These kisses are completely safe.'"

Mullane received a lot of letters after the column, most of them opposing his point of view. To his credit, he excerpted several of them. One letter writer, a member of the tech crew, wondered what was so much more threatening about *Rent* than some of Volpe's previous productions. He wrote: "*Sweeney Todd* was about a barber who slit throats, and then his landlady baked [the victims] into pies. *Parade* was about a young girl who was raped and murdered, and a man who was blamed because he was Jewish and was lynched because of it. *Guys and Dolls* had the theme of gambling and drinking. Even *Romeo and Juliet* was about suicide."

SPRING AWAKENING, WITH SOME OF THE
AUDIENCE SEATED ONSTAGE.

ARE YOU ALL FROM
THE KNITTING CLUB?

The *Spring Awakening* cast assembles on a morning in early August for the first day of rehearsals. It is blistering hot outside. Most of the boys are wearing shorts, the style that falls to their midcalves. The girls wear tank tops. Volpe shows up in a purple polo shirt and white shorts. "Nice legs, Volp," says Colin Lester, a senior and Bobby Ryan's heir as the troupe's resident wise guy.

The kids take seats in the auditorium, spreading themselves out in the first several rows of the center section. A few minutes after nine A.M., Volpe delivers his sort of first-day mission statement. He tells them that being selected for a pilot is both an honor and an obligation. Can they fail? Well, not exactly. MTI is not ever going to say the show was terrible. But the company executives will all come down from New York, and if it's not to their liking, it might be the last time they set foot in Levittown.

Many of the students go immediately from rehearsal to late-afternoon shifts at their summer jobs. When school starts in a few weeks, rehearsals will move to the afternoons. Students will have to juggle the show with their homework, some will still be working, and some of the seniors will have college applications and essays to begin. Volpe knows how quickly it all happens. He needs to get their attention—but not paralyze anyone. He didn't mention, for example, that they can expect the show may be reviewed by Broadway.com and possibly other national websites and theater publications.

"Remember, because this is a pilot for Music Theatre International, the show is going to be seen by a lot of people—people outside Truman, outside Bristol Township," he says. "They want to be able to sell it to other high schools. They have entrusted us with this, and all of you should be very proud of that. But in the end it doesn't change anything that we do. We come in here every day and we work and we trust each other and try to make this the best it can possibly be."

Any musical is a spectacle, a great outpouring of music, dance, and drama, staged with propulsive forward momentum, infused with appropriate measures of wit, comedy, and tragedy, all orchestrated to come together as a single piece, a story that coheres. *Spring Awakening* has its own particular challenges. The music is by no means easy, but Fleming believes it is within the cast's capabilities. The show's split context—an imagined punk-rock universe layered over nineteenth-century Bavaria—is its point of greatest interest and, for the actors, its most formidable aspect. They have to live in one time period and emote in another.

"We'll have all these pieces, all this stuff we're doing," Volpe says that first morning. "You'll think, *Oh my God, this play is never going to come together. It's so big, it's so grand.* And then eventually it does. I don't know how exactly. That's the magic. It becomes a play, and then it becomes *our* play. We start with this show called *Spring Awakening*, and over time, we make it our own."

They start by learning "The Song of Purple Summer." Significantly, it is the last number in the show—a fixed point, something in the distance they can see. "I want you to just think about this one song, not all of *Spring Awakening*," he says. "That's too overwhelming right now. This is a baby step."

Rehearsals, especially in the beginning, will go slowly. They might even seem tedious, he cautions. They'll master one thing, move on to the next, then backtrack. One step forward, one step back. Because "The Song of Purple Summer" is the finale and the whole cast sings it, they all are involved throughout this first rehearsal. Fleming sits in the front row of the auditorium with a keyboard in front of him, teaching the parts.

Baby step or not, this song involves some of the most difficult harmonies of any song in the show. The more the cast struggles, the more quietly they sing. Fleming suddenly stops. "Guys, you are really making me nervous. If that's all the sound our three lead boys can make, we're in trouble. This is the time to make mistakes, but I can't correct them if I can't hear you."

The girls are better, but only marginally. Carol Ann's innate talent is not matched by any previous training—no singing in church, no vocal direction whatsoever until this moment. The harmonies trip her up, and she stumbles on where to come in. "Can you do it again, the beginning?" she asks. A few minutes later, she says, "Where are we at? I'm totally confused."

It's understandable. She has never done this before, and yet she has been given the part of Ilse, perhaps the most vocally demanding of the female roles. Her voice is being counted on to soar above, to carry lesser voices. She laughs uncomfortably after one of her slipups. "Sorry, my laugh is really horrible," she says to the girl sitting next to her, Brittany Linebaugh, a junior and a veteran of two Volpe musicals.

Brittany sometimes has her own moments. By Truman Drama's demanding standards, she is considered a little drama-y, given to "crying faucets," as Volpe says, when things do not go her way. But she is an acknowledged talent, a wholesome-looking blonde with a powerful singing voice and a big stage presence.

Brittany puts a hand on Carol Ann's shoulder and rubs it gently. "It's cool," she says. "We're all family here."

A couple hours into it, "The Song of Purple Summer" doesn't sound half bad. You can tell the cast feels a sense of accomplishment.

Volpe sends them up onstage and does some rudimentary staging of how the finale might look. Mostly, it's to get them singing and moving at the same time. He gives direction as Fleming plays and they sing. "Stop." "Move." "Slower." He wants them to hit certain spots at particular points in the music and to form a stage picture at the end, with all of them visible and arranged in a pleasing shape. "It would be fabulous if Melchior [Luke] finds his spot on the word *born*. You know what I mean? Ryan, let's start over and try that."

There are twenty-one of them up there. It will take some ongoing work. Carol Ann is still uncertain and skittish. She sounds terrific, but she sways as she sings. "Just try to stand up straight," Volpe says.

More than anything else, the rehearsal is a demonstration for the newcomers of what can be accomplished in even just one day of sustained focus. They sing the song one more time before breaking for the day. They hit their spots and form a sort of V onstage.

"Voilà! Final stage picture. Standing ovation," Volpe says. "It looks gorgeous."

Volpe and Krause have to find some sort of work-around involving one of the show's signature songs. Its title is "Totally Fucked," which even on Truman's stage is problematic language, though not a complete no-go. The song is a very funny number about an unfunny situation: Melchior has impregnated his girlfriend, Wendla. The real issue is not so much the title as the excessive and repetitive use of the word itself. "Totally Fucked" is a celebration, an ode to the granddaddy of all Anglo-Saxon four-letter words.

It begins with Melchior singing, "There's a moment you know you're fucked, not an inch more room to self-destruct." The sentiment is amplified, riotously, by all the rest of the boys onstage, who come in with: "Yeah, you're fucked, all right, and all for spite. You can kiss your sorry ass good-bye."

And so on. As staged, it's a teenage rant. The boys are hopping around, going crazy. Great fun and hilarity all around. You want to know how to get high school boys in a play? Put on a show where they can throw their heads back, put their arms in the air, and shout "Fuck" a whole bunch of times.

Except that they cannot, exactly, play it that way. Volpe explains on the day the song is introduced, "We're still trying to figure out a way to do it because we can't say *fucked*, or we can't *keep* saying it. So we're thinking about how we're going to get around that. We're going to learn it first with *fucked*, and then we're going to take *fuck* out."

Everyone is laughing. Volpe is laughing.

Except Tracey Krause, who tells me, "I'm nervous about *Spring.* I want the principal's signature on everything." Volpe is far less concerned. It is part of what makes him and Krause a good team—one of them is usually available as a calming influence. "What Lou worries about, I don't spend any time worrying about," she explains. "What I don't worry about, he's frantic about."

They rehearse the song several more times, unedited, then Krause steps in with instructions on how they will proceed. She starts by going through a short history of the word as spoken on Truman's stage, a local and highly specific etymology. How many times it was said in *Rent.* How many in *Good Boys.* How many in *Blood Brothers*, where the line "Go fuck yourself" somehow survived.

"We can say it twice and still be PG-13," she says, referencing the informal guidelines of the Motion Picture Association of America's rating system. Krause is a trove of arcane factoids, most of them accurate. But how this one relates is not entirely clear, since high school theater performances do not get MPAA ratings. She says they will start with three *fuck*s, then "lose one" later.

Three of the boys, Melchior (Luke), Moritz (Tyler), and Hanschen (Colin), will say it when it first occurs in their parts of the song. After that, it will be sung with a hard *f* and nothing else. "So to review, we're doing three *fuck*s and that's it," Krause says. "After the audience hears it three times, we don't have to keep saying it. They'll get it when we say the hard *f.*"

Everyone practices hard *f*'s—a chorus of "totally *f*! totally *f*!" Krause likes how that has gone. "Okay," she picks back up, "from this point on, other than those three boys, you are never, ever, for any reason, to say the *f*-word in that song. Everybody hear that? Not on a closing night, not as a slip, never—and I'm not fucking kidding."

The summer rehearsals stretch to six or more hours, with a break for lunch, which for most of the kids consists of grabbing a sandwich from one of the nearby convenience stores. Colin is late coming back one day and trips and falls running in from the parking lot. He hustles back up onstage, like nothing has happened, until Brittany Linebaugh says something like, "Yecch, Colin's elbow is all bloody." Someone else suggests that he clean himself up and maybe get a bandage.

Krause says, "Let him suffer. He was late."

There is one area in which Krause claims superiority over Volpe: her understanding of Truman Drama's impact on students. "The one thing I get better than him is the kids' perspective, because I was one. I know what it's like to be a student in this program and to be his student. I know how it changes your life."

One day during *Spring Awakening* rehearsals, a 2007 graduate named Keith Webb stops in to visit. It happens all the time. Former students settle into seats in the auditorium, watch until the end, then talk with Volpe and let him know what is new in their lives.

A mixed-race kid, very handsome, Webb had played basketball at Truman before winning the part of Radamès in *Aida* in his senior year. He took a handful of college courses, but mostly has been working as an actor at the Sight & Sound Theatre near Lancaster, Pennsylvania, which puts on a year-round schedule of Christian-themed shows, with titles like *Behold the Lamb* and *Psalms of David*, as well as a hugely popular Christmas production.

The theater is a for-profit operation that draws eight hundred thousand patrons a year, most of them arriving by bus and paying $32 for a ticket. It provides that rarest of things for its actors: a steady paycheck. Webb describes it as a kind of gilded cage. He has a nice life, friends, a car. He doesn't have to sweat his monthly rent check, and how many young actors can say that?

He tells Volpe he is thinking about leaving and trying his luck as an actor in New York, but is unsure if it's the right move. "I'm really comfortable where I am," he says.

Volpe is never a blurter, someone who speaks out of turn or inappropriately. But he is spontaneous. His opinions can seem to burst forth without a great deal of forethought.

He nearly explodes at Webb. "You're what? You're *comfortable?* Keith, how old are you now?"

Webb replies that he is twenty-three.

"I'm sorry, but *comfortable* is not a word that I think should be in the vocabulary of a person who is twenty-three years old."

That's it. They go on to talk about a few other students Webb is in touch with from his high school years. About the challenges of *Spring Awakening.* Webb gives Volpe a hug and walks back out to his car.

When I call him eighteen months later, he is living in New York, getting work as an actor—mostly theater, a little film—and doing some modeling. He has been in several regional productions of New York shows, including a lead role in *In the Heights.* No big breaks yet, though he did get a callback after auditioning for a recurring part in the television show *Glee.* "I haven't been comfortable since I left Lancaster, but I'm living an actor's life," he says. "Mr. Volpe was right. I'm too young to go for the safe thing. If you're comfortable, then you're doing something wrong. You have to be in it for the heart."

I ask Webb if he had made the move based on what Volpe said. "In a way, yes. I was leaning that way already. I knew what he would tell me, but I needed to hear it."

Krause made the initial edits in *Spring Awakening*, changes intended to make it more suitable for high school audiences and actors. In addition to seeing the show in New York, she had watched a DVD of it countless times. For three years she and Volpe had been talking about producing it at Truman, and *how* they would do it, so she is intimately familiar with his thinking. Even so, she says, "for him to trust my judgment [to make the initial cuts] was huge for me. He had never asked me to do that before."

After they sent the suggested revisions to MTI, Volpe met with Freddie Gershon and John Prignano in New York. They let him know that the cuts had been approved, with just a couple of exceptions, by Duncan Sheik and Steven Sater. Volpe was struck by the casual aspect of his visit. Gershon gave him a knickknack from his office, a deck of playing cards commemorating the wedding of Prince William and Kate Middleton. He told him again what a great job he did with *Les Mis* and *Rent* and said he was not worried in the least that *Spring Awakening* would be another great success.

In New York, they talked about the possibility of modernizing the setting—moving the children's world forward from nineteenth-century Bavaria—to make it more accessible, but decided the very strangeness of that is an essential part of the show's allure. Volpe also feared that such a change would violate *Spring Awakening*'s structure, which he considers "perfectly balanced, almost Chekhovian in that way. If you brought the time period closer to the rock score, you would lose that. We realized it should stay as is."

The meeting in New York was flattering and made Volpe feel that he was being regarded more like a professional in the theater than a schoolteacher. But he was also daunted by the expectations. "We have this standard to uphold," he said, "and we have to meet it, and yet this is such a different kind of show."

Good Boys and True was a surprising play to see on a high school stage but, in most other ways, a traditional story. It had a clear moral through line, expressed by the mother, who must make clear to her son how reprehensible his behavior was. *Spring Awakening*, by contrast, is anarchistic in spirit. The grown-ups are in charge but shouldn't be. They're vile. They hoard information and lord their power over children, to disastrous results. Along the way, a lot of really awful stuff happens. An unwanted pregnancy. A botched back-alley abortion. A suicide. Amid it all, there is plenty of humor, much of it bawdy. (For instance, a piano teacher and object of fantasy named Fräulein Grossenbustenhalter—"Miss Big Brassiere.")

The music in *Spring Awakening* bares the chaos of the adolescent soul as hormones rage and the emerging adult self goes to war against parents and all other forms of authority. The characters break out of their "nineteenth-century confines," the production notes of the show state, "pull hand mics from their pockets, and rock out." By mixing the time periods—the German teens rebelling to a musical beat still almost a century into the future—the show suggests that its themes are timeless, fixed over the course of generations and human history.

"The part about power, with the grown-ups having all of it,

I totally get that," Colin Lester says. "It's what I go through every day of my life. What I love about the show is it doesn't lead you to just one place. There's nothing that makes you feel like, This is what I'm supposed to think. It's not like that."

Krause's edits had mostly to do with language. The greater challenges were in the realm of staging and direction—for example, what to do about the number "My Junk." It's a great song, a hilarious scene. But it takes place as one of the characters is masturbating, a pretty common activity for a teenage boy, but not one you usually see onstage. "It was shocking in New York," Volpe says. "Shocking." The actor's hand was inside his pants. "You can't show that to a high school theater audience. There's got to be a line. But you have to let the audience know what's happening with this boy, or you lose the whole scene. It becomes pointless."

This was the essence of Volpe's challenge. Bringing great theater to Levittown, up-to-date stuff rather than musty standards, also entails importing a whole lot of stuff that just cannot be staged at Truman or any other high school. Some of the scenes become *more* difficult to play than in New York, not less, and require more craft from the director and actors.

The scene leading into "My Junk" unfolds as Hanschen (Colin) is behind a closed bathroom door in his home, reading an erotic story aloud. The story is ridiculous: "One last kiss . . . those soft white thighs . . . those girlish breasts . . ." His father calls out to him. "Hanschen, you all right?" "My stomach again, Father. But I'll be fine."

With Volpe's coaching, Colin would play it with a quavering voice that makes clear what is going on without the need for a graphic physical demonstration. His voice is perhaps a little over the top, but it has to be, because his hands, so to speak, are tied.

In Truman's version of *Spring Awakening*, a "transparent dress" (stage direction in the original script) becomes just a dress. A gun that Moritz puts in his mouth in the Broadway version will be seen, but just briefly before a blackout—Tyler never aims it at himself. The line "Roll me a smoke" is excised, because Truman students would interpret it as "Roll me a joint," and references to drug use onstage are a clear red line.

But the story is the story, and Truman's version has to stay true to it. A couple of times, in the weeks he is rehearsing the show, Volpe brings up a high school production of *Avenue Q* that we had seen together. On Broadway, the puppets of *Avenue Q* are inappropriate. They're dirty. In the high school version we attended, they were so sanitized that the musical lost its edge. "That's what I can't let happen here," he says. "It's my biggest fear. I have to make *Spring Awakening* something we're proud to have on Truman's stage, but I don't want to lose the teeth of the play."

Volpe's students like doing plays that feel relevant to them and that they know are off-limits to other schools. Their own lives, in so many cases, are not ordered or pretty, and Truman theater lets them consider disordered worlds that are not their own.

Most of them, though, are drawn at first to Volpe's program for the same reasons that have always attracted kids to high school drama: They want to be onstage. Their friends are already participating. They suspect they have singing or acting talent, or someone told them they do. They are shy or awkward and hope drama will help them emerge from a shell.

Tyler Kelch is small and wiry, a bundle of nerves and self-doubt.

He's quirky. You can't always tell if he's *trying* to be funny or if he's just being himself. One day when he has a cold, he goes through an entire rehearsal with a big tissue box hanging from a string around his neck, like a pendant. He likes acting, he explains, "because it's good not to have to be me for a couple of hours every day. I'm a really insecure person. I have, like, zero confidence, so I like being onstage pretending to be someone else."

He is in part a techie, the kid who likes to take cameras and phones apart to see how they work. "My other favorite part of being onstage is wearing a microphone and being under lights. It's, like, the coolest thing ever."

The historical aspect of *Spring Awakening* appeals to Tyler, particularly seeing the things that do *not* change as time marches forward. The teenage characters in *Spring* "have the same hang-ups we do," he says. Many of the controversies and concerns expressed in the show—sexuality, abortion, teen suicide—are entirely current. "It's just interesting to think about when you consider the original play was written in, like, 1890-something. I'm pretty sure nobody in the audience is going to feel like it didn't give them something to think about."

The boys' first scene has them sitting in Latin class as they are terrorized by their instructor. The teacher walks from desk to desk, demanding precise pronunciation and shouting directly into the ears of students who do not get it right. He is a despot, far more brutal than any educator is allowed to be now.

One of Volpe's primary jobs is to bring his students context they do not have. In rehearsal one day, he tries to make them understand how having a teacher like this might feel. "I went to a Catholic high school, and I remember the priest would walk around the classroom, just like in this scene, and you could feel him coming up behind you," he says. "And you didn't want him to stop and make you be the one who had to answer the question. Until he passed your desk, you couldn't breathe. You felt like you were going to suffocate. That's how I want you to be. Even as you're sitting, I want to see your whole body tense up."

Mike McGrogan, the wrestler and future Marine, is playing the teacher as well as all the male adult parts. (It's the way the play is structured; a junior named Marilyn Hall is playing the female adults.) He is struggling to catch on, to get to that essential place where he will begin to construct a character who is not himself. Onstage, he seems like, well, Mike McGrogan—a big guy with a scruffy black crew cut and not a great deal of affect. He has the bearing of someone a bit older, which may be the quality that made Volpe want to put him in the role, as well as a reputation as one of the school's Lotharios. Some of the girls in the cast gravitate to him. Krause, at one point, asks him if he is still with the twenty-three-year-old Brazilian woman he was said to be dating.

"Date?" he says. "I don't *date* girls."

He reminds me a little of Zach—the aura of the Big Man on Campus. But he is not as invested in Truman Drama or as receptive to direction. Volpe tries his best to prompt him. "You have to show your dominance. You're invading his personal space," he tells him on how to play a scene with Moritz, who is faltering in the Latin class. Mike stands a little closer, but nothing in his voice or body changes. "Think of the worst, meanest teacher you've ever had. How is your wrestling coach when he's mad?"

Krause gets involved. "You know why I hate this teacher?" she says to him. "It's just a job to him. He's just in it for the money. He doesn't like kids."

Mike nods. He plays the scene again, a little better. He is a nice kid with a lot of responsibilities. "You know, he's got, like, two or three jobs," Krause tells Volpe. He misses a rehearsal one day to drive his grandmother to a doctor's appointment. He misses another on a day he has to get a physical for the Marines. Everyone is rooting for him, but it's not clear what will happen. He is a challenge to one of Volpe's core convictions—that as a high school director, he can make any athlete into an actor.

Volpe tells the kids one day about what he has in mind for the set—something very spare but with visual images projected on big screens at the rear of the stage. The pictures will change from scene to scene, or even *during* scenes. He has put Robby Edmondson in charge of gathering the images and mastering the projection system, which will be high-tech, high resolution, and expensive enough that the projectors and screens will come in late because they can afford to rent them for only a short time. It's high-risk. Robby will have to quickly make it all work, and Volpe won't get a real look at it until perhaps a week before the production.

The cast members, often more traditional in their thinking than their sixty-four-year-old teacher, do not much like this idea. They have in mind that a set must consist of big pieces, stuff that gets hammered together and painted and then is moved all around during the show.

I never saw Volpe reprimand a student or express irritation when questioned about his directing decisions. He welcomes it (why else would he teach all those theater classes?) and treats the kids as his artistic partners. Julia Steele, who is playing the very difficult role of Martha—her character is abused by her father—is probably a little more pointed in her questioning than most of the others and sometimes pushes the limits of Volpe's equanimity. "Let's make her assistant director in charge of God," he jokes to Krause one day.

After he introduces the idea of the projections, she says to him, "I think that will be really distracting. Won't people be looking at the pictures instead of the play?"

It's a reasonable concern, Volpe says. He'll try to make sure it doesn't happen. They'll look at everything once the system arrives and the images are loaded and tweak it if they have to—even though there won't be a lot of time.

Revisions in the script must be approved by the authors, but the staging is where Volpe, as the director, gets to express himself. The production doesn't have to look like it did on Broadway and, in fact, shouldn't. "I want to do something different," he tells them that day. "When the New York people come to see our production, I don't want them to think we just copied them. I'd rather try something and fail than not try at all, you know what I mean?"

They move on to the day's rehearsal, starting with one of the more haunting scenes, in which Julia's character reveals to the other girls the secret of her father's abuse. "Think about where you want to go with these lines," Volpe says. "I don't want to say to you, 'Move four feet and then turn to your right.' Take a chance and go somewhere. It's a big stage, and there's just four of you on it. Let it just happen."

What follows is the unsettling "The Dark I Know Well," sung by Julia, with Carol Ann, playing her friend Ilse, coming in about halfway through. "You say all you want is just a kiss good night, and then you hold me and you whisper, 'Child, the Lord won't mind.'"

Ryan Fleming coaches the vocals, but Volpe is the one who helps them see what is beneath the lines.

"When I'm singing this, am I supposed to be angry, or am I sad?" Julia asks.

"It's a myriad of things going through her mind," Volpe responds. "She's repulsed, because he abuses her. But she has love for her father, for her family. She doesn't want to be turned out of the house, yet she's got to get out of that house. It's such a difficult song. As you go through it, it will open up more and more to you. You'll find the right way, but it's really not one emotion that you're getting to. It's all these different things coming together, and they're in conflict with each other."

He has another idea. What if the father, near the end of the song, approaches slowly and stops right behind her? Volpe walks up onstage and demonstrates the movements. As she sings, he runs his hands along her body—he doesn't actually touch her, but just outlines the contours of her shape. It is creepy, and I recoil a bit the first time I see it. But Volpe is unafraid. It's theater, a deeply disturbing scene. He figures, let's make it even more so. The song is a meditation on family secrets and shame. It's *supposed* to be unsettling.

"Do you like it?" Volpe asks. "Should we do it this way?"

Yes, everyone agrees. It's effective. They go through it one more time, with Mike McGrogan stepping back in for Volpe.

They talk some more about the show's content. It has a minimalist aspect that he likes, but he tells them that it places an extra burden on the actors to fill in the empty spaces by building full-blooded characters. "This is a really difficult play because it's such a simple play," he says. "There's nowhere to hide. You can't hide behind the scenery, or within your costumes. It's just you and the material."

· · ·

A re you all from the knitting club? C'mon! Is that where Volpe recruited you from?"

Danielle Tucci-Juraga, the choreographer, has arrived. She is another former Volpe student, from the same 1993 graduating class as Krause (as well as Nicole Sabatini, the Bravo executive). Tucci teaches at the dance school she owns just north of Levittown, choreographs shows at local theaters and high schools, and still performs professionally—in shows, on cruise ships, wherever there's work. She had a cameo in the recent film *Silver Linings Playbook* as a dancer in the background of a scene.

She is the classic dance dynamo. If she weighs a hundred pounds, I'd be surprised. She is never called Ms. Tucci, Ms. Tucci-Juraga, Danielle, or Dani. It's just Tucci, her maiden name before she married her Serbian husband.

She had been at a rehearsal the previous week and installed the choreography in several of the numbers and is now expecting to see progress. Volpe has already warned everyone, "You better be on your game. You do not want the wrath of Tucci. She will be on your ass."

The boys start by rehearsing "The Bitch of Living." It follows a scene in which Moritz (Tyler) lets Melchior (Luke) in on a secret—that he's been having horrific nighttime dreams, erotic thoughts that rob him of sleep. Female legs in stockings and so forth. "Have you ever suffered such . . . mortifying visions?" Tyler asks.

Moritz's education is in shambles, his whole world a wreck, because he can't concentrate on anything but these thoughts. Volpe keeps stressing that the musical heart of the show is hard-driving rock. It embodies all the anger, all the chaos of teenage minds.

"I don't want this to be choral," he says about "The Bitch of Living." "It's got to rock out. This is where the play becomes very electric."

One of the darkest aspects of the show is that so much of it really *is* funny. The scenes with the boys and their preoccupations with sex are played for laughs, and should be. But the adults respond so poorly and brutally that everything spirals into tragedy. To Tyler, Volpe says, "Don't fear you're going over the top with this character. Let's face it: He kills himself later."

The boys are to jump on top of their school chairs and belt this song into handheld microphones. This quirk, the mics pulled from the woolen jackets, *was* taken from the Broadway production; every time they come out, it's like the dusty drama has been preempted by a Sex Pistols concert. But Tyler looks uncomfortable standing on his chair, like he might be afraid of heights.

"C'mon," Tucci says. "You're kidding me, right? You're, like, a whole two feet off the ground. Get over it! Don't complain about it. Just do it."

At the end of the number, they jump back down, then turn and kick the chairs over. It's the "last word" they give the audience on the song, Tucci says, so it has to pop. She wants the turn to be fast and emphatic, not slow and leisurely like some of them are doing. "You can't do it like that," she says, demonstrating the incorrect form. "It's garbage." She's also irritated that they're kicking the chairs too delicately. "This isn't hopscotch, you know. There's not any hopscotch in this whole show."

The dancing in *Spring* is not about gracefulness. It's "Fosse-like," according to Tucci—modern, athletic, violent-looking at certain moments. (On Broadway, the musical was choreographed by Bill T. Jones.)

Tucci and Fleming have a push-pull between them. He needs

them to sing, and they're still getting the hang of that; she needs them to *move* while they sing. At an especially exertive juncture in the choreography, Fleming looks up from his keyboard at her with an expression of despair. Instead of responding to him, Tucci turns to the boys and says, "I'm sorry, but this is musical theater, guys. Okay? You've just got to do it all."

They go through "The Bitch of Living" a last time. "Your whole body has to be in it, not just your arms and your legs. And your soul, too. It's very hard to teach. Just watch me. Copy me. There's nothing wrong with it. I learned from every teacher I ever had, except if the teacher sucked."

Tucci tells them she will stop prompting them from the side. They're supposed to know the dance by now. But she can't stop—in the moment before they make each move, she demonstrates it. "I'm sorry, I know I said I wouldn't cue you, but I have issues with control."

She talks with Volpe as she packs her bags and hurries out. They agree this is a particularly fast-learning group. She says they're picking it up as quickly as she can teach it. Volpe says, "It's all there, but the attitude is too soft."

She explains later that her mission at Truman is to run "a really fast boot camp." At other places she teaches, kids' minds sometimes drift. Not in Volpe's rehearsals. And since she's from Levittown, she knows the terrain—knows, for example, that there are never any parents poking their noses into the auditorium, looking at their little ones rehearsing before buckling them up in the family sedan and driving them home. I never see kids get picked up; they walk, get a ride from a castmate, or take the late buses for those involved in after-school activities.

The Truman Drama kids have not been raised as delicate flowers. The community has deficits, but also strengths. "It might seem like I'm pushing them really hard," Tucci says, "but it's what they want. I could do it a different way, but the show would be crap, and nobody would be happy about it."

The three people most intimately involved in assisting Volpe all have their different styles. Krause, the one most constantly by his side, is the profane den mother. Tucci is the drill sergeant. And Ryan Fleming, the vocal director, is the gentle soul. It's not that he has a soft touch with the kids. He is as demanding, but in a different way. The kids want to reach the level he is driving them to, and if he just says "C'mon, guys," it has the same effect as Tucci calling them to attention in her way.

He tells me about his career one day over burgers and a couple of beers at a bar and grill up the road from Truman. He does a little bit of everything—directs the music program at Emilie United Methodist Church in Levittown, where he's due in a couple of hours to lead choir practice; gives his private lessons; and sings professionally with the Crossing and the Opera Company.

He is not a former Volpe student and not originally from Levittown, or really anywhere in particular. His father was a pastor in the Church of the Brethren, one of the "peace churches" along with the Amish, the Mennonites, and the Religious Society of Friends (Quakers). His family moved frequently, whenever his father was assigned to a new church. Fleming's peripatetic career has been by choice. He attended Westminster Choir College in Princeton and has a degree in secondary education, but has passed up offers to teach full-time.

Like everyone I have ever known who has made a life in music,

Fleming believes deeply in its powers. The evening news is playing on the TV in the bar. We ignore it mostly, but one story catches his attention: a hopeful piece on Gabrielle Giffords, the Arizona congresswoman who was shot in the head and suffered devastating injuries. It says that she is relearning how to speak by singing songs she had learned as a child, a common therapeutic method for traumatic brain injuries. "What would happen if she didn't know any songs?" Fleming says. "Does anybody ever think about that stuff?"

A student who lands a role in a Truman musical can get up to four years of Fleming. In that time, Fleming can pass on only a fraction of his huge storehouse of musical literacy, but he runs his own fast boot camp. Combined with four years of Volpe, it is potent.

When the cast was chosen, Fleming knew that it had strong voices, even beyond Carol Ann. There is Brittany Linebaugh—"That girl's got some power!" Fleming says—who in addition to strong pipes has a magnetic stage presence. People tend to remember her after a show, even when she doesn't have the most prominent part. Julia Steele and Shannon Harron are innately musical, if not trained, and Fleming can easily work with them.

The girls are deep enough in vocal talent that Volpe gave Marilyn Hall the nonsinging adult role, even though Fleming considered her his best voice. "Wait a second, you're going to take my best singer and not have her sing?" he said at the casting meeting. Volpe said he had no choice; Marilyn was the only one who could play the part convincingly.

Tyler Kelch, Colin Lester, and Luke Robinson, by high school standards, are pros. The two new boys (besides Mike McGrogan), whom Fleming had been skittish about, are making steady progress with lots of one-on-one tutoring. He just wants them to be listenable, that's all. There are others to uplift the production.

Fleming doesn't figure anyone in this cast is going to sing on Broadway. "Not this year," he says. Antonio Addeo, the 2007 Truman graduate, is knocking on the door of that level of success in New York. But it's becoming tougher for Truman kids with the music program being decimated in Bristol Township. Vocal performance is like violin or basketball; you just don't take it up as a hobby at sixteen years old and reach the heights. Fleming thinks Tyler Kelch could be great fronting a rock band. Carol Ann, too. But her voice, for all its power and layers of meaning, probably went untrained for too long to compete for vocally demanding professional stage roles.

Before he has to go off to rehearse the church choir, Fleming tells me about another local high school, one with a killer music department. "It's fifteen minutes away and it's like night and day. Another world," he says. The school has a couple of vocal teachers, a music theory teacher, and instruction across the whole range of orchestral instruments, including strings. Their musicals are "technically perfect, or as close to that as a high school can be," he says. But they do not rise to Truman's level.

"I'm sorry, but they just don't," he continues. "Someone could say, 'Oh, he is part of Truman Drama, so of course he is going to say that.' But look at the acclaim Truman Drama gets, all the honors. MTI is not going to these other schools and asking them to do these pilots. The ambition at Truman is higher. The intensity is higher. Our kids feel these shows so deeply. That's Lou, forty years of Lou."

MEMBERS OF THE 2013
CAST OF *GODSPELL*, IN T-SHIRTS
COMMEMORATING FOUR DECADES
OF VOLPE'S PRODUCTIONS AT TRUMAN.

IF YOU HAVEN'T
DONE IT, IMAGINE IT

A few weeks into the school year, the cast hits a plateau. It happens part of the way through every production. They know their lines (mostly) and the choreography (mostly), but opening night is still off in the distance and they've already been at it for a while.

The excitement of being chosen for the pilot, the newness of first coming together, has dissipated. Little things begin to bother them. One day the auditorium is not available and they have to move to the cafeteria, where the football team has gathered to consume a spread that's been set out for them—sandwiches, chips, soft drinks, cookies. "We're the ones who are the best in the country, and they're the ones feeding their faces," Lindsay Edmondson, Robby's sister, says.

Even Volpe shows flashes of grumpiness. He sits in the auditorium and observes as a scene is rehearsed, one he's had to tone down. "Sometimes I wish I could do this the real way," he says. "It would be so much funnier." It's the only time I ever hear him complain about the limits of being a high school director or express a wish that he could work at a higher level of theater.

He tells the cast that the following week, two days of rehearsals will be lost because he and Krause are attending a conference of high school theater teachers in Chicago. The kids don't like it. They may be getting a little weary, but they'd still rather rehearse than not. "Is this something you have to do, or you go because it's fun?" Colin Lester asks.

He is launching into one of his bits, as Volpe knows. Colin is one of the school's top students as well as a serious actor planning to pursue theater in college. He is distinctly a character actor type, a little guy with a tuft of blond hair and a face that reads irony and attitude.

"Oh, it's fun," Volpe says of the upcoming conference. "We know lots of the other teachers there."

"So it's like an ego thing, too? You like it when people say, 'Oh my God, there's the great Lou Volpe'?"

"Yes, that's exactly how it is. We eat fancy hors d'oeuvres, and they buy me expensive champagne and praise me in elaborate toasts."

The production itself could use some of the snap of this repartee. Part of the problem is that not everyone is fully off book—they have not yet memorized the whole of their parts.

"You will *never* have a character when you're reading from a script," Volpe has to tell them. "The play will never work."

He segues into the rhetorical tic I've heard before, his own call and response. "Am I mad? No. Is the show awful? No. Is it good? No.

Right now, we're stuck in neutral. If you're satisfied with that, fine. We can do a very neutral show and the audience will applaud politely and forget the whole thing one minute after they leave the theater. But if you want to do better than that, you've got to get rid of the damn books. Do you hear me?"

It is a sort of first warning. If anyone has imagined his patience is infinite, they now know it's not.

M ost of the challenge of *Spring Awakening* resides in the sheer difficulty of the show itself. Volpe's young actors could do teen angst and anger once they learned the music and got the hang of the story's punk-rock spirit. But sexual awakening, the other thread woven through the musical, is more challenging.

Melchior, Luke's character, is a recognizable figure from any era: the righteous young man, seized with intellectual passion, whose ardor migrates from his brain to his loins. He defends the academically faltering Moritz against their authoritarian teacher, explains the concept of sex to the other boys, based not on experience but on his deep reading about the subject, and makes arguments against the evils of the onrushing Industrial Age.

Wendla (Georjenna) is fetching, socially concerned like Melchior, but painfully and tragically innocent. As the show opens, her sister has just had a baby. "I'm an aunt for the second time and I still have no idea how it happens," she tells her mother, who replies, "I honestly don't know what I've done to deserve this kind of talk!" Melchior and Wendla like to meet in the forest and talk. He tells her that he worries over the future of the peasantry and fears that "industry is fast determining itself" against them. "Against us all," she replies.

It's maybe not the most suggestive courting language, but one thing leads to the next. They make love in a hayloft. On Broadway, the scene, as played by Lea Michele and Jonathan Groff, is explicit. The script includes such directions as *Melchior starts to unbutton Wendla's dress. He gently reaches up her legs. Melchior reaches inside Wendla's undergarments.*

It cannot go that way at Truman. The easy thing for Volpe would be to just let everyone off the hook and allow them to play it as chastely as possible, but that is not his style. Georjenna and Luke, friends since grade school, get together one Saturday to try to get this scene right. Each of them brings a friend. They spend a good half of the time joking and talking. The rest of the time, they practice wrapping themselves around each other in ways that might seem convincing. The following Monday, they do the scene at rehearsal. Volpe is unimpressed. "I know you're trying, but I'm sorry, this looks like two friends in the park on a Sunday afternoon."

He tells them it has to "sizzle" and reminds them they are *acting.* Yes, the Truman version of this scene will be PG—or PG-13 at most. Fully clothed. Hands in proper places. But it can still convey something of the real thing.

"If you haven't done it, imagine it," he says. "That's acting. It's what we do here." He makes a reference to the previous year's musical, *Dirty Rotten Scoundrels.* "After all, Georjenna ran around like a Texas cowgirl firing a six-shooter, and she had never done that."

It's a funny line. But everyone understands the point. Their director will protect them by staging the show appropriately; he's never done otherwise. But they can't be afraid of it.

. . .

A reporter from the *Bucks County Courier Times*, the paper whose columnist went after *Rent*, is expected at a rehearsal. He wants to write a story about Truman landing another pilot. The school district's public relations director suggested the story on a list of other feature ideas she hoped might put Truman in a positive light. Krause's response to this impending visit: "You have to be fucking kidding me."

She fears a disaster. The reporter will surely Wiki the show and learn about its elements of sex and rebellion, abortion, sexual abuse, a little homosexuality, a hint of S&M—maybe without understanding that the Broadway version is not what will be produced at Truman.

Every one of these aspects, however, does remain in the play, if muted in some cases—even a whipping scene that Volpe dislikes and believes has "no theatrical purpose." (To understand what it must feel like for Martha to be beaten by her father, Wendla asks Melchior to bend her over and lash her with a switch he picks up in the woods, which he does, hesitantly at first, then with some enthusiasm. In the revisions that Volpe and Krause sent to New York, they cut this scene; it is one of the few edits that the authors rejected.)

Volpe expresses no worry over the reporter's visit. On the day he is to arrive, the rehearsal schedule includes "Totally Fucked," which Volpe proclaims "no problem at all" because it is, after all, one of the best songs in the show. Why shouldn't he get to hear a great number? This is a Volpe I did not know when I was his student—and who maybe didn't exist then: the person who really gets a kick out of stirring the pot.

The reporter walks into the auditorium halfway through rehearsal and watches the cast go through about the last thirty minutes of Act 2. He's missed "Totally Fucked," which Volpe later acknowledges was a good thing, saying, "I've already got too many challenges with this show."

It may also be that the reporter's computer does not access Wikipedia. "What's the play about?" he asks after the snippet of rehearsal he watches. Volpe gives him a pretty PG version of *Spring*—a bit about the music, a riff on the lessons that this era's youngsters might take from those who lived in the nineteenth century. It's not quite *Rebecca of Sunnybrook Farm* he describes, but it's cleaned up. Volpe will stand one hundred percent behind what he puts onstage, but he is not eager, as was done with *Rent*, for elements of an upcoming show to be cherry-picked and criticized in advance.

After the reporter leaves, Ellen Kelleher, Bristol Township's PR chief, has a much more pointed discussion with Volpe and Krause. "I'm afraid this will be known as the abortion play," she says.

"The word *abortion* is never even used," Krause responds.

In Act 2, Wendla gets pregnant—of course she does; the basic facts of life have been kept from her—then is taken by her mother to the oily family doctor, who leads her to a back-alley abortionist. He botches the operation and she dies. Her gravestone will say that she died of anemia. The point of all this is the dire consequences that ensue when information is withheld from children. The show is a comment on sex—it's powerful, it can't be bottled up—but not on the issue of abortion.

Krause says some people in the audience may not even realize what leads to Wendla's death. Musicals, especially one as raucous as this one, are not the most linear forms of storytelling. A person could easily miss it. Kelleher does not seem mollified. She's just very concerned, she says.

"I'm sorry, but we can't run away from the content, Ellen," Volpe says. "That's not what this program has ever been about."

He tells her this in an even tone, but with a clear resolve. She smiles, looks resigned, gets up, and leaves. It puts me in mind of what Jim Moore, the principal, said: "He can do what he wants. He's Lou Volpe."

With four weeks left before opening night, the Mike Mc-Grogan experiment ends. Volpe calls the cast to the front of the stage before an afternoon rehearsal. "I'm sure you already know this," he begins, "but I'm going to tell you straight out. I talked to Michael this morning. I told him I was replacing him. He was very good about it. I'm replacing him with Steven, who will now play the male adult roles."

Steven is Steven Dougherty, a junior who has been in past shows and was in the ensemble in this one. He is not the ladies' man that Mike is and, though well-liked by the cast, is considered a little odd. Tall and thin, with short black hair and an angular face, he has a bit of a hunched posture and a lurching way of moving. Everyone considers him highly intelligent, but when a class doesn't interest him, he won't always bother doing the work. He's not a kid who seems to care about chasing high school popularity.

When Volpe makes the announcement, Steven's castmates applaud for him. He smiles and says, "Thanks for the birthday present. It's my birthday today."

Volpe told Mike that he hoped he would stay in the show, as part of the ensemble, but that he would understand and respect whatever decision he made. Like the rest of the cast, Mike has already given up part of his summer and devoted about 150 hours to rehearsals.

As the rehearsal gets under way, he is nowhere in sight, at least not from the seats in the auditorium. About an hour in, Volpe gets a text from one of the girls onstage: Mike is in the wings, watching. Volpe walks up onstage and around the curtain to talk to him. About ten minutes later, Volpe comes walking back to his seat and Mike takes a place in the ensemble—where he will stay right through closing night.

Everyone but Steven is off book. He has a script in his hand, but he barely needs it. He knows the blocking. Knows most of the lines. He had observed and listened closely from the ensemble. The characters he must play—Herr Sonnenstich, the malevolent Latin teacher; the fathers of all four of the boys; the family doctor who hands Wendla off to the abortionist—are out of another era, authority figures at a chilly remove. Steven's otherness serves the roles well. "Steven, you did well. Thank you," Volpe says as rehearsal ends. The cast gives him another ovation.

With opening night beginning to come into view, the production has already started to gain momentum. Fleming and Tucci have worked their magic. Adelbert, one of the boys in his first Truman role, has one solo song. He has to hit some high notes. He's not amazing, but he's tuneful enough. "Sort of hard to believe, right?" says Fleming, who has been working closely with him.

The casting change accelerated the progress. It wasn't Mike's fault. He was, quite literally, miscast. As soon as Steven took the role, it was clear he should have gotten the part—not that he was a finished product, any more than the rest of them were. Volpe had to spend some time editing his mannerisms. A few days after he starts, Volpe asks him to please stop standing onstage with his feet splayed. "It's like you have clown feet," he tells him.

Steven says he finds it easier to stand that way. "I'm not interested in easy or in your comfort," Volpe says. "That's part of being an actor. Discomfort."

A few days later, he notices another issue. "Maybe you don't realize it, but you look like you're chewing sometimes when you're onstage."

It turns out Steven *is* aware of this. It's just something he does when he's bored or nervous.

"Well, stop," Volpe says. "Number one, you're driving me out of my mind. And number two, your character does not chew, so therefore, you don't chew."

Steven had the misfortune of being elevated to the main cast at just the point when little things were starting to be noticed and corrected. Everyone else was getting the same scrutiny.

Volpe stops a scene halfway through.

"Luke!"

"Yes?"

"Do you have a beach ball or something in your mouth?"

"Uh, no. Why?"

"Because every time you say *bourgeois*, I hear *boardwalk*."

Volpe gives the word its proper French pronunciation. Luke repeats it, pretty close to correct. They do it one more time and the word sounds just like Volpe said it.

"From now on, that's the only way you say it, right? No more *boardwalk*."

. . .

Volpe keeps asking, pushing, demanding. No detail is too small, no theme too big or too frightening. The work rate of the kids is impressive. They don't take days off, don't complain, don't drift. If they give less than full effort or attention, they're called on it, either by Volpe or one of their castmates. Excuses are not accepted. "Luke, your focus has been at best ordinary," Volpe says one afternoon. "You like to have a good time. You're a jovial, great guy. But you have to be Melchior every moment you are on-stage, and Melchior is not a jovial guy."

The dark soul of this play comes more easily to some than others. Perhaps the angriest words in the angriest song ("And Then There Were None") are sung by Tyler, right after Melchior's mother has declined his character's request for money so he can flee to America. "Just fuck it, right? Enough, that's it. You'll still go on, well, for a bit. Another day of utter shit."

Tyler could pretty much sell this from the beginning, not because he is a despairing person—he isn't—but he has an aspect that allows him to reach down to that level. Each of the cast members took their own meaning from the material. Tyler didn't see playing a character who kills himself as uplifting, but he believed it was a *useful* role. "Look at what happens afterward. All the sadness, the people who miss him—if somebody was thinking about doing that, he would see the devastation it causes."

To Georjenna, the show is a rumination on the struggles of life, something Truman students already know well. Their difficult lives may, in fact, make them better onstage. Our best actors, after all, often do not come from backgrounds of privilege and tranquillity. Volpe's students have taken some knocks. They have experienced life. Their soulfulness, combined with spending a few years in his program, is potent. Georjenna doubts that the richer schools nearby—"fantasy lands," she calls them—could do *Spring Awakening* even if they were allowed. They'd be too afraid of it. "We have something inside of us for this kind of theater," she says. "It's indescribable, but Mr. Volpe can touch it and bring it out of us."

It took some longer than others to find their characters, but that's why Volpe builds in as much time as possible, especially when the material is demanding. As the performances approach, the show sounds good, it looks good, and the actors have wrapped their minds and hearts around their roles. This is the point in the process when he always ratchets things up: the stakes, the bonding of the cast, the emotion. When it's finally good, he twists it all a little tighter, hoping to make it great.

The cast, all twenty-one of them, including the ensemble, gather on the edge of the stage. "In August, when we began, this play was a possibility," he says. "That's all it was. Now it's real. I opened that door for you. But you walked through it. You made that choice. You didn't have to rise to the challenge, but you did. You've become so good that every mistake you make has a spotlight on it. In a couple of weeks, it will be gone. It disappears, and it's a memory."

"No," Georjenna calls out. (Just as Courtney did in Nebraska.)

Kids do not much like finality. They don't like to consider the end of things. This is one reason that teenagers are such natural procrastinators—there's always more time. But the concept does focus their attention.

The last time Georjenna and Luke rehearsed the hayloft scene,

Volpe pronounced it vastly improved. He told them how proud he was that they had given it more layers, made it more emotional, more believable.

Georjenna says now, "But we can make it even better. It's like he says, we've gotten it to a good place, but now it's up to us to go far-ther. I think the whole show can get better if everybody just takes more risks."

I ask how she would define a risk. "Trying something you haven't done before. Saying a line a different way. Adding humor to it, maybe. Just anything to make it more complex."

Dozens and dozens of small matters still need attention. The hayloft scene, for example, has a whole tableau built around it—a stage picture, with other couples singing in their own romantic poses. Volpe likes how Adelbert has his head nuzzled against Julia's neck, but cautions him not to do it in such a way that all his micro-phone emits is static.

Moritz's last solo before he shoots himself is performed in front of a stand-up microphone. Ryan Fleming wonders why he meticu-lously lowers the mic stand after the song, observing that it seems like an unusual piece of housekeeping in the instant before com-mitting this act. Volpe disagrees. He mentions an incident he knows about—a young woman, the daughter of a friend, who spent hours in her garage, straightening up each shelf, before throwing a rope over a beam and hanging herself. "Sometimes people tend to seem-ingly mundane details before committing suicide," he says.

Maybe this sounds macabre. Why is a teacher sharing this in the middle of a rehearsal, or at all? But the interesting thing to me, watching the cast, is how intently they are listening. Volpe spins out these kinds of digressions as they occur to him. They always con-nect to something. They're quick, and he moves on. I've yet to look into the faces of any of these kids, who spend hundreds of hours with him, and think a single one of them wants him to shut up. Their teacher is more compelling to them than their friends are, which is no small feat.

He turns back to the show. The big thing he wants the cast to think about is pace. Everything about *Spring* is quick, almost violent. The music, the dancing, the story. It's a cascade. He says they have to start thinking about the transitions between scenes. Whatever they think of as fast, they have to make it faster. There are no big set pieces to move around, no excuse for dawdling. "You lose the mood, you lose the play," he says. "Am I worried about that happening? No. Is it something we have to pay attention to? Yes."

Even in Truman's no-drama drama troupe, stuff happens. It's a high school. No week goes by that Volpe doesn't have to deal with something on the periphery of the show.

This cast, in general, is more academic than the *Good Boys* group. It doesn't have the same alpha figures among the boys or the girls. Colin is one of the school's top students, but he is not a natural leader in the same way as some of the previous year's seniors. Leading up to one of the Saturday rehearsals—which are crucial, because the cast gets all day to practice—he calls another student in a class an "asshole." He is sent to the discipline office, where the punishment meted out is "Saturday school." While the cast rehearses, he will do time in the library.

"I want you to know I did this for the show, not you," Volpe tells Colin when he informs him that he was able to bargain the sentence down to lunch detention.

The cast and their parents have been selling ads for the program. It's not easy to get merchants to write checks, even for just
$50 or $100. They get requests constantly—from school clubs,
sports teams, volunteer fire companies, fund drives for kids sick
with cancer. It's endless. And there's not much money in Levittown's
flattened economy. Volpe has even had to lower ticket prices. He
used to charge $15 for shows like *Rent, Les Mis,* and *Beauty and the
Beast* (the "power shows") and $12 for other musicals. Since 2008
the top ticket price has been $10.

A father of one of the cast members comes walking in with a big
sheaf of ads. He hands the papers over to Volpe, who leafs through
them, then separates two from the pile. He doesn't laugh, doesn't
get upset, but just says calmly, "You have to know that I can't take
these, right?"

The ads are from local strip clubs.

The father is a former Volpe student and cast member who was
a munchkin in a long-ago production of *The Wizard of Oz.* "C'mon,
Lou," he says, "you've got people in this show having sex, killing
themselves, and you can't take an ad from a tittie bar?"

Truman's *Spring Awakening* has a couple of crises still to overcome. The first is Homecoming Weekend and its associated
revelry—a bonfire, a competition between the different grades to
build the best floats, sixty minutes of screaming in support of a
perpetually losing football squad, and late-night parties following
the officially sanctioned school events, all on a couple of cold, damp
nights. Rarely have I seen Volpe truly angry, and never this angry.

Some of the kids are already battling colds and upper respiratory infections. A Saturday rehearsal follows the Homecoming blowout, with a pit orchestra accompanying them for the first time rather than just Ryan Fleming on keyboard. It's an important moment. But the cast is exhausted and bedraggled. Hacking coughs rise above the harmonies.

They are to run through the whole show, both acts, twice—once in the morning and again after lunch. The musicians are on the clock, with their pay coming from the theater department budget. After they start out a little too soft, Volpe stops everything for a moment to remind them that the show must be powered by a hard-driving beat. He seethes through the morning session, then starts in on the cast. "In the beginning maybe it was partly the band's fault. I wanted them to sound like Led Zeppelin and they sounded like Bread. But they fixed that. You didn't fix anything." (The kids don't get the last part of that reference, but this is not the moment for anyone to say, "Who the hell is Bread?")

Poor Luke. He has the most important male role and has grown into it beautifully. When he is at his best, the promise of his stunning audition looks like it will be fulfilled. But he can be inconsistent and not always laser-focused. An earnest, enthusiastic kid, he wore his voice down to sandpaper by screaming at all the Homecoming events, and he was *already* sick.

"Luke, really, I don't want to bring you down, but you were so bad this morning I hope you got it out of your system," Volpe says. "All I saw was a boy trying to act. There was no character going on anywhere in your body today. I wish I could say I feel sorry for you, but I don't."

Luke coughs. Pulls a wad of tissues from his pocket. "And go to the doctor. *Please* go to the doctor."

The girls had arranged themselves in straight lines in some of their scenes, one of Volpe's big peeves. "If you're behind somebody, you're behind somebody! I love it that you all want to be in the spotlight but you're ruining the scenes. Are you getting that?"

Volpe liked one number the whole morning, "Touch Me." It's a mellow song, so it fit the mood, "but unfortunately, this show isn't called *Mellow Awakening.*"

The cast couldn't even execute proper stage slaps. Late in Act 1, Steven has a scene in which he slaps Tyler, but it looked like a love tap. Krause says, "If you can't do any better, just slap him for real."

Volpe had recommended that the cast leave the Homecoming festivities just before the game started, so they would get enough rest—guidance that many of them disregarded. "I feel great," he says. "I was in bed at nine-fifteen. But you don't feel great, do you?"

One thing about working with kids: They do stupid things, but also recover quickly. Some of them use the lunch break to take naps on the couches in B8, the theater classroom. The sick and weary are revived. Miraculously healed.

The afternoon rehearsal is the opposite of the morning runthrough—it's tight and energized. Steven takes Krause's advice and slaps the hell out of Tyler. Looking on from row eight of the auditorium, I feel like it snaps *my* head back a bit. Tyler is unfazed. It's Truman theater—not for wimps.

The final hitch, the last hiccup before opening night, is Volpe's concept for the set—his idea to project images onto big screens at the back of the stage. Julia Steele ("assistant director in charge of God") and some of the girls had questioned him when he first brought it up, fearing the pictures might divert attention from the actors (i.e., *them*) and the show itself.

Two months later, when the idea is translated into reality, it seems they had a point. The rented equipment arrives eight days before the show, in time for the last Saturday rehearsal. Robby Edmondson and Tony Bucci mount three big screens behind the existing set, which is minimal—the school desks and chairs in the class scenes and very little else. The setting is to be represented on the screens by a changing gallery of images, which Robby has been assembling since Volpe gave him the task in the summer.

He programmed the images into the digital projection unit, and they start rolling as the morning rehearsal begins. A pregnant abdomen for the opening number, "Mama Who Bore Me." Pages from an antique Bible. Two hands clasped. Pictures of forests you imagine to be in Bavaria. An ancient stone wall. An old church. Stained glass. A field of wildflowers. Lovers, embracing.

The pictures evoke the action on the stage—some directly, others more abstractly. Volpe leans in my direction and says, "What do you think?"

I tell him what he already knows: It's bad.

"I know," he says. "We're not watching the show, right?"

Images are flashing on and off the screens with great rapidity. Krause says, "Do you think we'll have to put something in the program to warn the epileptics?"

Just a few of the individual images bother Volpe—a woman with heaving cleavage that looks like it belongs in *Maxim*; a kiss with too much tongue in the frame; a rainbow projected onto the screens timed to a gay interlude between two of the male characters, which he deems much too obvious. "Why don't we just spell out G-A-Y?" he says.

But overall, the pictures have been thoughtfully curated. Several of them are quite beautiful. There are just so many that the musical feels secondary to the slide show.

As a student, Robby ascended to the highest level in Truman Drama: artistic collaborator with Volpe. He is adept with all the technology, but what animates him is thinking about how to use it to tell stories onstage. He likes his job running the lights at the pro hockey games, but it's just that: a job, a way to earn his tuition money. He is at community college, soon to transfer to the University of the Arts in Philadelphia. "I don't belong here," he says of Levittown. "I want to do theater for the rest of my life, in New York."

He listened to the *Spring Awakening* sound track over and over to discern the "internal meanings" of the songs and culled the pictures (all in the public domain) from the Internet. He knows Volpe's methods and has heard his maxims: "Go out there as far as you want, and I'll pull you back in if it's too much." "Less is more." Both axioms apply here, but the unfortunate thing is that Volpe has had to impose them so late. They talked all through the process, but there was no way until now to see how it would look.

"It just kind of sucks," Robby says. "I've been at this since August. I went through, like, five thousand pictures. I don't know if he understands that. But whether I like it or not, I have to do what he thinks is right for the show."

Volpe asks him to edit the pictures way down, so that the images don't change more than once a scene. He says he appreciates all the work that went into it, still likes the concept, "but it's too much right now."

Robby will spend a couple of days going back through all the images, removing about 60 percent of them. It makes a massive difference. Only the best and most telling images remain. At the dress rehearsal, the projections match Volpe's initial concept—they are a stand-in for the set, not a slide show. "Gorgeous," he tells Robby, invoking one of his favorite words. "I absolutely *love* it."

The whole dress rehearsal gives everyone a huge confidence jolt. The cast is healthy. The show rocks forward at an urgent pace, one of Volpe's primary goals. "It has all fallen into place," he says to them. "It was a difficult show to do, a lot harder than I thought it was going to be. But you're there. You should be looking forward to having a lot of fun this weekend. You've worked so hard, and now it's time to reap the rewards."

On opening night of Truman High's *Spring Awakening*, the sign in the parking lot at Cesare's Ristorante says WELCOME MUSIC THEATRE INTERNATIONAL. I smile when I see it—it's so small-town—but it also fills me with pride for my old English teacher, Mr. Volpe. Levittown is far removed from any notion of success. Its moment in the vanguard was a half century ago; its last good times were in the 1980s. And yet Volpe and his kids perform at such a level of excellence that the world takes notice.

Drew Cohen, president of the company and second-in-command to Freddie Gershon, has made the trip from Manhattan, along with John Prignano, MTI's senior operations officer. They are seated at a big round table that includes two agents who work overseas for MTI—one who licenses shows in Australia and another in the United Kingdom. They figure that *Spring Awakening* will be attractive to high schools in their sales territories and want to see its debut at Truman.

It is Prignano's second time at Cesare's. (No more cold cuts in the front office; Krause now arranges proper pre-theater dining for visiting dignitaries.) A former dancer who grew up in Paterson, New Jersey, he refers to the restaurant's tomato sauce as "gravy," as it is called in many Italian neighborhoods and families. "It always makes me so happy to see a Lou Volpe show," he says. "It's one of the best parts of my job."

We drive over to the high school and arrive about thirty minutes before curtain. The parking lot is filling up. You can feel a buzz, a sense of nervous anticipation. *I'm* nervous.

The atmosphere around Volpe and Truman Drama is always a mix of the sacred and profane. (The work is sacred; everything else, not.) On show nights, he and Krause traditionally have dinner together in B8 late in the afternoon while the cast is getting in costume and doing makeup. It's just takeout, nothing special, but it's their moment together. Volpe shows me the texts he received when he let the kids know he was eating and where he could be found if anyone needed him. One says, "OK," the second, "Whatever," and the last, "Fuck you."

"Isn't it wonderful how they express their love for me?" he says.

The throng waiting to enter the theater is a mix of Truman students and parents as well as people from the community whose children are long past school age. People I have not seen in decades are among them: a local pastor and his wife who are the parents of childhood friends of mine and rarely miss a Volpe production; an old neighbor from my section of Levittown; a friend from my graduating class, now teaching at a high school up-county, and another regular on show nights.

Some of the students here are from neighboring high schools. The cast did "cuts" from the show at a school assembly during the week—a preview, essentially—and it created a buzz and an explosion of Facebook posts. Word went out beyond Truman.

Backstage, a few minutes before curtain, Volpe tells the cast, "People out there are excited. I'm excited, because I can't wait for them to see this play. We have people who have come to see this from New York, and that makes it special and exciting. But the main thing is that you have created this together, and that's what you will remember forever."

He takes a look at Tyler, whose hair has been frizzed out and tinged with purple. "Perfect," he says. "You look like Beethoven on acid."

The play begins with Georjenna alone in a spotlight, singing the difficult "Mama Who Bore Me." It's a pure solo. Not much orchestration. She would never, like Zach, say, "I brought the heat, Volp!" but she accomplishes the same thing—she nails a difficult opening and sets everyone else at ease.

Volpe momentarily puts his head in his hands during a number halfway through Act 1, as Carol Ann and Julia sing the unsettling "The Dark I Know Well." He is overwhelmed by it. Later, he says, "It actually gave me chills to think how far they had taken that song. It is one of the most difficult songs, emotionally, that I have ever asked high school students to do."

At intermission, he walks into the room where the cast gathers backstage and says, "Could it be any better?" He describes their pacing and transitions as "liquid."

As if the cast needs any more of a lift, Christy Altomare, the actress who played Wendla in the touring version of *Spring Awakening*, walks in right behind Volpe. "You guys are amazing!" she says. "You're doing everything right. Every choice you've made is the right choice."

Volpe always tells the kids "it's theater," meaning something will always happen you don't expect. Lines missed, props missing, a costume change not made. It's part of being an actor. You don't panic; you just find your way back.

Part of the way through Act 2, you can hear a noise, almost a growl, that seems to come through one of the microphones. It is brief, not that loud, and not obvious what it is. Later, we learn it was Carol Ann. Her challenge was beyond the relatively simple matter, say, of a dropped line. She has a fever and flu symptoms. She vomited into a trash barrel, then ran back onstage. Perfectly timed. Didn't miss a line, a scene, or a song.

She was not among those who wore themselves out at Homecoming, and as she said later, "I don't go to parties, I don't drink, I don't do any of that, and I'm the one who got sick."

Carol Ann put any initial doubts about her dependability (based only on her being an unknown) to rest. She is, if anything, sicker for the next show, but performs. Her voice elevates the show, in solo and harmony. "If she doesn't go on, I have no idea what we would do," Fleming says. "For her to be that sick and carry on—amazing. I could maybe tell a little difference in her voice, but no one else would notice."

As the curtain comes down on opening night after "The Song of Purple Summer," that very first number they learned in the beginning of August, the crowd rises to its feet. The cast takes its bows to a loud and long standing ovation. When it subsides, Volpe asks the MTI executives to come up onstage and thanks them for "entrusting" the show to him and Truman High.

Drama people are, of course, dramatic by nature. But John Prignano is genuinely overwhelmed. "I am so moved," he says, his voice trembling. "This is beyond anything I thought I would ever see."

Drew Cohen, the MTI president, says that Steven Sater and Duncan Sheik were reluctant at first to make their show available to high schools. They wanted it in front of young audiences, but feared it could not be done with its integrity intact. When they asked MTI who could direct it, "we immediately told them that Lou Volpe would be the only one we could ask to take this on."

He thanks the Truman cast and Volpe on behalf of the high school directors and the young actors who will now get to do *Spring Awakening*. "We must also commend this community for being so open-minded," he says—the only time I had ever heard those words applied to Levittown.

Jesse North, the national editor of the website Broadway.com, watches from a seat in the second row. The following day, he posts an online video about what he calls the "boundary-pushing theater" he witnessed at Truman. It was, he says, "so much better than any high school production I have ever seen."

To this cast—to any Truman cast—the words that matter most are Volpe's. The ovations subside. The theater empties. He gathers them backstage.

He tells them how proud he is that the performance pleased the people from Music Theatre International. That they would come to Truman from New York, he says, "is like icing on the cake, but what matters most of all is this production, this piece of art that we made. *Spring Awakening*, all of us being together for these last three months, changed my life, and it changed your life. We can say that. It always does. You are not the same person as when we began."

The show was a challenge, he says—maybe the most difficult material ever attempted by Truman Drama. But they got there. The audience saw the show, not the struggle. He tells them that their performance could not have been better. It far exceeded any expectations he had when he took on the show.

"It was," he says, "totally Truman."

VOLPE STANDS ON TRUMAN'S STAGE AND
LOOKS OUT INTO THE AUDIENCE AFTER
THE CLOSING-NIGHT PERFORMANCE OF
GODSPELL, HIS FINAL TRUMAN MUSICAL,
ON MARCH 9, 2013.

EPILOGUE

Volpe's calendar was marked with the dates of all that he presided over at Truman High—his fall and spring productions, prom, the senior class trip, and various other traditions added in over the years, like an annual holiday formal for students. These events carried him forward, year after year, decade after decade. The milestones in his own life came up with less predictability and often took him by surprise. A door would open, revealing a path forward he had not anticipated.

Not long before rehearsals began for *Spring Awakening*, Volpe decided to move out of the town house he had lived in since his marriage ended. He bought a house, bigger and with more privacy, in a new development less than a mile away. The first person he told was Marcy. "But I don't want you to think I'm abandoning you," he said on the evening he walked over to let her know. "I'm not. I'm just going to be right down the road."

He bought packing boxes well in advance and began the excavation and sifting that is part of every move. He unearthed a photo album of his father with his buddies at a Marine base in 1943, and sat there just transfixed at how handsome his dad had been. A porcelain lily given to him by a friend when his mother died (her name was Lily) made him think of the wedding gown his mother had sewn for his sister, Rosemary, even with her hands racked with rheumatoid arthritis. He opened up Tommy's sports bag. The cleats were still caked with mud. His bats, batting gloves, and caps were stuffed in there just as he had left them after his final high school game. Volpe had never wanted to shine or clean any of it. His mind flashed from Tommy playing T-ball at five to making the Holy Ghost varsity in tenth grade to winning the baseball award when he graduated and then being inducted into his high school's hall of fame. It was a fast reel of his son from boyhood to young manhood.

The first items he placed in the packing boxes were nonessentials of a certain kind: playbills from shows he had seen in New York; photos; thank-you notes and gifts from his casts; a big album of photos and mementos from Truman's *Rent*. The porcelain lily was handled with particular care. Somewhere in the anticipation of his move and the tactile handling and sorting and bubble-wrapping of these objects, he came to realize that he was going to leave Truman High. He had not soured on teaching, high school theater, or his students. But he wanted to try something new while he still could—maybe take a shot at directing in a regional theater or teach some college courses or even see what role there might be for him at MTI.

In the summer of 2012, he announced that he would retire at the end of the upcoming school year. The musical in March 2013 would be his finale, the last big Volpe production on Truman's stage.

He had previously directed several religious-themed musicals—
Children of Eden, Godspell, Jesus Christ Superstar. (His oeuvre really did
mix the sacred and the profane.) He didn't repeat himself much,
but *Godspell* was a notable exception—Volpe produced it three
times, though the last was back in 1990. It was a Biblical story, but
one told with enough sass and humor as to feel entirely current to
his young cast, and a true ensemble piece, with room for many different actors to shine. It wrestled with leading and following, inclu-
sion and exclusion, suffering and redemption, through the story of
an alpha male (or was he?) and his acolytes. Volpe decided it would
be his last Truman musical. "It makes people happy," he explained.
"I do like to make people happy."

The final night of *Godspell* was a celebration and a homecoming.
All 864 seats in the auditorium were filled, and hundreds of
people who called for tickets were told it was sold out. Former students of Volpe's came back, many from decades past and some from
substantial distances. A friend from my class of 1974 flew in from
Los Angeles. For two others from my era, it was the first time they
had set foot in the school in forty years. Volpe's current actors
looked on wide-eyed at a reunion a few days earlier, as members of
the casts from Truman's 2001 *Les Misérables* and 2008 *Rent* stood
atop cafeteria tables and did impromptu numbers from their shows.

Levittown rarely felt like a small town, a cohesive place where
people were connected to one another. It was sprawling and diffuse,
and even more so in the years after its anchors—U.S. Steel's Fairless
Works plant, the public pools, the churches and synagogues—fell
into decline. We had all emerged from this town of mass-produced

and nearly identical-looking houses. Volpe bound us to one another, to our pasts, to a particular moment when we had first felt intellectually and creatively alive.

Everyone who walked into the theater on closing night passed under a freshly unveiled plaque that said LOU VOLPE AUDITORIUM, the theater's new name as decreed by the Bristol Township school board. It included two pictures of him, bookends—his photo from the 1968 yearbook and the upcoming 2013 edition. Bucks County's elected leaders declared the day of the last show "Lou Volpe Day" throughout the whole county—north *and* south of the Route 1 divide. "Does that mean I get a free cup of coffee at Starbucks?" he asked.

John Prignano of Music Theatre International traveled back to Truman (stopping first for dinner at Cesare's) to present Volpe with MTI's inaugural Lifetime Achievement Award. In honoring his "incomparable" contribution to theater education, MTI also announced guidelines for future honorees—among them, that they be teachers who "use theater to promote discussion [and] debate, and to challenge traditional assumptions."

Volpe fretted that his kids would feel overwhelmed by the pressure of performing in his last show, but their closing-night performance was free and exuberant and up to Truman Drama's standard of excellence. When the curtain came down, Tyler Kelch, who moments before was Jesus in *Godspell*, stepped forward and asked everyone to stay so the cast could thank the teachers and others who helped them. Tracey Krause, though not yet formally appointed, was soon to be given the formidable task of succeeding Volpe. As she stepped up for her gift, Tyler handed her a plastic bag from the Wawa, a local convenience store. "To the only woman in the world who doesn't like flowers," he said. "Krause, here's your hoagie." She pulled it out of the bag and looked genuinely pleased.

When Volpe climbed the steps to the stage, the crowd stayed on its feet for nearly two minutes. Most of the cast wept, and so did many in the theater. Volpe was dressed as . . . well, Volpe—in a pair of black-and-white madras pants, a white shirt, and a black velvet sport jacket. He noted that the audience was filled with his former students and fellow teachers, many of them long retired. He said he didn't want to call out too many names, but pointed out that Roger Vaserberg—"my original Snoopy, from my first musical in 1975, *You're a Good Man, Charlie Brown*"—was in the theater and that his niece, Carol Ann Vaserberg, had been Mary Magdalene in *Godspell*. "It's a family we have here," he said. "That's who we are to each other."

Volpe thanked several other people, including Marcy, who was sitting in the third row. He said that in the month between when he sold his old house and when the new one was ready, she had insisted he move back in with her. "Who does that?" he said. He asked Tommy to join him onstage and delivered his remarks with his right arm draped over his forty-year-old son's shoulders. It may have been partly for support, though Volpe was one of the most composed people in the auditorium. He had his own standard to meet—he was on Truman's stage, and therefore not about to break down in a puddle of tears. His program, after all, was all about composure, discipline, craft.

He spoke, as always, without notes. Summing up the breadth of material he had produced at Truman, he said, "We have traveled the world together. From the barricades of Paris to an enchanted castle where a beast fell in love with a beauty to a crazy British guy who baked pies to the East Side of New York and those bohemians who were dealing with AIDS and drug addiction. We covered so many subjects, some of them very happy and some of them extremely profound. And it has been a great ride. I have had a blessed and enchanted and almost spiritual experience at this high school."

In 2012–2013, nearly three hundred Truman students took Theater 1 courses—just about one in five students at the school. Many of them would want to continue into the other three courses in the sequence, which meant that in addition to replacing Volpe as director, another theater teacher would have to be hired or identified from within the district.

Volpe used the occasion of the MTI award to thank the school board for its support, but also to hold them to their commitment to offering arts electives. In the case of the truncated music program, it was perhaps a plea for a *renewed* commitment. "I accept this on behalf of arts education, the band and the music program and visual art and photography, and those teachers in math and the sciences—everyone who helps provide our kids with a full education," he said. "When I leave here, I know that our students will not just be skilled or trained. They will be *educated*, and that's what's most important to me."

The *Godspell* cast did not give Volpe his gift onstage. They presented it to him at a dinner about three hours before the final show. In a picture frame, under glass, were two ticket stubs to the original 1984 Broadway production of *Sunday in the Park with George* with Bernadette Peters and Mandy Patinkin in the lead roles. In the frame and just below the tickets was the *Playbill* for the show. Volpe put his glasses on to read the handwritten note on the cover of the *Playbill*. It said: *To Lou Volpe, thanks for inspiring so many young people—Stephen Sondheim.*

He seemed at first like he might hyperventilate. No words came forth. Finally, he said, "He signed it."

"To you," Krause said.

He asked the kids how they had gotten the reclusive Sondheim to write to him. The answer was that they had found a home address for him and sent him the *Playbill*, which they had purchased on eBay. They wrote Sondheim a letter about their teacher, never knowing if he would receive it, read it, or send the *Playbill* back.

"This is the best present I ever got," Volpe said. "I never got a better present in my life." For a few minutes, that was all he could say—variations on that same theme. "Tomorrow I will be putting this up. There is nothing in my house that will be more valuable. There is no other present that could be comparable. It will hang in my house until the day I die."

He told them that what touched him more than the gift itself was the thoughtfulness and love required to give him a present of such deep meaning. "I will leave here tonight so completely fulfilled, so completely realized, as a teacher and as a person. Part of it is the gift, but most of it is you."

He asked them, "Do you all understand what this means to me? This musical changed my life. When I walked out of this musical, I was not the same person. That's how much of an impact it had, and to this day, it still does. I can barely get through it in one piece. I went to see it in New York again a few years ago. I thought, *Okay, I've seen it twenty-five times, it won't happen again.* And it did."

Volpe might have continued, but a cast member in *Godspell*, a bright, self-possessed senior named Tamera Cato-Walker, rose up from her seat and took a step in his direction. "Mr. Volpe, it's kind of funny that you're telling us that this play and this character changed your life," she said. "Because that's exactly who you are to us. You're that person who changed our lives."

ACKNOWLEDGMENTS

It's an unusual experience to return to your own high school, and not just to visit, nearly forty years after graduating. The two years I spent back at Harry S Truman High were enriching and rewarding, sometimes in ways I never expected. I am grateful to Jim Moore, the principal at Truman High, Sam Lee, superintendent of schools in Bristol Township, and the members of the district's school board for granting me full access to the school. They gave me the chance to dwell fully, which is an essential element for any work of nonfiction. I'm proud of the staff card they issued me once I passed my background check.

Much of this book is told through the dozens of student actors and actresses, as well as members of the technical crew, whom I encountered in Truman Drama. I found them remarkable and inspiring, and there was not one day I spent at the school that I didn't love being around them. To all of you boisterous and rigorous Truman Drama kids: Thank you for letting me into your lives. Your energy and exuberance are infectious; don't lose that.

Tracey Krause, Ryan Fleming, and Carol Gross were my interpreters in the land of modern-day Truman High and Truman Drama, and along the way, they became friends. Carol, the documentarian of Truman Drama, took many of the photographs that grace this book.

I am indebted to Marcy Volpe, Lou Volpe's former wife, and their son, Tommy. They helped me understand the man at the center of this story and did so with an abundance of heart and courage that I will never forget.

This book is mainly a work of on-the-ground observation informed by my own memories and reflections of my childhood. In the passages on the earliest days of Levittown, David Kushner's *Levittown: Two Families, One Tycoon, and the Fight for Civil Rights in America's Legendary Suburb* helped further my understanding of the violence directed at Levittown's first black family.

Writing a book is a solitary and sometimes lonely endeavor. I have been buoyed throughout by a circle of support from family, friends, and professional colleagues. Bruce Martin has been my closest friend and steady truth-teller since junior high. Together with Darryl Hart and Hillar Kaplan, he helped confirm or debunk my Levittown and high school memories. He and his wife, Lorie, opened their home to me often on my many reporting trips.

My daughter Sofia Sokolove and my friend and former editor in Philadelphia, Avery Rome, read drafts and offered valuable guidance. My father, Leonard Sokolove, faithfully showed up at every Truman production during my reporting, and clapped heartily, because supporting a child is a lifelong endeavor.

I am fortunate to have a home base at *The New York Times Magazine*, which for the last dozen years has sent me to far-flung places and beautifully displayed my work. Hugo Lindgren, the editor, and Dean Robinson, my longtime story editor, were gracious in allowing me to step away for a while. Every writer needs a close writer friend to whom he can turn for urgent editorial guidance, gossip, or general griping about how difficult the business can sometimes be. For me, Jonathan Mahler is that comrade.

I benefited immensely from the editor's sensibility of Scott Moyers, at the Wylie Agency, who helped shape my idea into a proposal. When he returned to publishing, I was taken on by Andrew Wylie himself, who is the ally and advocate every writer deservers.

Geoff Kloske saw the potential in this project immediately, applied a deft editing touch to the manuscript, and was there whenever I needed him over nearly three years. I am also indebted to the team at Riverhead Books, including Jynne Dilling Martin, Katie Freeman, Elizabeth Hohenadel, Helen Yentus, Casey Blue James, and Laura Pereiasepe. Kate Hurley did the vital work of copyediting and spared me errors and made improvements.

The reader and editorial partner I value most is my wife, Ann Gerhart, a fine writer and editor herself. It was she who pushed me to tell this story, then talked me through it, lifted me when I faltered, and read early and late drafts. Her ear, tone, and judgment are exquisite. She elevates everything she touches, including, she has just reminded me, these acknowledgments.

Finally, Lou Volpe. He first taught me in 1972. He opened a realm of words and stories and ideas and gave me my first inkling that I might be able to inhabit such a place. To be back by his side, so many years later, has been one of the great joys and honors of my life. He bravely and openly shared stories that he had told no one else, and he did not want to read a word of this book until it was between hard covers. I am overwhelmed by the trust he put in me, and the faith he had in me, to tell the story as I saw it, and I hope that what I have written is worthy of it.

One day before auditions, he told the group: "We're going to need to see how far you can go. We need to see the fire. If it's anger, if it's pain, you can't be afraid to go to that place. I'm not talking about shouting. I mean something you find deep inside."

With that, he had taught me again, something I needed to know more fully, which I didn't realize until months later.

That is his profound gift, to me and to all he has touched.

PHOTO CREDITS